Commando

COMMANDO

A ROYAL MARINE'S STORY

GEOFF NORDASS

with Ralph Riegel

LUME BOOKS
A JOFFE BOOKS COMPANY

Revised edition 2024
Lume Books, London
A Joffe Books Company
www.lumebooks.co.uk

First published by O'Brien Press in 2009

This paperback edition first published in Great Britain 2024

We love to hear from our readers!
Please email any feedback you have to: feedback@joffebooks.com

Cover design by Imogen Buchanan
Cover images © Alamy

ISBN: 978-1-83901-586-1

To the Nordass and Hall families, for their unstinting support over the years. And to my boys, Aaron (RIP my boy) and Morgan, With all my love, Geoff and Dad.

CONTENTS

PROLOGUE 1

1 FROM THE WOLDS TO DARTMOOR...................................... 11
2 FORGING A COMMANDO.. 15
3 YELLOW RIVER TO HONG KONG NEON 34
4 SNOW, SKIS AND NORDIC BEAUTIES 48
5 PROVING MY METTLE 60
6 THE CRUEL SOUTH SEA 74
7 STERN TRAWLER TO COCHON ISLAND 94
8 FEARLESS TIMES 118
9 HALLS OF MONTEZUMA – SHORES OF TRIPOLI 130
10 ROMAN CANDLES.. 139
11 SAME WAVES.. 151
12 FROM POTATO PEELER TO BODYGUARD........................ 162
13 FLIM STAR OR MARR 172
14 JELLY SHOTS AND BROKEN YACHTS................................. 175
15 SADDAM'S REVENGE.. 186
16 FALLEN COMRADES 202
17 ENDEX . . . OR NOT QUITE.. 228
18 PIRATES 233
19 THE NEXT CHAPTER.. 248

AFTERWORD 251
APPENDIX 255
ABOUT THE AUTHOR 271

PROLOGUE

25 MAY 1982

The Skyhawks swept down through the clouds over San Carlos Water in the Falkland Islands and sped towards the distant islands on the horizon. Lieutenant Ricardo Lucero of the Argentine Air Force warily scanned the sky above and behind his twenty-year-old US-made jet. The Royal Navy's Sea Harrier jet fighters had already come as a nasty surprise to Argentine aviators over the Falkland Islands – and several Argentines hadn't returned to their distant base in Patagonia as a result. Worst of all, the Sea Harriers had claimed a Mirage, one of Argentina's best fighter planes, as one of its victims. Lucero wasn't going to make the same mistake; this mission was already dangerous enough without the Sea Harriers from HMS *Hermes* and HMS *Invincible* showing up.

Lucero glanced around at the other jets in his four-aircraft flight from Grupo 4. The flight was led by Capitán Garcia and to Lucero's left and right were his friends Tenientes (Lieutenants) Paredi and Isaac. The four Douglas A-4 Skyhawks were heavily laden with more than 2,000kg of ordnance each, and all four pilots knew their mission was crucial if the Falklands/ Malvinas were to be held.

The Skyhawk was a fine fighter-bomber; the Americans even nick-named it the 'Hot Rod' because of its light weight and sparkling handling. But that was almost thirty years ago – and the Skyhawk had got heavier with age as it was updated with extra weaponry, while air-to-air missiles

1

had grown vastly more lethal. Some of the Argentine pilots joked among themselves that the Skyhawks were actually older than some of the young conscripts now preparing to fight off the British on the Malvinas.

Lucero was also acutely aware that the diminutive jet was close to the edge of its effective range, with its base more than 600km away across the desolate South Atlantic. The Skyhawk's theoretical range with a full bomb load was almost 1,500km, but its single J65 turbojet engine, he knew, burned aviation fuel rather than theory. Not to mention the fact that combat flying burned jet fuel at an alarming rate. He and the other Argentine pilots were well aware that they were a long way from a safe runway. Heavily laden with 5,000kg bombs, the Skyhawk aircraft had enough fuel for perhaps two passes over the islands before it had to break away to head back to Argentina across the freezing ocean. A nimble and quick aircraft when unloaded, the Skyhawk was so heavily laden today that it had all the manoeuvrability of a beached whale. So it was crucial that Lucero and his flight located the British task-force ships as quickly as possible – and cripple them before they could deliver their deadly loads of planes, men and materiel to the Malvinas.

It had been a good war so far for the Argentine pilots. Operating under horrendously difficult conditions, they had fought hard to prevent the British from establishing air supremacy over the islands, and particularly from landing and launching their aircraft from carriers. The previous day, flights of Skyhawks and French-built Dassault Super Étendards had furiously attacked the British landing areas and had hit three ships, HMS *Coventry*, HMS *Antelope* and the *Atlantic Conveyor*. Also, the day before, a Delta Dagger plane had shot up a British landing craft with its 30mm cannon. But it was the loss of the *Atlantic Conveyor* that had shocked the British fleet commanders. It had been hit with a French-built Exocet missile and, though Lucero and the Argentine Air Force didn't know it, the ship had taken a huge portion of the British assault forces' support helicopters and ammunition to the seabed. What Lucero did know was that if further damage could be inflicted on the British fleet today, it would ease pressure on the Argentine army forces now dug in along the Falklands' main bays.

The air attacks hadn't been without cost. The capabilities of the Sea Harrier came as a nasty surprise, but it was the missile threat that now preoccupied most Argentine pilots. Several Skyhawks had already failed to return to Grupo 4's base and it was feared they had fallen to a new British missile system, which probably equipped some of the escort frigates and destroyers. Yet the aviators had inflicted losses and were determined to succeed where the Argentine Navy's surface ships had patently failed.

The war hadn't been so good for Lucero's army and marine colleagues ashore, of whom many were conscripts. The British, who were professional soldiers, had, despite the odds, already established a vital toe-hold on the islands. South Georgia, the largest of the Sandwich Islands, was already back in British hands and the battle had moved up to the main island. Everyone knew that the elite British Special Forces, the Special Air Service (SAS) and the Special Boat Service (SBS), were now operating behind the Argentine lines, and the ships now offshore planned to unload units of Royal Marines and battalions of Parachute Regiment (Paras), the best-trained soldiers the British could field. If they got ashore with their equipment at San Carlos Water, the likelihood of the Malvinas reverting to being the Falklands was extremely high.

San Carlos Water is a long inlet on the north-west coast of East Falkland Island, the main island of the group; the extreme eastern end of the inlet is around 70km from Stanley, the largest settlement in the Falklands.

The seas around the Falklands were now indisputably British. The sinking of the Argentine ship, the *Belgrano*, an ageing former US cruiser, had seen to that the previous month. Everyone wearing an Argentine uniform still cringed at the horrendous losses involved – more than three hundred men dead – and was aware that the Navy now would not, could not, attempt to intervene directly with the British task force. It was up to the Air Force now.

No one had expected the British to actually fight to take back the Malvinas. The military junta chiefs had calculated that Britain would negotiate a deal. After all, the islands were located just off the Argentine coast; surely, no one doubted that they were rightfully governed from Buenos Aires? And no one had thought the British would send an entire task force across the world to retake these godforsaken rocks.

Lucero scanned the skies around his aircraft again as he continued to lose height. The islands were now fast filling his bombsights and the Royal Navy ships would be in one of the several bays facing him. The Sea Harriers, he knew, wouldn't be too far away either, but his fellow fighters from other units, in the Mirage and Dagger squadrons, were trying to lure them away. His Skyhawk was now virtually skimming along over the waves, trying to stay below the Royal Navy radars and buy time for a surprise attack. Lucero knew that some planes would try to attack British positions ashore while others would target the task-force ships. But how many would make it back to Argentina to swap stories in the cantina tonight? Lucero focused on his instrument panel while again scanning the sky with cool efficiency.

The four Skyhawks now screamed ashore about 70m above the water. Suddenly, there they were in San Carlos Water where the British task-force ships had bunched together to offer mutual fire support. The picket, or sentry, ships were the destroyers and frigates, but the logistic ships, carrying troops, equipment and fuel, were the more valuable targets, closer to shore. Garcia gave the signal to attack, and then it was every pilot for himself. The Skyhawks manoeuvred for their bombing runs – and suddenly it appeared as if the very gates of Hell itself had been opened.

Rising towards the Skyhawks was a wall of lead as every British ship and land position opened fire on them. Cannon fire, machine-gun fire and anti-aircraft tracer rounds tore through the sky, and the pilots cringed at what they were about to fly through. Every British soldier and sailor with a weapon had opened fire on the incoming planes. The weight of fire was so great that, after the air raid, British commanders were worried that troops and sailors would be hit by spent rounds falling from the sky having missed an Argentine aircraft, and they had to issue an order limiting anti-aircraft fire. They were also worried that the large volume of fire might interfere with vital defence systems, such as anti-missile-targeting radars.

The four Argentine aviators were very concerned by the threat of missiles. The modern Royal Navy warships in the Falklands were equipped with the new generation of missile defence systems – Sea Dart and Sea Wolf – which could target not only incoming Argentine aircraft, but also enemy missiles. The ship-borne missiles were both radar- and heat-seeking, and were a vast improvement on the guidance systems from the Vietnam-era missiles, which were both crude and unreliable. An Argentine aircraft targeted at optimum altitude by any of these modern British defence missile systems was invariably either damaged or shot down. Missiles meant certain death for the graceful but delicate Skyhawk planes, and the pilots couldn't manoeuvre properly while so heavily laden with 5,000kg bombs. The anti-aircraft fire was intimidating – but it was missiles that the pilots truly feared. The problem for the British was that many of the Royal Navy ships were not equipped with the new missile systems.

Lucero was vaguely aware of a single smoke trail speeding towards their formation. The Argentine lieutenant didn't know it, but he was unlucky enough to be singled out first by the missile search radar of HMS *Yarmouth*, one of the picket ships for the landing force. The smoke trail now heading towards his aircraft was a Sea Dart missile capable of reaching Mach 2 (twice the speed of sound and more than three times the top speed of a Skyhawk) and boasting a 22kg blast-fragmentation warhead. If the Exocet was the nemesis of warships, the Sea Dart spelled similar destruction for aircraft. Fully committed to his attack, Lucero had no choice. He couldn't avoid the missile and he couldn't outrun it in his Skyhawk – not at this altitude. The tiny computer in the missile was as remorseless as it was lethal – anything that came within its electronic targeting envelope instantly triggered a greasy black cloud of high-explosives, shrapnel and flames that reached out for more than 50 metres and spelled the end for pilot and plane alike.

Suddenly, there was an enormous explosion and a blast of heat and pain. Amid a deafening roar, Lucero's plane began to disintegrate around him. Eject, eject, was the only thought screaming through his mind as his combat training took over. Reaching overhead and ignoring the spreading waves of pain, he yanked on the ejection handle and, with a roar of exploding bolts and a blast of icy wind, he was catapulted free of the burning wreckage.

Lucero's burning Skyhawk cartwheeled into the sea as the other three aircraft continued their bombing runs amid a hail of gunfire. The Skyhawks were now also attracting Rapier and Blowpipe missiles, having come too close to the Royal Navy ships for the effective use of Sea Dart or Sea Wolf missiles. But they pressed their attacks regardless, conscious that the next forty-eight hours could well decide the outcome of the war.

Lucero – by now semi-conscious and suffering shrapnel wounds and shock – drifted gently down towards the icy waters. Seconds later, it was all over. The cluster of 5,000kg Argentine bombs missed their targets and three Skyhawks screamed back out towards the safety of the open sea. But seconds later a Rapier missile – smaller than a Sea Dart but equally lethal – sped after the fleeing fighter-bombers. The missile exploded to the rear of an Argentine Skyhawk and its cloud of razor-sharp shrapnel inflicted fatal damage on the graceful jet. Spotters on the British ships reported seeing a plane disappear out to sea, trailing a cloud of smoke. Like Lucero, the flight leader, Garcia, was forced to eject from his burning aircraft and trust to his parachute and survival raft. A second missile also exploded to the rear of Paredi's Skyhawk, but he was luckier than his two colleagues: his fuel tanks were hit and constantly leaking aviation fuel as he struggled to fly back to Argentina. Only the availability of a KC-130H Hercules, a four-engine turbo-prop aircraft adapted to act as an air-to-air refuelling aircraft via a special pipe connector, allowed him to keep topping up his tanks for most of the trip home, and he made it to base. The fourth pilot also made it back home unhurt, his plane undamaged.

Back in San Carlos Water, Royal Marine Geoff Nordass was focused on his job. Attached to 3 Commando Brigade's 1st Raiding Squadron, he was returning to HMS *Fearless* to refuel his Raider, a seventeen-foot fibreglass-hulled craft. Geoff had just spent the morning working as a coxswain, escorting troops and vital materiel ashore. It was a desperate race against time and the Royal Navy needed to get the troops and materiel on to land before the Argentines could sink their transports. And everyone knew that if any of the two aircraft carriers – HMS *Hermes* or HMS *Invincible* – was sunk, the entire operation could face catastrophe.

Tired, cold and hungry, Geoff began to climb the rope ladder to board *Fearless* when suddenly he heard a roar from above – and seconds later realised another Argentine air attack was underway. Bloody hell, do the buggers ever give up, the exhausted Commando thought, recalling the British losses the previous day. Seconds later, the flight of Skyhawks roared overhead. Automatically, Geoff craned his neck to follow the path of the departing jets. He then registered the scream of several Rapier missiles rising to the sky in reply, as well as the ongoing barrage of anti-aircraft fire. The missile units were part of 3 Commando Brigade, and their brigadier was determined to get all the vital units and equipment ashore as soon as possible.

Seconds later, Geoff heard the distant thunder of an impact and wondered what had been hit. As he stared at the retreating Argentine jets, he heard another roar from the top deck of *Fearless*. 'Pilot down, pilot down – get a boat out to recover that man.' Without thinking, Geoff dropped back down the ladder and into his Raider. At least this should be better than humping equipment ashore, he thought.

The Raider's single 140hp engine surged into life and the craft arrowed out into the bay, just ahead of both *Fearless* and *Sir Galahad*. Geoff could see the smoke drifting from the sea surface where the stricken Seahawk had obviously impacted. The immediate thought that crossed the Commando's mind was that the Argentine pilots were taking another hammering with more than a dozen jets shot down in only a week. Just ahead of the *Sir Galahad* bows, Geoff paused. He could make out a descending parachute. Less than a minute later, he was easing his Raider alongside the Argentine pilot who was still strapped into his ejection seat, partly shrouded in his own parachute, and bobbing in the freezing water.

The ejection seat was specially designed to remain buoyant, but the pilot had become partly tangled in the trailing lines from the parachute canopy. Geoff could clearly see that the pilot was badly injured. Lieutenant Lucero was now in a combination of shock from his ordeal and the impact of the freezing water. As the adrenalin rush from his narrow escape from death began to ease off, the pilot became aware of a mounting wave of pain from his numerous injuries.

Geoff grabbed hold of the ejection seat bobbing in the water, but realised he would have to cut free the lines around the pilot to be able to drag him on to the Raider. 'I eased my combat knife out of its sheath and leaned over to try and cut through the harness and the parachute lines. That's when he freaked out,' Geoff recalled. Lucero, confused through the combination of shock and pain, believed the muscular British Commando was simply going to cut his throat. Not surprisingly, he decided to fight for his life.

Flailing wildly in his seat, Lucero prevented the Commando from getting close enough to cut the harness and the parachute lines just as a larger British craft pulled up alongside them. The result was that the Argentine pilot was dragged underneath the ramp of the British Landing Craft Utility (LCU) by its wake, and only reappeared several seconds later at the stern of the craft. By now, Lucero was weakening and Geoff, having repositioned his Raider, was finally able to grab the seat and start slashing through the lines that trapped the Argentine. Seconds later, he was free. Geoff held grimly on to the wounded man as the LCU crew came alongside to help. Between them, they managed to ease the limp pilot onto the LCU where he collapsed on deck.

To make the man more comfortable, Geoff eased off his battered white jet helmet and tossed it back on to his Raider. That'll make some souvenir – only place for that is the mantelpiece back in Flamborough, he thought, and smiled to himself. When Lucero looked up, the fact dawned on him that he wasn't going to have his throat cut. He was alive – a prisoner of war, yes, but alive. But his British rescuers weren't taking any chances and the Argentine aviator still had an SLR assault rifle pointed at his head to ensure he remained calm. Lucero was now grimacing in pain as the scale of his injuries drove home, and Geoff realised from the blood seeping through the man's trouser leg that his kneecap was almost certainly shattered.

'We'll take him in,' the LCU 2nd coxswain helpfully offered. By this time, the pilot was moaning in pain and beyond caring who brought him to the command ship. Geoff didn't argue because it was clear there was far more room on the landing craft and he couldn't both cox his Raider and keep the pilot under armed guard at the same time. He shrugged and wearily climbed back on to his Raider. The LCU powered up and within seconds began to head back towards HMS *Fearless*. Geoff turned to the Raider's console and decided to have a closer look at his booty, the Argie's helmet. Except, the white helmet wasn't there! He glanced behind him and spotted a cheeky smile on the 2nd coxswain's face as the LCU disappeared back across the swell towards the fleet. 'Thieving bastards!' he shouted, realising that others had the same ideas about souvenir hunting. And with that, Geoff knew there was nothing for it but to head back to *Fearless*, finish fuelling the Raider and try to scrounge something warm to eat.

If I ever get my hands on that corporal I'll kick his arse, the furious Commando promised himself. The thought offered a sop of savage comfort, and Geoff promised himself that their paths would cross again. The Raider's engines fired instantly at his command and the craft sped back to the task force amid the expectation of further Argentine air raids before the day was over.

Two years later the two Marines met up in the Royal Marines base in Poole, Dorset, but decided to go for beers instead and were regulars on Poole Quay after that. And are still affable today. Last seen, the helmet was adorning the Royal Marines Museum's South Atlantic trophy cabinet.

Ironically, the final tragic script of the day's fighting wasn't written until almost a year later. While Ricardo Lucero was being dragged from the sea by Geoff, his badly injured flight leader was hauling himself on to a survival raft far out at sea. Capitán Garcia's plane had crashed out of sight of land and no one from either side realised he had survived. Badly wounded, exhausted and freezing, Garcia had no idea how to reach land and no radio or way of alerting either Argentine or British forces as to his location. The pilot ultimately died at sea. In 1983, twelve months after the final shots of the campaign had been fired, his body, still on his survival raft, was washed ashore at Golding Island in the Falklands.

1

FROM THE WOLDS TO DARTMOOR

I have always reckoned that I come from Viking stock. A strange thing to say, I suppose, when you've been born and bred in Yorkshire. But my part of Yorkshire – Flamborough Head – has had a very storied past. Roman legions fought the Picts here; the Angles and Saxons arrived from Germany to conquer Roman Britain along this coast; and the Viking armies in the tenth century used Yorkshire as a beachhead in their drive to invade Saxon England. They ultimately made York, just inland from Flamborough, the capital of their Viking kingdom – in fact, Flamborough was once known as Flaneburg, Norse for 'arrow fort'. William the Conqueror may have claimed the English crown at Hastings in Sussex where King Harold died in 1066, but the Normans still had to burn Yorkshire almost to the ground in the so-called 'harrying of the north' before their rule was finally accepted. I am proud of this heritage and I like the feeling that I come from generations of independent-minded people.

Even my name, Nordass, is Norse in origin and means 'North Hill'. My guess is that eleven hundred years ago a footloose ancestor of mine arrived in England as part of an invading Viking army and left me an inheritance not only of a Norse surname, but of a wanderlust ingrained in the blood. That, and a hankering for the military life. There is also a long-standing and proud military tradition in my family, so I guess I was bound to end up in uniform.

Flamborough was a marvellous place to grow up. We were never more than a stone's throw from the sea and almost every family either had a boat or had access to one. Flamborough was sheer heaven for young boys. While most youngsters of the era played cops and robbers or cowboys and Indians, we played Viking lords and Norman knights, mostly around Dane's Dyke.

Just as the Vikings would rather burn books than have to read them, I didn't fancy myself as much of a scholar. I think everyone knew I was simply putting down time till I could leave school. It didn't help matters that I was constantly appearing before the headmaster for fighting. The problem was that trouble had a knack of finding me. By the time I was fifteen I was already one of the biggest lads in the school. That meant that any smaller guy who wanted to earn a reputation as a tough nut felt he had to measure himself against me. There were times, I have to admit, when I was only too happy to oblige and beat a little sense into them. Ultimately, it meant that my teachers were only too happy to see the back of me.

By the time I was sixteen I was already testing the water, quite literally, for life beyond school. I got a job on a ten-metre fishing coble which went out from nearby Bridlington. The hours were long, the conditions tough and the work hard. But, compared to the classroom and homework, I felt like I had been released from prison. I really liked the work and revelled in the camaraderie of the fishermen.

For the most part, we fished for cod. The highlight of our work was when we were paid to take coal miners out for a day's fishing. The men worked for the National Coal Board (NCB) pits, and always arrived pretty tanked up on bitter or Newcastle Brown Ale. They were a decent bunch and very generous to us working on *Our Freda*. Predominantly from Barnsley and Leeds, they were known colloquially as Wessies, as coming from the West Riding of Yorkshire, but the cod were usually safe – the miners spent more time puking over the side and feeding the fish than actually getting them on a line! What I loved about the job was the freedom.

But I already knew what I wanted for my future. I think my dad was the first to guess that I was headed for a life in uniform and seemed to welcome the prospect. He himself had risen to the rank of chief petty officer in the Royal Navy, the navy's equivalent of sergeant-major. He had served, primarily, on landing craft tanks (LCTs) in the fight against Hitler and the Third Reich. These lumbering, slow craft were the backbone of every wartime marine operation, from North Africa to Normandy.

Maybe he felt that a little discipline was precisely what his son needed. I remember sitting down with him in early 1978 to talk over my options and what surprised me was that while he spoke really highly of the Navy from his time in service, he didn't push me to follow his path. I think he figured that I wanted to carve out my own path in life, not just try and replicate his career. He also sensed that I wanted something that would really challenge me. That's when the possibility of the Royal Marines cropped up. Dad had seen these guys in action during the war and had been very impressed. Winston Churchill's demands had led to a subtle shift in the role of the Royal Marines. From being merely battle-hardened soldiers attached to His Majesty's various warships they suddenly became Commandos – an elite, highly trained and highly mobile strike force that would not only lead the Normandy landings but would be at the forefront of the drive to take the war to Hitler's Berlin.

Serving with LCTs, my dad dealt with Royal Marine Commandos at close hand and he recognised them for the elite that Churchill wanted them to be. 'If you want a challenge,' he said to me, 'why not the Commandos?' It was an option I hadn't really thought about and so I immediately went to find out more about them. In the end, I narrowed my choice to two options: the Royal Marines or the Parachute Regiment. But I had injured my ankle playing football as a youngster and wondered whether it would stand up to the rigours of repeated parachute drops. And I liked what I heard about the Royal Marine Commandos – that they were always eligible for global assignments and were usually one of the first into action. Little did I realise that the physical demands in the Commandos were as bad, if not worse, than in the Paras.

In the end, my choice was simple. If I wanted a career in uniform, did I opt for land or sea? In the end, I decided to go for both, and the Royal Marines' famous motto, 'By Sea, By Land' ('Per Mare, Per Terram'), became the guiding path of my life for the next four decades.

2

FORGING A COMMANDO

Three weeks into basic Commando training at Lympstone in Devon I was dreaming about going back home. Here I was, seventeen years old and supposedly full of energy and fight, but after just twenty-one days in the Royal Marine Commandos I was exhausted, bruised, cut, wet and miserable most of the time. I was beginning to wonder what the hell I had let myself in for. Worst of all, I had joined in autumn – Halloween, in fact – which meant that my basic training ran over the winter months, with the prospect of weeks roughing it outdoors in the rain, frost and snow, not to mention cross-country treks in heavy kit through the bleak gloom of Dartmoor and Woodbury Common.

Signing up hadn't been easy. Everyone seemed to be telling me that I'd made a mistake and should instead go for the easier options of the army or the navy. 'You'll do nowt with the Marines, lad,' one local sage warned me. 'John [so-and-so] down the road didn't make it with the Marines and he's bigger and tougher than you are.' But stubbornness is definitely a trait in the Nordass DNA, so I persevered, though I'd be a liar if I didn't admit that doubts still lingered at the back of my mind.

My parents took me to the train station in Hull, just south of Flamborough, and waved me off on my epic journey. I had never left East Yorkshire on my own before. I caught six different trains to cross England and arrived at CTCRM, or the Commando Training Centre Royal Marines, in Lympstone in Devon, just outside Exmouth and on the fringes of the great brooding mass that is Dartmoor. I should have read the telltale signs as the train pulled into the Royal Marines' own dedicated train station on the main Bristol line.

As I arrived from Exeter, in the mudflats below the station by the River Ex, a squad was being taken on a 'mud run' while the tide was out. This involved running through mud and sucking sludge that often came up to your knees.

As I sat on the train and looked at the struggling, miserable and exhausted troops, I didn't realise that it was my first glimpse of 'beasting', the age-old process by which corporals and sergeants assess their new recruits, test their limits and gauge their leadership abilities. To add a little pride to the exhausting exercise, the recruits were being forced to use their footprints in the sticky mud to spell out the name of their unit, '124 Troop' or '238 Troop'. What I didn't know then, but would quickly learn, was that the poor bastards, covered from head to toe in muck and slime, would have to combat-march back to their billets and then restore their kit to pristine and gleaming condition via the 'static tank'. This was a vast concrete tank of freezing water where troops had to dive in and wash off excess mud. It was also used as part of the assault course, with soldiers in full kit having to crawl across a five-centimetre-thick rope suspended over the tank – they had to dangle from the rope over the water and then 'regain' their position at the top of the rope and cross to the other side of the water tank.

To the left of the train, the ground rose in a steady hill towards a complex of five-storey concrete buildings. The assault courses, for which the Commandos are famous, were clearly visible from the train, and they were already covered with young men in combat fatigues marching, running and doing press-ups while being screamed at by ferocious-looking members of the training cadre. Three weeks later, I wondered why I just didn't stay on board the train and keep going. But in reality, I knew precisely why I shot off the train like a scalded cat and reported to my recruit corporal, and why I stayed over the next nine months no matter how tough the training became. Where else would I go? I wanted to be a Commando and nothing they could throw at me or do to me was going to change that fact. They could send me home if I failed the course, but I would not quit.

The Royal Marine Commandos, like the British Army as a whole, take a very different approach to their soldiers than, say, the French Foreign Legion, who are notorious for bullying and brutalising their trainees into efficient fighting machines. They will make you a soldier, sometimes whether you want to be one or not. In the Commandos, it was all about training you to become the best soldier you could possibly be. Sure, discipline was sometimes enforced at the end of a fist or boot. But the corporals and sergeants really wanted to train you rather than bully you. They weren't going to force you; if they reckoned you couldn't cut it or weren't up to scratch, you simply didn't make the King's Squad, the select bunch of recruits who actually go on to become Royal Marines and wear the famous Green Beret.

The Commando training centre at Lympstone was world-famous for a number of reasons. The assault courses here were judged the toughest in the world, and basic Royal Marine recruit training was also the longest and most detailed of any combat infantry unit within NATO. It was also the only specialised infantry training centre where ordinary ranks and officers trained over precisely the same assault courses, except that officers were expected to perform the same tasks faster, better and under more stress than the men they were to command. Many of the Commando tasks and assault courses dated back to World War II and Churchill's famous demand for a seaborne elite infantry striking force. They hadn't changed much, largely because old salts reckoned that if these courses could produce soldiers good enough to fight the crack German SS divisions, why bother changing them?

I was a junior Marine in a recruit troop, number 124 troop. There were around fifty of us, drawn from all over England, Scotland, Wales and Ireland. From the very beginning, we had to re-learn everything we thought we knew. How to shave. How to iron. How to keep your kit and gear clean and tidy. How to dress. How to make your bed. How to wash. How to shower. At one point, a training corporal took us into the shower block, stripped off in front of us and proceeded to wash every nook, cranny and orifice he had in a flurry of soapy lather and water. We stood, wide-eyed and open-mouthed, as he told us in no uncertain fashion that this was precisely how we would shower in future. There was only one way of doing things from now on – the Commando way.

We were basically taught how to do what we would ordinarily have thought impossible. How to go beyond the bounds of physical endurance and psychological tolerance. It started slowly and then built up to the hell of true Commando training. The first fortnight was all about memorising everything you needed to know about how the Marines operated. How to salute, how to march, how to clean and fire your rifle.

One of the funniest things was the medical screening procedure. Every recruit had to receive various inoculations for things like tetanus, or the bugs they might be likely to encounter in various deployment zones around the world. Our individual medical histories were checked and then we were all marched down to the medic's office for a series of jabs. All the inoculations were given in one go. It was hilarious to see this group of superbly fit, potentially elite soldiers nervously standing outside the medic's office, and then see one or two collapse with fright at the thought of receiving so many jabs.

We were each also assigned an SLR 7.62mm assault rifle, basically Britain's copy of the famed Belgian FNA1 rifle. We had to memorise the serial number of the rifle and ensure that it was always in gleaming condition. 'Your rifle is an extension of your arm. Treat it with the same respect,' our drill instructor roared at us. We also learned to strip that weapon down to its component parts and reassemble it in seconds. When I arrived in Lympstone, the SLR had already been in production since 1953 and, because of its weight and size, was slowly in the process of being replaced by the much lighter SA-80. But that wasn't much comfort to us recruits, lugging the 4.45kg SLR weapon around in the ditches, marshes and mudflats of Devon.

For the third week, we moved towards the outdoor training segments that the Royal Marines had made world-famous. In fact, the phrase 'Commando assault course' originated from the extreme physical training programmes devised here. These courses were aimed at testing both man and equipment to the very limit. If you couldn't pass these courses, you couldn't become a Royal Marine. And it was gauged that Royal Marines should be able to live and operate outdoors irrespective of the weather or season. The first thing we learned was to get used to being wet and miserable. Our initial exercise was called 'First Step', and we lived for days on end in freezing bivouacs on Woodbury Common, a large area of gorse and woodland bordered by the River Ex, about 7km inland from Lympstone. On one occasion, we were forced to break the ice in frozen potholes to shave because our drill instructor didn't want his recruits letting down the honour of the Commandos by having stubble on their chins!

It didn't help that the winter of 1978 was extremely harsh, with heavy frosts and frequent snowfalls. The only hot food we had was cooked in situ in mess tins, using Hexamine blocks, basically like an intensely hot firelighter. While the hot meals were really welcome, we grew to hate the routine of having to clean the cooking utensils which, because of the Hexamine, were left coated in a thick, tar-like substance. Adding further misery was the fact that, because our operation was deemed to be a realistic field exercise, we had to leave absolutely no sign of our presence. Camp areas had to be pristine when we left, and any waste carried with us. It was a very steep learning curve and fresh recruits like us made lots of mistakes. Looking back, I reckon we left a trail through Woodbury Common like a herd of wild elephants. A blind man could have tracked us. But the drill instructors weren't forgiving, and mistakes were heavily punished. Slowly but surely, we began to learn.

Our second exercise was called 'Hunter's Moon', a very fanciful name for an operation specialising in pure misery. It was just before our Christmas leave in 1978 and there was a heavy hoarfrost on the ground. 'Hunter's Moon' was a non-tactical exercise and was to cover basic patrolling techniques as well as camouflage and concealment. One night, we were brought to the main training team's tent and told to sit around and enjoy a so-called 'sod's opera' – this is where the team and the recruits can lampoon each other's personalities. Some of the lads unwisely did too good a job of aping the training team, and paid for their cheek afterwards in the various drills and exercises. The corporals got to show us a lighter side to their otherwise stoic exteriors and put on a good show.

The whole affair was designed to build us into a team or a family of men. There were some lads sent out to keep watch in a sentry position and we were all introduced to the 'martial art of Spoons'. This is probably one of the favourite social exercises for corporals – and their way of getting revenge on any of the recruits who are a little too clever for their own good. The game involves two recruits being taken out to the front and blindfolded. They each then have a dessertspoon placed in their teeth and take it in turns to tap each other on the head with the gripped spoon. What one unlucky recruit doesn't realise is that when he bends his head for his turn to get whacked, one of the corporals has a heavy ladle concealed behind his back, and he steps forward and gives the lad a whack. Thirty years on, I can still hear the 'crack' of the ladle on skin and bone. Take it from me, it bloody hurts. The recruit who has just been hit is then determined to inflict the same pain on his unwitting opponent. I have seen lads chip teeth because they think the opposite guy is a better hitter than they are.

From the very beginning, we realised that if one of us in our team screwed up, we all paid the price. Punishments were meted out to all the troop, not individuals, though a personal cock-up would also be greeted with a punch or a boot for good measure. It taught unit solidarity. None of us wanted to let down our mates. But mistakes were inevitable. Once, at Okehampton on Dartmoor, we were told to dig trenches as part of an elaborate defence exercise. It was back-breaking work, because you had to contend not only with rocky soil, but gravel and compacted clay. I almost lost the top off my finger after an accident with a knife while heading out on the exercise; by the end of the week, the finger was stinking like I had gangrene because I chose not to see a medic for fear I would miss the exercise. The corporal later came around to check the depth of the fire trenches and the camouflage arrangements. He had a long metal pole for checking the trench depth, and my foxhole, unfortunately, came out a few centimetres too shallow. 'Take your helmet off,' he ordered. I immediately complied and took off my tin helmet, wondering precisely what was coming next. Without blinking, the corporal swung the heavy metal pole over his shoulder and cracked it down on my skull. Dazed, I staggered and fell to my knees, blood oozing from a cut on my scalp. But I never again dug my foxhole too shallow.

Mistakes on exercises were generally dealt with on the spot. I once screwed up a perimeter instruction from my corporal who, just to underline the importance of listening to instructions, carefully sprayed CS gas straight into my face. As I writhed in agony, tears streaming from my burning, reddened eyes, the suddenly sympathetic corporal provided a canteen of water for me to wash my face with, knowing full well that water merely prolonged and worsened the irritation. It was sadistic, but that was how you learned not to make the same mistake twice.

Other mistakes around the base resulted in recruits being told to use blunt knives to strip the white paint off copper toilet fittings back at their billet and polish the brass work underneath. When the fittings were finally gleaming, the recruits were told to paint the fixtures white – and the process started all over again.

Keeping equipment in order was like a religious commandment. During exercises, if even a slight trace of food or tar from the Hexamine cooking tablets was found on a mess tin, it was thrown into the deepest, thickest gorse or bramble bush. The offending Marine was then ordered to retrieve the mess tin from the thicket on his hands and knees. Trust me when I say you learned not to make that mistake again.

The errors that seemed to freak out the drill instructors most were the perceived offences against hygiene. I guess the thinking was that if you couldn't comply with simple instructions about personal cleanliness and kit maintenance, how the hell could you be trusted with millions of pounds worth of equipment and, ultimately, decisions about life and death in a combat zone? If you were sloppy in the small things, the chances were you would be sloppy in the big things. During one spot inspection, a young lad was caught hiding some underwear that he had not washed properly and in accordance with regulations. The offending underpants were pinned to a noticeboard near the main parade ground and the poor chap was humiliated in front of everyone. But that recruit – and everyone else who witnessed the punishment – ensured afterwards that their kit was always clean, washed and put away in the regulation stowage area and folded to the regulation size and shape.

The worst time was the mornings. At five o'clock, when it was pitch black, wet and freezing outside, you'd open your eyes, look at your watch and think: Oh Christ, not any more, not again. You desperately wanted it all to end, but there was no end in sight. The trick, I found, was to try and keep it all in the day. Dreaming about home or Christmas leave seemed to make matters worse, so I kept focused on taking each day as it came and getting through the training.

I also learned why the older Commandos used the slang phrase 'Nods' for us young recruits. The woollen cap comforters that kept us warm on the moors and made Commandos famous in World War II, became a torture when worn in the classroom because the heat they generated made it all the more difficult to stay awake. Their shape is made by a three-way fold, and as the itchy fabric worked its way loose, they were a dead giveaway for sleepy recruits. When the rubbernecking started, the floppy unfolded and the woollen garment bounced all over the trainee's head.

What I was amazed to discover was that most people who quit or failed basic training did so because they couldn't handle the mental side of things. They could successfully negotiate brutal assault courses and deal with all of the heavy physical demands thrown at them. But they simply couldn't take the constant assault on their mental processes that the Commandos reckon is an even greater part of training – the unrelenting series of impossible demands, the constant search by drill instructors for mental weaknesses, and the seemingly unfair, often arbitrary way that some recruits were singled out. Like sharks sniffing blood in the water, the Corporals would sense a weakness or personal failing, and slowly increase the pressure until the recruit either cracked or proved he could hack it.

All this combined to slowly take its toll. Some men can cope, some cannot. It was years later that I fully understood that the Commandos wanted the training to be bad, stressful, unfair and gut-wrenchingly difficult so that when it came to combat, soldiers would be able to cope admirably. In most cases, and I mean this quite honestly, soldiers welcome combat rather than training because in the former, the support systems are there to work in your favour rather than to make your life more difficult, as in training.

The most daunting thing at CTC, was seeing so many injured guys hobbling around the base. There were recruits with casts on their legs or on their arms, and even a few with their heads bandaged. Virtually everyone seemed to be showing a bruise of some kind. One of the endurance marches was nicknamed the 'Nutcracker' by Commandos because, having completed it, recruits had so many blisters and sores on their feet that they walked gingerly around like a cowboy from *Brokeback Mountain* who had had a date with a donkey. The poor bastards hobbling around on raw feet also looked like they'd just been castrated. 'The only other time in your life when you walk like that is when you've been kicked in the balls by a combat boot,' one sergeant wryly observed.

You also learned to think like a Marine. Midway through basic training, we heard that some Royal Navy guys were in a billet near ours at HMS *Raleigh* in Cornwall. Being young and stupid, we got involved in a pillow fight for the honour of the Marines. Some of the pillows burst and made a mess that was impossible to clean, as the carpets seemed to be made from Velcro. When our drill instructors returned to base from having been on the piss in Plymouth, they heard all about it and decided to make an example. The entire training cadre were really annoyed, as if our actions were a direct reflection on them. We were all ordered into combats at three in the morning and, with full kit, ordered on to the parade ground for a series of marches, assault-course runs and a variety of press-ups and stress exercises. It continued until we began to collapse, one by one. By five o'clock we were screaming with the pain of having to use muscles that were tied in knots with cramp. But we were ordered to keep going and when our bodies began to fail us, the drill teams cut loose with their fists and boots. 'Next time don't use pillows like a bunch of fucking girls,' one sergeant seethed.

A mate of mine was singled out as one of the ringleaders and, when he couldn't perform any more press-ups in front of the base petty officer, he got a kick full in the face from his troop Officer's boot. The following morning, as we all hobbled to the parade ground, the same Officer challenged him about the mangled condition of his face. 'What happened to your face?' the officer inquired. 'You booted me, Sir,' came the reply through bruised lips. The instructor bellowed again, 'What happened to your face?' The startled recruit answered, 'You booted me, Sir, on the parade ground.' The instructor now levelled his face with the recruit and, eyeball to eyeball, screamed, 'WHAT HAPPENED TO YOUR FACE?' The penny suddenly dropped as terror kick-started the recruit's brain. He answered: 'I fell, Sir.' 'Very good, move on,' came the Officer's satisfied reply.

We made it through an urban warfare/riot control exercise called 'Coiled Spring', which was supposed to prepare us for the harsh reality of Northern Ireland.

One aspect of it basically consisted of us recruits donning shields, riot helmets and protective equipment and then having another troop of recruits, brought up specially from Lympstone, pelting us with bottles, stones and bricks. For us the highlight of Coiled Spring came when the same bullying Officer ignored his own instructions and strayed too close to the rear of our ranks during the riot phase. He wasn't wearing proper protective gear and took a brick full in the head; the Green Beret he was wearing wasn't as bullet-proof as he thought it was. He was hospitalised for so long that he missed the rest of our training programme, all the way to the passing-out parade.

Our biggest enemy was always exhaustion. My lowest moments came when I was physically wrecked and feared that I couldn't take much more. The instructors had the exhaustion factor down to a fine art. Every recruit would be singled out for stress and attitude testing immediately after a major exercise – at times it resembled a pack of wolves circling a hapless sheep. You knew what was coming and couldn't do anything to avoid it. But I understood precisely what was going on, and I knew that, once they were finished with me, they would move on to the next recruit. The key factor was not to react; just do the best you could to comply with their orders and remember that many of the tasks you were being given were impossible to fulfil. And the troop sergeants knew that. Slowly, I learned to try and see beyond the pain and misery. Throughout it all, you prayed that you'd be accepted into the Marines and make King's Squad.

Funnily enough, parade-ground drill itself was a welcome relief. The Royal Marines take enormous pride in their parade-ground precision, and hours upon hours are devoted to fine-tuning the craft. Drill Leaders (DLs) are also natural comedians, though you didn't need a sense of humour to find our initial efforts absolutely hilarious. Most of us struggled just to tell our left from our right and at the start, any attempt at a mildly complicated manoeuvre would inevitably end in chaos, with recruits going the wrong way and tripping over one another. But at least we could laugh at ourselves, and that lifted the overall mood of training. In the end, we looked forward to parade-ground drill as a welcome relief from the misery of Woodbury Common, Dartmoor and the assault courses. And, as the hours of parade-ground practice progressed, we got better and better, though we all hated standing around on cold and frosty mornings, shivering while we were being inspected for minutely detailed errors in dress and bearing.

Because I was so young – some of the other recruits were five years older than me – I was given two chances to opt for quitting during my training period. Most recruits were only afforded one chance to quit training, about midway through the programme. But, because I was only seventeen, the policy was to give me two chances to quit. I rejected both within a second of them being offered. My biggest fear was no longer the demands of training but of failing the course and being sent home to train as a brickie, a carpenter or an electrician.

My billet, known to Marines as "Grots", comprised five other lads, and the six of us were trained to operate as a single unit. We ate together, worked together, suffered together and bled together. We came from varying backgrounds – tough inner-city lads, middle-class guys who just wanted to prove themselves, and me, from a quiet part of rural Yorkshire. After five months of training, I was the only one of the six to make King's Squad. Of the fifty-odd lads who gathered at Lympstone train station that Halloween day, just twenty-four of us ultimately made it into the Royal Marine Commandos.

By the middle phase of our course we had lost so many recruits from 124 Troop that we were going to be amalgamated with the troop who were one week behind us in the training schedule, 125A Troop. We were told that we did not have to go through this lost week again in order for them to catch up; instead we would have a so-called 'buffer week', which would be fun and relaxed. We would have a really enjoyable time, we were told – and most of us were stupid enough to believe it.

We were going to do a sports 'free-fall' at the Royal Marines Free Fall School in Honiton, Devon. We were also going to Portsmouth to see the Royal Marines Museum at Southsea, as well as doing the helicopter 'dunking drills' at HMS *Vernon*. This was where the Navy pilots learned how to get out of capsized, sinking helicopters designed to simulate a ditching at sea. And, finally, we would do a small navigation exercise to practise our map-reading skills. This was to be a week I would never forget. 'Compass Rose' was the exercise, and though it might sound romantic and exciting, it proved to be yet another pit of misery because of rain, snow and freezing temperatures. It was my first experience of what it is like to be in genuine fear of not getting through the night alive. Our kit was deliberately taken from the previous Royal Marine generation, which meant that it was heavy, was in no way waterproof and functioned only half as well as the kit issued to Commando units. The central facet of Compass Rose was being able to map-read and navigate at night. Needless to say, we got hopelessly lost and ended up trekking miles farther in the pouring rain than we should have, and sleep was something you did on leave periods.

On return to our bivouacs in the middle of the forest, we were supposed to strip the outer layers of water-sodden clothing and get into our dry outer layers from our large pack – the 'large' pack should actually be called a very small pack. The black bin liners were not adequate as waterproofing bags and so the clothes inside were wet through as well as the ones you were wearing. You were meant to have a dry night in your sleeping bag (slug), but that was not waterproofed either, and was now very wet, extremely heavy and annoyingly uncomfortable. It did teach me one thing that night, wet or not, it is better than nothing at all. I spent the whole night wiggling my toes to keep them warm, listening to the rain falling on my two-man 'bivouac' and avoiding the droplets coming through the holes in the not-waterproof poncho liner that we used as the tent material.

You do feel very alone up to the point when the sentry gives you the famous 'foot shake' to let you know it is your turn to go outside, put back on your original set of wet clothes, now even more thoroughly drenched, and go back out into the night to stand sentry – on the lookout for the 'enemy', played by the training team, who, because it was raining, didn't bother that night.

It was also in this week that they gave us a live chicken to look after – at the end of the week we were supposed to kill it and cook it for supper, with some potatoes and onions. In the end our corporal killed it for us – and, to make a point about being tough, he didn't wring the poor chicken's neck or even cut its throat with his combat knife; no, he ripped its head clean off with his teeth.

The parachuting was a disaster because it was exceptionally windy. Hours were wasted being made to do silly things to each other for the sadistic amusement of the training corporals, and half of us never even got to jump. Portsmouth, however, was good and a welcome relief, while the Royal Marines Museum (now closed) in Southsea, joined to the then Eastney barracks, reminded us precisely why we had opted for the Commandos as our chosen path.

The helicopter 'dunking drills' were something entirely different. They were also something we were simply not ready for. At HMS Vernon, in Old Portsmouth, we went into a huge circular water tower and got into some old overalls, a life-jacket and a helmet. In groups of six or so, we sat in the shell of an old Wessex helicopter, suspended on robotically operated hydraulic arms and strapped ourselves into the seats. We were briefed as to what to expect and what to do once the cycle was underway. We were to hold on to a window exit for orientation, so you knew how to get out, and as the water slowly passed your chin, you were supposed to take a deep breath, wait until the simulator was completely submerged, stopped and upside-down! Then you followed your arm, pulled yourself out and swam to the surface. You had to do this three separate times. The water was freezing and the one 'deep breath' before submerging became lots of panicky small ones.

On our first attempt, one lad was a bit apprehensive and so was given a dry bag to wear. This is a suit that keeps you totally dry inside and traps any excess air, therefore creating a more buoyant approach to the surface from the bottom of the tank. But he took off his strap as the chopper started to rotate, totally panicked and, not knowing where to get out, just ran around in the chopper as it slowly sank to the bottom of the tank. Because of the air in his suit, he was pinned to the roof of the chopper in its upside-down state and had to wait till it surfaced again. We all just sat there, apprehensive, scared and cold, but we knew we had to follow the instructions. People like him could have caused us all to panic and, in real life, we might all have drowned because of one man. The next six recruits went down and under and we saw them all escape and swim to the surface with a single exception – a recruit called Simmo was stuck inside, and neither he nor the safety diver could get his seatbelt released. So the poor guy just went down and back up throughout the whole cycle, strapped inside the flooded helicopter. When it came to the surface, he was just sat there as cool as a cucumber – you just had to admire his cojones. What was supposed to be a fun week ended up being one of the worst of our entire training cycle.

Basic training took a total of thirty weeks, aside from a brief period of Christmas leave, Easter leave and not including the extra 'Fun week'. The real crunch came in the twenty-eighth week. The entire seven days were devoted to a gruelling series of Commando tests, and if you failed any one of these, you had to go 'back troop', which meant returning and repeating the entire basic training programme again from the point where the next troop coming behind were at. I don't think I could construct a single worse nightmare than having to repeat basic training. Even now, thirty years on, it's enough to make my hair stand on end. The bottom line was that everything we had endured since 31 October 1978 had led up to this single week in June. And we would now discover precisely why Commando assault-course training had become a by-word globally for military fitness and efficiency.

There were five major challenges: a ground-assault course and a Tarzan-style aerial assault course, both of which had to be completed within a specific timeframe; a combined Tarzan-assault course; fourthly, the dreaded endurance course; and finally, a fifty-kilometre forced march over Dartmoor that had to be completed in under eight hours (something that our troop was the first to re-instigate). If anything, it was the endurance course that was the ultimate measure of Commandos and was judged to finally separate the men from the boys. It tested physical strength, endurance and teamwork. Even experienced Commandos didn't take the challenge lightly. The fact that it came at the end of an exhausting series of tests only made it more difficult.

The endurance test, as was usual, took place on a Saturday morning. We wore relatively light kit, weighing 'only' 14kg, with the SLR rifle another 4kg. We walked to Woodbury Common, about 6km from the base, where the course and test began. The recruits were paired off and released on to the assault course at timed intervals. The entire course was 10km long and studded with bone-jarring obstacles and challenges. The first was a series of twenty-metre-long tunnels, buried deep into the ground. The tunnels were so narrow that it was only with great difficulty that a soldier wearing full kit could push his way through. Your rifle had to be carefully tucked alongside your body – if it wasn't, it would snag on the tunnel roof or sides and block your progress. To make matters worse, jagged rocks were set deliberately into the floor of the tunnel to ensure you were cut and bleeding by the time you finally emerged from the end.

And you had to work as a two-man team. After several more obstacles, you then reached a chest-deep bog, known to Commandos as 'Peter's

Pool'. You had to carry your rifle over your head to protect it. You also somehow had to use an overhead rope to slowly drag yourself through the clinging mass. When you emerged wet, sodden, chafing and tired, you ran for a further kilometre or so before you faced an obstacle that was universally dreaded – the flooded tunnel. This was basically a length of wide piping, whose entrance was underneath a gushing pool. The only way to negotiate it was for your teammate to grab you by the collar and physically stuff you underwater and into the flooded concrete tube. By shoving and pushing your legs, he also helped you get through the tunnel.

This was a hugely daunting challenge for virtually every recruit, especially for those uncertain about water or enclosed spaces. Most recruits who failed to complete the endurance course failed at this obstacle. Luckily, I found the worst part was going underwater and just being shoved into the pipe. Once you were inside, the water pressure pulled you through quite quickly. The instant you exited at the other end of the tunnel, you had to drag yourself back to the entrance and repeat the shoving and pushing favour for your teammate. Only when both of you had successfully gone through the tunnel could you go on to complete the course individually.

The boots of thousands of Commandos who had completed the endurance course over the decades had gouged deep tracks near some of the water obstacles, and these gullies sapped the remaining energy from your battered and bloodied limbs. The actual endurance course distance was just 3km, but it felt much more like 20km. Once back through the Woodbury copse, you had to run the 6km back to Lympstone. At the base, you raced to the firing ranges, checked your SLR to ensure the barrel was clear and then fired ten rounds at pre-arranged targets. Seven of the ten rounds had to be within specified target limits. If they were – and if your time was within the eighty-minute endurance course limit – then you had passed the single most gruelling Commando challenge.

Needless to say, no one was content to allow us to savour the moment. The very next day was the scheduled speed-march – 50km (30 miles) across the hills, dykes, streams and bogs of Dartmoor. This had to be completed in full combat kit and within a strict eight-hour limit. But any thought we had of feeling sorry for ourselves was tempered by the realisation that anyone undertaking the corporal's promotion course in years to come, had to undertake a similar march, but with each group of six carrying a telegraph pole, euphemistically called a 'log', between them for good measure, though not for so long a distance, admittedly. Thankfully, it would be another eight years before I'd have to face that task. I think most of us were so relieved to have completed the endurance task that we got through the speed-march on a rush of adrenalin. Anyone who had problems with the previous Commando task programme still had a final chance at redemption: the day after the speed-march, anyone could retake the courses that they had just failed. But it had to be done within twenty-four hours – a Herculean challenge if ever there was one. If you failed, you were 'back-trooped'. My mate Simmo attempted the march twice over the course of two days – and failed it both times. He was back-trooped and had to repeat a major section of his training rota, which he eventually managed after a total of 150km and three attempts.

That speed-march saw me truly come into my own. I think I finally realised that I'd made the grade, and the military career I had dreamed about for so long was suddenly within touching distance. Being young, I was bouncing back from the physical demands much better than some of the other lads. During the march, I found myself helping a few lads who were struggling, assisting them with their weapons and their kit. Some of them were so shagged they could hardly stay standing, let alone speed-march with their kit. It would have been very easy to say 'fuck them' and leave them behind, content to focus on preserving my own energy. But I'd sweated blood and tears with these guys and I desperately wanted all of us to make it. It never even entered my head to abandon them, so I dropped back and helped the lads, dragging them bodily along at times as we raced to make it back within the time limit.

The training cadre noted what was happening and, when the names were confirmed of those who had made the grade and were rotating to King's Squad, I was thrilled to discover my name was among them.

31

Better still, I was being awarded a special Commando medal for having met the best training traditions of the Royal Marines. I discovered later that the Commandos take ferocious pride in never leaving a man behind in combat – and, without knowing it, by dropping back to help the stragglers in the speed-march I had done precisely what the training team were trying to teach us. We were no longer individuals, we were Commandos, who were expected to live, fight and, if necessary, die together as a single, proud unit.

I would pass out the next week in full-dress blues and with the honour of being the recruit displaying truest Commando spirit among my intake and was awarded the commando medal in front of my parents. King's Squad is basically what we had all spent the previous twenty-nine weeks dreaming about. To be in King's Squad means that you have made it through training; you are officially deemed worthy to be a Royal Marine Commando, and now you are simply being polished up for your induction parade. The week was spent on kit preparation and elaborate parade drills for the Lympstone ceremony. King's Squad also had certain privileges denied to ordinary recruits and, after the misery and pain of the previous few months, I can still recall the pride and satisfaction of that one single week.

Having my parents present for my passing-out parade was an added bonus, and I was especially proud for my dad because I knew he under-stood from his Royal Navy days exactly what I had just achieved. When the famous Green Beret was finally placed on my head, I thought my chest would burst with pride. I stood ramrod straight on the parade ground, determined to savour every last second of the ceremony. All my teenage doubts seemed to vanish as I revelled in the fact 'the best of the best' thought me worthy of being a member. I had taken the worst the training team could throw at me – and come through it all with honours.

After all the uncertainty of school and wondering about finding my true niche in life, I had finally arrived. The world was suddenly my oyster, and, still just seventeen, I felt virtually bullet-proof. Yet the funny part was that, once I had been assigned to my unit, Four-Two Commando, the pace was hard to deal with because it was so slow compared to what we had endured at Lympstone!

And I am the first to admit, when looking back at those first few months, the slow pace and mundane routines of run, range, NAAFI break and kit inspections set in a large amount of lethargy, hard to shake off.

3

YELLOW RIVER TO HONG KONG NEON

Having passed out with King's Squad and finally become a Royal Marine Commando, I felt I had fully paid my dues. I had taken the best that the training team could throw at me – and I hadn't quit. I'd been bruised, cut, exhausted and frozen to the point of hypothermia. But I'd stuck with it. And now, officially, I was a Commando. Only someone who has gone through these extreme courses can understand the pride you take in putting on that famous Green lid and wearing those Royal Marine Commando shoulder flashes. What I didn't realise was that to both Royal Marine officers and, even more importantly, to the sergeant majors, I was still just one step above a raw recruit. Marines who had been in Units for a few years were called 'sweats' and we lads, fresh from the factory, were just 'sproggs' or 'skin', until the bristle was rough and new lads from the recruiting base kindly took your place.

The major issue that arises after your passing-out parade is your first Commando assignment. The Royal Marines were divided into various distinct and specialised units. My drafting options were with Four-One Commando, based in Malta, now disbanded; Forty Commando, which was the jungle warfare unit, then based in Crownhill, Plymouth; Four-Two (42) Commando, the Arctic warfare unit, based on the edge of Dartmoor at Bickleigh; or Four-Five (45) Commando Group, which undertook Arctic warfare as well as general support duties, based in Arbroath, Scotland; and 3 Commando Brigade, based in Stonehouse barracks, Plymouth, Devon.

I reckoned that I'd get whatever assignment I opted for. After all, I had just received my troop's 'Commando Medal'; surely, if anyone was to get a preference it would be me? Unfortunately, my plans didn't quite gel with those of my commanding officer. My first preferences were for a warship detachment or assignment to Forty Commando for jungle warfare training, because of its exotic and exciting reputation. But I wasn't alone in this – virtually all the lads wanted to join that unit. After a winter spent marching around in the mud, slime, frost and snow of Dartmoor and Woodbury Common, I had seen enough Arctic conditions to last me a lifetime. Today, in hindsight, I laugh at how my Royal Marine career has been inextricably linked to cold, wet and miserable conditions. Back in June 1978, I fancied that jungle warfare would be an interesting challenge and, I reckoned, at least I'd be warm most of the time and I'd deploy overseas which, at seventeen years of age, was my dream.

The assignment I was praying for was on board a warship. I thought a ship deployment meant two things – you always had a comfortable billet on board and, because the ship was on deployment, you got to see a pretty big slice of the world. If you were really lucky, your warship could be attached to a major exercise in the Far East, the Pacific or the Caribbean, and you'd get your shore leave somewhere exciting. It might sound a little simplistic, but that was a huge issue for me. I knew, however, that warship assignments were generally given to more experienced Commandos – probably because older, wiser salts were less likely to cause the mayhem in port that a seventeen-year-old like myself would revel in. There was also the problem that a ship assignment did not lend itself to the practical infantry instruction that every young recruit was expected to focus on. In later life, I'd learn that a ship deployment was the polar opposite of exciting, and actually dreaded by most experienced Commandos.

Needless to say, it was sod's law – and I got the one assignment I didn't want: Four-Two (42) Commando and long periods of Arctic warfare. 'Get married quick and have kids before your balls freeze off,' was the advice of one veteran when he saw the appalled look on my face. The only silver lining I could think of was that at least I would be taught how to ski, which was some small consolation. Four-Two Commando is based at Bickleigh barracks in Plymouth, Devon, so the only other consolation – and a very small one at that – was that at least I wouldn't have far to relocate from Lympstone, as Bickleigh was just down the road. However, somewhat ominously, it was also located right on the edge of Dartmoor which, despite its wild and desolate beauty, I had by now come to hate with a passion. Little did I know I would effectively operate here for the next eighteen years.

Of course, what all new soldiers want is action, and what I didn't fully realise was that the Arctic warfare units were, in reality, the front-line troops, and the most likely to deploy if Britain ever got involved in a shooting row anywhere in the world. They were also the units that supplied most of the men for the specialist Royal Marine assault groups as well as the water-borne equivalent to the SAS, the Special Boat Service (SBS). And I would be a liar if I didn't admit that joining this elite group was the dream of every young Commando worth their salt.

I arrived at Four-Two Commando at a time when the unit was somewhat depleted. When the Commandos were being deployed to Northern Ireland it had become the norm to transfer experienced soldiers from other units to bolster the detachment going to Ulster. When I left Lympstone, Forty Commando was heading to Northern Ireland for an extended tour, at a time when the so-called 'Troubles' were reaching previously unimagined levels of violence and bloodshed. The IRA were becoming lethally efficient and British units deploying there weren't taking any chances. So, to ensure that the maximum number of Marines undertaking the tour had vital experience, older Commandos were temporarily transferred from Four-Two to Forty. It was a process dubbed 'mothering' for the younger recruits, many of whom were undertaking their first tour of Northern Ireland.

As a consequence, the majority of recruits leaving Lympstone were diverted to Four-Two Commando as direct replacements. I arrived in June 1979, and my biggest fear was that I'd be on a training rotation for a year or more before securing an overseas deployment. I was assigned to K Company and my first few weeks were spent integrating. I was in with a decent bunch of lads, and a mountain leader (ML) who was as tough as nails, but scrupulously fair. I'd heard over the years – especially from my dad – that the sergeants and petty officers were the backbone of the British armed forces. I was beginning to learn that a good sergeant was worth three good generals. These guys turned orders into reality, and most seemed to be chiselled from the same block of granite. You made an enemy of a sergeant at your peril – and, secretly, I knew that one day I too wanted to make that grade.

Initially, we did a lot of running, a lot of live-fire exercises and a good bit of classroom work focused on tactical stuff: how to detect an ambush, how to lay an ambush, how to respond to a flanking move, how to secure a beach head. Great emphasis was also placed on FIBUA (Fighting In Built-Up Areas) exercises. We all knew that, in the long run, this meant that they were blooding us for a tour to Northern Ireland. The other major training we undertook was called 'SpearHead', and this is undertaken by every British unit in line for imminent overseas deployment. At any given time, at least one major unit is on SpearHead and ready to ship out at a moment's notice. We knew that once we were on SpearHead we could go anywhere, and more than a few of the older guys kept a wary eye each evening on developments in Northern Ireland on the BBC News. Being young, I was getting sick of all the training and wondered when I would get the chance to put it all into practice.

While the training was tough, it was nothing like as ferocious as at Lympstone. I also began to make a few friends – and we now had proper leisure time to ourselves. For the most part, I went into town on leave at weekends with the other lads and did what young soldiers do: got pissed, got into the odd scrap and did my level best to impress the local ladies. I wasn't one of those who went looking for a brawl every time he got pissed, but I wasn't going to stand by either and watch a mate get whacked without going to help him. Again, my size was my biggest enemy – whenever there was a row in a bar or club, anyone looking for aggro tended to target me. I'm not sure if they thought there were extra bonus points from fighting the biggest guy in the room. Of course, if someone acted the dick and wanted to prove how tough he was to his mates, I was happy to oblige and send him home bleeding.

As the trips into town became the highlight of our social life, some of the lads started doing steady lines with local girls. There was a tradition dating back almost four hundred years of soldiers and sailors marrying local girls – and I doubted if there was a single family here that didn't have some connection to the military. But I had no intention of getting serious with any lass no matter how good-looking she was. I was only starting out on my military career and, to be blunt, any female company I wanted was on a strictly no-strings-attached basis.

The major advantage of being in an Arctic warfare unit was that they had an almost annual deployment cycle to Norway. Bit of a no-brainer really – if you want to fight an Arctic war, you have to train in the Arctic. I heard that Norway wasn't easy; the training was tough, the conditions were harsh, there was an endless succession of near-Himalayan mountains that had to be climbed in full kit and you finished your deployment with a massive manoeuvre exercise that involved the pride of the Royal Norwegian Army, the Royal Dutch Marines, the Royal Marines and usually a strong detachment from the US Marine Corps. The inter-service rivalry was ferocious and unit pride was taken very seriously.

The unspoken attraction of a Norwegian deployment, we all knew, was Norwegian women. The Royal Marines traditionally deployed to northern Norway, usually around Narvik, the site of the famous World War II battle between Franco-British forces and German troops. These places were extremely remote and the local female population usually found several hundred love-starved and testosterone-laden Commandos a very welcome diversion in the depths of the grim Nordic winters. Apparently, our guys weren't too popular with the local Norwegian lads, which was perfectly understandable given the fact we were shagging their women. But, we all knew that Norwegian women were, by any standards, breathtakingly beautiful and surprisingly generous to young Marines.

Hence, I was praying for Norway and dreading Northern Ireland when, in August, we were all stunned to learn that we were, instead, heading for the heat and humidity of Hong Kong. Apparently, the People's Republic of China (PRC) had eased border security around Hong Kong and it was causing an illegal immigration deluge, nightmare.

It appears that the PRC were getting sick of waiting for Britain to pull out of Hong Kong and wanted to remind London that Beijing regarded the colony as a festering sore that would only be healed once it was firmly back in the PRC fold. I'd later learn that Beijing considered it a national disgrace that Hong Kong was being governed by Britain and wanted the colony back to save face. A handover date was apparently in the process of being confirmed, but Beijing clearly thought that a flood of illegal immigrants flowing across the border into Hong Kong might make London accelerate the timetable. I guess, from Beijing's point of view, anything that caused the Brits problems in Hong Kong was too good an opportunity to be missed.

The word about the easing of border security quickly spread and, within a matter of weeks, literally tens of thousands of Chinese immigrants were trying to flee across the border, attracted by the prospect of a new life away from hardline communist dogma in the PRC. What had started as a trickle quickly became a flood so dramatic that it threatened to undermine the very economy of Hong Kong. Immigrants were swimming across the Yellow River and scampering through the New Territories into Hong Kong city, while others were grasping anything that could float and trying to negotiate the harbour approaches to Kowloon. None of this could have happened without the tacit approval of the old men who had won power after the death of Mao Tse-Tung.

The Governor of Hong Kong, Sir Murray MacLehose, was very worried and advised the British authorities that something needed to be done about border security. Sir Murray had been Governor of Hong Kong since 1971 and was an experienced politician who had shrewdly guided the fortunes of the tiny enclave throughout the chaos of the Cultural Revolution just across the Chinese border. His word carried a lot of weight and his assessment of the situation was endorsed by the military commanders on the ground. It was immediately decided in Westminster to beef up Britain's military detachment to Hong Kong until the immigration issue was resolved.

Because Four-Two Commando was on SpearHead, we were immediately assigned to the job. It was felt that the border issue was strictly short-term and the bulk of the Royal Marine detachment would be back and available for use in Northern Ireland, if required, within a few months.

I was absolutely thrilled; I felt like pinching myself just to make sure I wasn't dreaming. Just a year ago I had left Yorkshire on my own for the first time; now I was about to spend a few months in Hong Kong, a place that most people could only fantasise about visiting. The deployment was given such a high priority that we flew out on an RAF VC-10 rather than going by ship. On that flight I had my first experience of the dramatic difference between training and operations. As the pilot announced we were flying over the Med, one of the lads – a Liverpudlian, nicknamed 'Scouse Keogh', of course – got stripped off, down to a towel and flip-flops, carrying his wash bag, ready for a shower, just for a laugh! An irate crew member had to escort him back to his seat, but the commanding officer didn't seem to mind. In fact, I thought I spotted him laughing along with the rest of the contingent at the antics of the lad. The training establishment always took inflexibility to new heights; but I learned that when you were on an operational deployment, senior officers tended to turn a blind eye to escapades that helped ease tension and didn't threaten discipline, security or the reputation of the Corps.

It reminded me of the famous story told about Julius Caesar when politicians from some Roman town came to him to complain about the drinking, brawling and whoring of soldiers from his crack Ninth Legion, who were off-duty and camped nearby. Caesar listened to their complaints before simply replying: 'My Legionnaires fight just as well when they're stinking of wine and perfume.'

Four-Two Commando deployed to Hong Kong that September with

four full companies: L, K, M and Support Company. My company, K, would work alongside M and Support Company on security along the border with the People's Republic. L Company would assist the Royal Navy and Hong Kong police in securing the colony's maritime approaches and would be based on Stone Cutter's Island in the harbour. Within one week of arriving, I was on patrol in the New Territories along the border with the PRC. I felt I was a real soldier at last. (Coincidentally, I celebrated my eighteenth birthday as we arrived in Hong Kong). We had been given a few days to acclimatise to the heat but, to be honest, they could have given us six months and we still would not have got used to it. I was assigned to observation patrol (OP) duties. Our job was to use sniper scopes and night sights to assess any movements along the border.

The numbers trying to get into Hong Kong were nothing short of astonishing. You could see thousands of people milling around in the hills and valleys on the PRC side – it was like watching an ant colony from a distance. Except that you knew these were people, checking out the best approach routes to get into Hong Kong. The border crossing was usually studied by small teams of three or four men, and we could clearly see them marking out their crossing route by the Yellow River. The illegal immigrants (II's in Marine parlance) usually tried to cross the border at night, they would then lie low in the undergrowth or reeds inside the Hong Kong border the following day and, once night had fallen again, they would try and sneak through to Kowloon, Hong Kong Island and Wanchai, which still lay another full day's march away. From what I could see, there was little or nothing being done on the PRC side to staunch the flow of immigrants.

Dozens of immigrants swam across the Yellow River with children strapped to their backs and their entire worldly belongings in a sack. Many of these poor people had travelled more than 3,000km to reach Hong Kong. The vast majority had walked most of the way, and what little money they had had been taken from them by the Triads for escorting them to the border. They were clearly desperate to get into Hong Kong in the hope of giving a better life to their children. But the minute they crossed the border and began to move around, we had them. The advent of individual weapon sights (IWS) and night-observation devices (NODs) had transformed the capabilities of infantrymen to operate in darkness. In future years, night-vision goggles would make operating at night only slightly more difficult than operating in full daylight, such were their capabilities. The second a Chinese immigrant began to move around in the reeds on the Hong Kong side, we zeroed in on them.

The policy then was to monitor them and, when they started to move away from the river and towards Hong Kong through the New Territories, we would move to intercept and detain them. A lot of them tried to run, but they simply had nowhere to go. There were so many coming across that you were almost guaranteed a 'catch' every night or day, depending on your duty rotation. We tried to be as gentle as we could because these people weren't criminals – they were simply trying to do the best they could for their families and children. In compliance with our orders, all detained immigrants had to have plastic handcuffs locked in place and the detained groups would then be loaded on to a Land Rover and driven back to the border crossing. In a curt ceremony, the immigrants would then be handed back to the PRC personnel. I have no idea what happened to these poor people afterwards – I like to think that they got a second chance to find the life they so desperately wanted, but I doubt it. There were too many stories going around about PRC guards setting dogs on them as they were unloaded from the trucks and herded back to where they came from.

We also never lost sight of the fact that the PRC undoubtedly had army teams watching us as intently as we were watching them. The hills on the Chinese side of the river were studded with military bases and observation posts, and everything that happened in Hong Kong was watched intently by the People's Liberation Army (PLA) commanders. The PLA may have outnumbered us by a factor of more than 100:1, but they regarded us as an elite infantry unit and we knew their watchers were determined to study our operating techniques, our weapons and our capabilities. There was no indication of confrontation – but none of us took that for granted. Just one accidental shooting could have sparked mayhem.

The hillside patrols themselves were monotonous rather than physically draining, but compared to Woodbury Common or Dartmoor, this was like a holiday camp. No one was intent on making your life a living hell, though a few corporals and sergeants still had their moments, particularly with us younger Commandos. I was fit enough and tough enough to handle the worst they could throw at me. Even though we didn't take any chances with security, we knew we weren't likely to experience any major threats from the job in hand. It was possible that an immigrant might be armed with a knife but, faced with an infantry squad armed with assault rifles, they simply tried to escape or, failing that, surrendered with the minimum of aggravation. The main problem we faced on a daily basis was the heat and the humidity. Even though we were issued jungle fatigues, we were still slowly roasting in our hillside perches. The humidity was something else – there were days when the heat and steam from the river valley made me suspect we were working in Mother Nature's very own steam room. Only by drinking litres of water could you avoid dehydration.

For the most part, we did stationary duty, watching the river – and proving a slap-up meal for the myriad of bugs and insects that swarmed all over the steaming terrain. Our OPs were usually logs arranged with camouflage netting over them to provide a disguised position. The monotony was broken by Commandos swapping duties. We even got a chance to work with the Land Rover on Quick Reaction Force (QRF) – the highlight of that duty was the cool air sweeping through the jeep as you drove around at breakneck speeds.

The other thing not lost on us were the contrasts. Here we were, trying to keep dirt-poor Chinese peasants out of the land of their dreams. The grim reality was that even if they managed to slip past our patrols they faced the 'joy' of a lifetime working in a Hong Kong sweatshop, a hotel kitchen or a laundry. And all for a few pence an hour. Yet, they would be in one of the world's greatest concentrations of wealth. Manufacturing, textiles, financial services and electronics had made Hong Kong one of the richest cities on earth, and everywhere you looked you could see evidence of that wealth. Some of the restaurants charged more for a single meal than I earned in an entire week. The local racetrack boasted some of the richest horse races in the world. And it was not unusual for wealthy Hong Kong residents to spend up to £1 million for a specialised car-licence plate simply because it was regarded as a lucky number. There were times when, as we sweated off the pounds in our sweltering hillside OP for our humble queen's shilling, I wondered who were the real mugs.

The main problem for the Hong Kong authorities was the sheer numbers involved in the illegal immigrant flood. At one point, there were almost four thousand people attempting to cross the border each month. If this was left unchecked, Hong Kong's economy would simply be swamped. There was also the sneaking suspicion that a few of those trying to get into Hong Kong might not actually be economic migrants, but political agitators operating to an agenda set in Beijing. This was 1979 and relations between Beijing and London were still quite cool. The PRC was determined to get Hong Kong back, and Britain was trying to negotiate a reasonable handover agreement, satisfactory to everybody before the old lease on the colony, signed with a nineteenth-century Chinese emperor, expired.

Within a few weeks of Four-Two Commando arriving, the flood of immigrants had been reduced to a trickle and the land border had been fully secured. In the space of just two months, Four-Two Commando had detained an estimated ten thousand illegal immigrants. The word quickly spread within the PRC that the Hong Kong border crossing was no longer an easy touch. When the question of II's began to threaten to hinder the handover timetable, Beijing suddenly started its own border crackdown.

Still, we kept watch, though the pressure eased. And we had some unusual experiences. One day, four of us were moving stealthily to intercept a group of immigrants spotted in undergrowth at night at the bottom of a steep hill. As we descended the hill, three of us were startled by a crashing noise behind us. We stopped and looked back, and realised it was the fourth member of our patrol crashing through the undergrowth with all the subtlety of an elephant with an erection. 'What the fuck are you doing?' the lance corporal hissed. 'I can't see a fucking thing – the whole thing's black,' the soldier replied. He told us he couldn't even see the outline of the path in front of him and was blundering into every tree and stump on the hillside. We thought no more about it at the time. Then, only a couple of years later, we heard the poor bastard was going progressively blind – his antics had been caused by the fact he had absolutely no night vision, something the Royal Marines had amazingly failed to spot.

Then, almost as soon as we had arrived, our deployment was over. We arrived in September and were ordered back home in late November. A few of the older lads were delighted – they wanted to spend Christmas at home with their wives and kids. Two of the older 'sweats', who had several years' experience, even managed to go into Hong Kong and get themselves measured up by one of the city's famed tailors for handmade suits. But, just for a laugh, they decided to go for flares, jackets with super-wide collars, and horrendous waistcoats made from what looked like tablecloth material, complete with an eye-watering design of green, yellow and red flowers. Even at the height of the 'flower power' craze in the 1960s, these suits would have brought a busy city street to a stand-still. But the lads didn't give a shit – it was all a great joke as far as they were concerned. Me, well, I wished the deployment had lasted a little longer. We had six days' free time before we headed back to Plymouth and a few of us lads had a lot of steam to let off. The booze was cheap and readily accessible and we made up for lost time. Unfortunately, I had enough free time to get involved in a savage off-duty brawl as Four-Two Commando members clashed with members of the Green Jackets, an army regiment who were also here on an assignment.

We had heard there was a ball at the China Fleet Club, so we headed there one evening for a bit of a laugh and to maybe pick up a few local girls. However, a Commando clashed with two lads from the Green Jackets in the ballroom. I have no idea what triggered it, but everyone had already been drinking for a few hours and, within seconds of the

Commando throwing a chair at the two army soldiers, a mass brawl erupted.

I was minding my own business, watching the brawl from the other end of the ballroom, when someone punched me from behind. I was lucky that it was only a glancing blow and I was able to turn, grab the guy by the throat and throw him onto the floor. I was a tough bastard when I wanted to be and I was determined to beat some manners into this fucker. Within seconds, I was punching him in the face, when suddenly a Green Jacket leaned forwards from the crowd and broke a beer bottle over my head. The world went dark for a few seconds before I realised that other Commandos were now pouring forwards both to rescue me and to exact a little revenge on any available Green Jacket. God only knows what the Chinese made of it all – the British seemed intent on doing their work for them and beating the crap out of each other.

The brawl raged on until the Military Police arrived and I was dragged off to the medic's office for treatment along with another Marine. He had suffered awful glass cuts to his face – I found it hilarious to hear him explain that he was a chef and, the minute the brawl erupted, he had jumped under the nearest table for safety; unfortunately, someone threw a bottle, which missed its target and shattered on the floor just in front of his table. The exploding fragments peppered his face and sliced a chunk of flesh from underneath his chin. I escaped with just a couple of stitches to a scalp wound and, with the scar on my finger from my Okehampton trench experience, had proudly earned my second Commando scar. It didn't spoil the fact that I had just successfully completed my first overseas deployment as a Commando, and I prayed fervently that it would not be my last.

The major success of the deployment was, in fact, a rigid, double-skinned fibreglass craft, fitted with a powerful outboard motor. This was the Rigid Raider, and at that time only the Royal Marines had it. The Raider provided a whole new capability to policing and protecting Hong Kong's Marine approaches, and L Company used them to incredible effect around Hong Kong waters.

The Raider is perhaps best described as the Spitfire of the sea. It was blisteringly fast, highly manoeuvrable and, when fitted with extra fuel tanks, had a decent range. It could operate in all but the most appalling weather conditions and was virtually impossible to outrun except by the most specialised of craft. Its success had not gone unnoticed back in Britain, and Royal Marine commanders were delighted with the potential of this cost-effective yet hugely adaptable new tool. They saw a whole range of potential uses for the Raider far and beyond Hong Kong's shores. They decided to set up a new Raiding Squadron that would work with and complement their existing landing-craft units. This was the birth of 3rd Raiding Squadron, which I would later join, and be the start of some of the happiest days of my life.

4

SNOW, SKIS AND NORDIC BEAUTIES

Within a couple of weeks of returning to Bickleigh, Hong Kong was a pleasant but fast-fading memory. I had been transferred into Headquarters Company of Four-Two Commando and, aside from a few weeks of welcome Christmas leave back home in Yorkshire, we were straight back into the training cycle that most soldiers grow to hate.

A soldier's life is an endless series of placements, then training, then another assignment, then training and so on. You're not on holidays back at base; in fact, training is always tougher than an assignment. I was only in the Commandos a year and I was already beginning to understand why older Marines cringed at the prospect of training cycles. Assault courses, cross-country runs, rifle drills, classroom briefings – the Royal Marines were determined that not a single minute of our time would be wasted. 'Idle hands make the devil's work' the old saying goes – and I reckon our commanders bought into the saying, big-time. Despite having served in Hong Kong, I was still regarded as a work-in-progress.

Yet I could already see the difference in myself. I had got off the train at Lympstone a boy – but I was already a man. And, in physical terms, quite a tough bastard to boot! I had always been well-built, but the intensive physical fitness programme had now left me lean, hard and with a pair of shoulders a Welsh prop forward would have been proud of. The assault drills had shown that I could hold my own with the toughest guys in the unit – and I was convinced that I had chosen well in joining the Commandos. Now I desperately wanted to be a Commando worthy of the name.

Even though I hadn't yet turned nineteen, I was already developing a loathing for whingers and layabouts, who took the pay but complained about the pain. I just couldn't understand how anyone could put on the uniform and then whine about doing what it took to be a Commando. We had to be fit because we were generally the first into battle – and we had to be tough as nails because we would go up against the best an enemy could throw at us. It may sound arrogant – though I suppose arrogance goes hand-in-hand with being young – but my view was that if someone whined, they should have joined the catering corps.

When I first joined up I was quiet and reserved because I was younger than virtually everyone else. If a sergeant screamed 'Jump!' at me, I rocketed to my feet and, as the saying goes, asked 'How high, Sergeant?' But I was slowly finding my feet – I had made a few good friends and was slowly growing in confidence about becoming a good Marine. I had a wicked sense of humour and was well able to laugh at myself, which helped break the ice with some of the other lads. I looked around me and saw the kind of men that I wanted to be – tough but fair, driven yet loyal, feared but respected. Slowly, I grew to realise that proving myself worthy of the famous Green Beret and Commando shoulder flash would become the defining constant in my life.

We then got news in January 1980 that Four-Two Commando was going on an exercise rotation to Norway. I had got over my dread of the cold – it was Arctic warfare training – and I couldn't wait. I was about to add a whole new cultural experience to my CV and another tick in the passport of life. Some of the older salts were a little wiser. They knew that Norway wasn't about fun and games in the snow. It was like Dartmoor with attitude – ball-breaking endurance exercises, all conducted in a potentially deadly ice-box. Yet Norway was still one of the most popular deployments within the Royal Marines.

Norway, in particular, was what Four-Two Commando was all about.

Every Commando sent to Scandinavia on his first training rotation had to focus solely on Arctic warfare skills. And every tour he subsequently undertook included at least three or four weeks of refresher work on Arctic warfare. You were taught how to live in the open for extended periods, how to build a snow shelter, how to make the elements work in your favour, how to dress for layered heat retention, how to ski, how to stay mobile in the most unforgiving terrain and above all how to fight in Arctic conditions. We were trained to turn an environment that could kill you into a battle asset.

It was physically exhausting. Arctic warfare exerts the toughest physical demands of any type of combat, and it is a type of fighting where mechanisation can do the least amount to help you. And it's all done in the most demanding environment Mother Nature can throw at you. The key to the whole thing is mobility and using the surrounding terrain as your ally. That, and not getting frostbite on your manhood!

Most Arctic warfare techniques and policies date back to the Russo-Finnish War just before World War II and the actions of Norwegian partisans against German forces from 1942 onwards. The Finns were vastly outnumbered by the Soviet Red Army in 1939 and they were heavily outgunned. Yet, using ski troops and Arctic warfare skills, they fought the Russians to a standstill. The Soviets even deployed their new KV-1 heavy tanks with 76.2mm gun and 100mm thick armour – and the Finns still found ways of neutralising their impact by attacking from the flanks. The Soviets were largely confined to the roads and railways, while the Finns exploited the forests, mountains and valleys to the full to cut the Red Army's supply lines, attack isolated detachments and cause chaos in the Soviet rear areas.

The world watched amazed as one of Europe's smallest armies held off one of the world's most formidable fighting machines with vast materiel at their disposal. The newsreels were dominated by black-and-white images of Finnish troops on skis flooding around the flanks and rear of the cumbersome Soviet armies. Adolf Hitler disastrously misread the lesson and, failing to learn from the Finns, fatally underestimated the Russians in World War II. In the end, the Finns were overcome by sheer weight of numbers when their main defensive line was breached by Soviet armoured units in February 1940. But it was a startling example of what a small group of well-trained and highly motivated troops could achieve, using the Arctic conditions in their favour and exploiting their manoeuvrability to the maximum degree.

The Norwegians themselves offered another example of the lethal challenge posed by Arctic fighters. Nazi Germany invaded Norway in April 1940 and within weeks resistance groups had formed whose operations forced the Germans to maintain very large troop detachments. The Norwegian resistance fighters became famed – and feared – by the Germans for their ability to appear from nowhere, strike troop convoys or strategic targets and disappear again on skis into the Nordic forests.

The technology might have changed in the half-century since then, but I would basically learn precisely the same skills in the snow and mountains of northern Norway. And we were learning Arctic warfare skills because the fear was that, should World War III erupt, the first thing the Soviets would try to do was block US efforts to reinforce and resupply NATO troops fighting in Europe and the easiest way to achieve this was to cut off the North Atlantic convoy routes. Scandinavia, as the Nazis discovered during World War II, strategically straddled the maritime approaches to Britain and Europe. Keeping Norway free and a NATO ally was critical, and that's why such emphasis was placed on Arctic warfare.

Yet the only time I had ever seen a ski was on TV. I hadn't even tried on a pair, let alone had lessons in basic winter-sports skills. But most of us Commandos were in the same boat; we were all novices. And, even if we had skied before, the Alpine downhill ski techniques that you'd learn in France, Austria and Germany wouldn't be much use here. We weren't learning downhill skiing, we were learning cross-country skiing, or *langlaufen*, which, believe me, is a very different animal indeed.

For a start, cross-country skis were longer and wider, to better help the skier negotiate hazards like rutted paths, streams and dykes. Their extra width dispersed your weight. They varied in length from 190cm to 210cm, depending on how tall you were. They were made of wood in the traditional way and were also slightly bowed so that a user had traction on level ground, and, if necessary, could walk rather than ski while wearing them. While elements of downhill skiing were applicable, cross-country skiing involved a different technique and was largely about stamina.

The skills we were now learning had been handed down from generation to generation within Norwegian families. The very first detachment of Royal Marines that deployed to Norway for NATO Arctic warfare exercises in the 1950s was actually trained by some of the volunteers who took part in the legendary Telemark Raid, the incredible attack on a Nazi secret research facility during World War II. The Norwegian team parachuted into the country from Britain and blew up a German heavy-water plant just outside Rjukan. That single operation sabotaged Nazi efforts to develop an atomic bomb and remains one of Norway's proudest military exploits, inspiring the film, *The Heroes of Telemark*. Several of the Royal Marines trained by these Norwegian resistance volunteers in Rjukan in the 1950s and 1960s went on to achieve military ski instructor (MSI) status within the Commandos. Several of our instructors were personally trained by these guys.

I must admit that I didn't find skiing easy. I was young, naturally fit and I was in good shape. But I still found it tough. I'd swear there is not a single patch of flat ground in Norway – it's hill after hill after mountain. Even a mountain goat would have found it intimidating. And if that is not bad enough, you have forests as far as the eye can see, as well as more mountain streams than there are sands on Blackpool beach. However, slowly but surely, we learned. Then, when it was assessed that we were relatively competent on skis, we were assigned to dedicated Arctic warfare training (AWT).

We started our training in the depths of the Nordic winter. At times, it went as low as minus 52 degrees outside – and what no one broadcasts is the fact that guys regularly die during training here. Funnily enough, the biggest danger is not hypothermia, but asphyxiation. To survive outdoors in temperatures as low as a blast freezer, you have to find shelter. Every Commando is taught how to dig a proper snow hole and erect a tent shelter big enough to provide shelter for himself and maybe two or three other guys. But, to allow for heat and cooking, an air vent has to be made in the roof of the snow hole or tent. If that vent is blocked, either by a partial collapse of the shelter roof or a heavy snowfall over the tent, everyone will die because of the noxious fumes that now have no way of escaping. In one case in 1993, a great friend of mine died because his group erected a tent as a snow shelter and their air vent was blocked by a twenty-five-centimetre fall of snow overnight. Their small cooker had been used to warm up a quick two-man hotch-potch of everything from their ration packs. This could include apple flakes mixed with stew – and some chilli peppers and curry added, just to spice the entire mess up. It was then first in with the quickest spoon. The cooker would be turned off, but sometimes it could still give off carbon monoxide. My mate – who was just twenty years old – was overcome by carbon monoxide and died without ever waking up.

Not that the cold should ever be underestimated either. The temperatures here were lethal, and the key to coping with them was 'layering'. You didn't just wear a warm jumper and heavy military jacket. You wore a T-shirt, a thermal vest, a pullover top, a Norwegian shirt, another heavier jumper, a fleece and then your waterproof military parka. As you got warmer, you peeled off an outer layer until you reached the correct temperature. As you got colder, you simply added another layer of clothing. The trick was to stay as dry as possible and as warm as possible. Wearing fewer items of heavier clothing restricted your ability to respond precisely to the heat and cold, and, if a critical layer of clothing got wet, you were pretty much unable to remove it. And that's what would probably kill you.

Another crucial factor was that more than six weeks before we deployed to Norway we received our full Arctic kit so that we had time to ensure that everything, from boots to combats, was properly 'worn in' and absolutely comfortable by the time we reached Norway. The last thing in the world you needed in a mountain wilderness was to have blisters or chafing because your boots weren't properly broken in. If you couldn't maintain mobility you were a danger to yourself and a liability to your unit.

53

By March, we were all maintaining our skis and equipment as if born in the Arctic. The skis were carefully waxed each day, the ties were checked and tightened, pole ends were sharpened and our goloks, a type of Arctic machete, were edged carefully. We Commandos took to the goloks with glee. However, they were eventually dropped as an essential part of Arctic kit. Norwegian conservationists complained about the number of small trees and shrubs being chopped down for overnight shelters by Royal Marines while out on manoeuvres! They were worried that our winter manoeuvres would permanently alter the Norwegian eco-system.

The Marines reaction to that criticism ultimately became so ridiculous that when we went for a shit we were ordered to bag the crap so we could take it away with us after the exercise concluded. The Norwegian tree-huggers didn't like the idea of stepping in defrosting Commando crap in the springtime! Trust me when I say that going for a crap in minus 50 degrees is no joke at the best of times – without having to contend with bagging what you've just produced while trying to ensure you don't get frostbite on your arse. The idea, apparently, was to produce a more environmentally-friendly type of soldier to fight the Russians if they ever decided to invade Norway over a boring weekend.

The process, needless to say, produced some of the funniest moments I've ever had in uniform. Once, one of the lads was taken short on an exercise and sprinted behind a bush to have a crap. He dropped his white camouflage suit to squat and do his business. Unfortunately, he had got his angles wrong and dropped his load into the back of his suit. He quickly pulled up his camouflage gear and proceeded on with the exercise – unwittingly carrying a load of crap with him. He only discovered what had happened that evening when his tent heated up and left no one in any doubt about what was in his suit.

The survival-skills lectures were even boiled down to a sort of 'Arctic Warfare for Dummies' format so that even the thickest guy could remember what was important. For instance, 'COLD' became an anagram for the essential anti-hypothermia rule: C = stay clean at all times; O = overheating to be avoided at all costs; L = layer clothing to promote proper body temperature maintenance; D = stay dry as much as possible. The last was easier said than done because Norway, having such an enormous coastline and with most inland areas not being too far removed from the sea, was always prone to rain. I lost count of how many gorgeous winter mornings started with heavy snow flurries, only to transform within an hour to icy sleet showers. The danger was that you'd get thoroughly soaked by the rain and, when darkness fell, the temperatures plummeted so fast that the waterlogged garments would literally freeze solid on you.

But the reality was that we were Royal Marine Commandos and we had to learn how to deal with these situations. There was nowhere to go to dry off, so how did you keep yourself alive in a snow shelter with wet gear? There was enormous emphasis placed on teamwork and we were expected to blend seamlessly together as a small unit.

Our first few weeks of exercises were entirely conducted among Royal Marine units. Our skiing skills were improving day by day and the Commandos took enormous pride in the ski race conducted every Saturday. It was like the assault courses all over again. Everyone wanted to prove their mettle and uphold the honour of their unit. Within three months, most of us were skiing as if born to it. Well, at least that's what we thought. The local Norwegian kids thought we were hilarious, and one of their favourite games was following us around and then playing in what they called 'the English holes' – the huge crater-like impacts created in the snow by a Commando after he crashed on skis with full kit.

Once we were deemed to be properly mobile, the cross-country deployments started. We practised laying ambushes, avoiding detection, reconnaissance, sabotage, unit extraction and even how to plan speed-marches across difficult terrain. It was exhausting and occasionally back-breaking work, but we revelled in it all. The added bonus was that, after such exercises, there was always a decent wind-down period in the base bar.

Northern Norway is no joke in the winter and the decision was made years ago to involve the locals in some of the Royal Marine social activities. I suspected that one of the major reasons was that the support of the locals would be absolutely crucial if NATO troops were ever asked to fight off a Soviet winter invasion. But, irrespective of the rationale, the young Commandos were simply thrilled that Norwegian women would flock to the base bar on a Saturday night. And what we'd heard about them was true.

It's no coincidence that so many Marines ended up married to Norwegians. I have been stationed in many parts of the world and I have to say that these girls are among the most beautiful on the planet. The parties on base became legendary. There were three thousand Royal Marine Commandos in circulation, there was cheap beer by the case-load, piped music and an open invitation to the locals to join in. Unfortunately, the main danger was that the local girls occasionally looked far older than their years. The combination of booze, testosterone and immaturity left many Commandos facing time in Norwegian jails for dalliances with girls they thought were seventeen or eighteen years old but who actually turned out to be only fifteen or sixteen. In some cases, the Commandos were only eighteen or nineteen themselves, but the Norwegian police took a very dim view of any liaisons with underage girls. The older Commandos always advised their younger colleagues, or 'sprogs', to take a long, hard look at their prospective Norwegian partners in the daylight and never to trust a judgement on age to a fleeting meeting in a club or disco.

Our entire Nordic odyssey came to an end with a massive winter exercise called 'EndEx' involving all NATO units deployed in northern Norway. Four-Two Commando were supported by Four-Five Commando and Two-Nine Army Commando, Royal Artillery who, in a conflict situation, provided our heavy firepower. Sometimes we even had Five-Nine Commando Royal Engineers. But the key components in the exercise were the Royal Norwegian Army, the Royal Dutch Marines (Korps Marinier) and the US Marine Corps.

To add to the realism of the winter war games, there were forward aviation observers and aerial support units for the Royal Norwegian Air Force and US Air Force (Europe). These observers could call in strikes by either jet fighter-bombers or even artillery. And if there was one thing every pilot had wet dreams about, it was catching an enemy infantry unit out in the open and effectively defenceless. The entire exercise was taken extremely seriously. We usually found ourselves fighting alongside the US Marine Corps.

It wasn't easy, as we were up against Norwegian soldiers and Special Forces (Jaeger Corps) who were born to snow fighting and knew every inch of every mountain and fjord. The scale of EndEx was such that it sometimes extended from Narvik to Bodø, or from Stavanger to Bergen (about 170km). The Royal Marines 1st Raiding Squadron – which I would shortly join – rotated to EndEx from their base at Ramsund in northern Norway. No expense was spared and the EndEx war game was usually observed by NATO's most senior commanders. The exercise typically started out with reconnaissance and manoeuvre, all small-unit activity. We were tasked with locating and identifying the enemy forces and then supporting a major infantry assault.

This climaxed in a set-piece battle where infantry units combined with naval and air-force strike detachments. More often than not, the Royal Norwegian Army won – after all, this was their patch and we were fighting the type of combat they'd trained for decades for. But we held our own, particularly given that most of us couldn't even stand up on a pair of skis just twelve weeks before.

Once EndEx was over, it was back to Bickleigh on one of the dedicated logistic ships, *Sir Galahad* or *Sir Percival*. The journey was pretty much over in a day, though carefully packing and stowing all our kit away was a major pain in the arse. The final few days before our shipping out was taken up with saying our farewells to any Norwegians we'd met and ensuring that none of the leftover beer went to waste. Some of the parties thrown in those days have rightly gone down in legend. And I learned that one of the best jobs on Arctic warfare deployment was 'rear party' – basically a clean-up rearguard. We were the last to leave Norway, usually about two weeks after the first units rotated back to Britain. While there was a lot of work involved in packing and stowing the kit, the huge attraction was that we had first call on all the beer that was left. Not to mention the fact that the same number of gorgeous Norwegian women were attending the bar, and now there were only a few dozen Commandos compared to three thousand just a few weeks before!

Once back in Bickleigh, it was straight out on the town to celebrate being home. Plymouth was a wonderful place at the time to be young – there was a great social scene there, some fantastic clubs and, well, some lovely ladies too. It was one of these female encounters that led to me earning my Commando nickname. The Royal Marines are no different to any other military outfit in that it has its own proud traditions and ethos. Nicknames are one of them. You were given a nickname and, for all your years of your service, that's what you'd be called by your mates. If you were Welsh, you would probably be 'Taff'; if you were Irish or had an Irish name you were 'Paddy'; Smith would be 'Smudge'; Edwards would be 'Nutty'; Reynolds would be 'Debbie'; and Miller would be 'Dusty'.

In my case, I was out on the town with a mate one night when we hooked up with two ladies. We were both in our late teens and these girls – well, suffice to say it had been quite a while since they had seen their teenage years. I also had no doubt that we weren't the first Commandos to have escorted these girls home. One was already pretty notorious within our Commando unit, not to mention the whole of Plymouth, for her antics. Incredibly, she was a vicar's daughter. I knew this girl was banned from one of the pubs we frequented because she had scandalised the owner – but delighted the Commando patrons – by drunkenly doing an impromptu sex show on a pool table. The bottom line was that if you were paying for the booze, she was game for virtually anything. This evening, the four of us returned to the flat after an entire evening in a local pub. My mate immediately retired to a bedroom with one girl who promptly threw up all over him. Drunk as I was, I made a mental note to tell all the lads the next day.

I was becoming amorous with the other girl and helping her out of her blouse and bra when she drunkenly asked me my name for about the fifth time that night. I replied 'Geoff' as I fumbled with her buttons, but she promptly giggled and called me 'Geoffrey Bubbles Bon Bon'. In 1970, Richard Beckinsale and Paula Wilcox starred in a British TV sitcom called *The Lovers*, which became hugely popular. Richard Beckinsale – who would die tragically young – was always trying to bed the Paula character and always failing. Paula's adoring nickname for Beckinsale in the series was 'Geoffrey Bubbles Bon Bon' and it had become a popular catchphrase. Back in the dingy Plymouth flat that night I couldn't care less if this girl called me Postman Pat or a Wimbledon Womble once she let me have my wicked way with her.

Unfortunately, my mate in the other room – now carefully trying to scrape vomit off himself while his lady friend dry-retched in the toilet – overheard what the girl had giggled to me. The next day he told everyone the story – and I was instantly christened Bubbles. Even now, thirty years later, I'm still called Bubbles by some of my best mates. And all thanks to copious amounts of Trophy bitter, Babycham and a middle-aged woman who liked teenage Commandos.

5

PROVING MY METTLE

Only the Irish could come up with a euphemism like 'The Troubles' for the sectarian carnage that at one point threatened to tear Northern Ireland apart. An order to deploy to Northern Ireland was never taken lightly by any British unit, particularly in the early 1980s when the entire province seemed determined to tear itself apart and the animosity towards us British military guys was savage. I suppose I was lucky that my tour to Ulster came as my third major deployment, with Hong Kong and Norway already having given me great confidence in my capabilities as a Royal Marine Commando.

After Norway, I returned to the normal training rotation and, in late 1980, was sent to Poole in Dorset, not far from Bournemouth, for my coxswain's course. Poole was a famous Royal Navy flying-boat base called HMS *Turtle* in World War II and boasts a magnificent harbour. This was a crucial bit of training for me because it meant that I would be certified to handle boats, a pretty important part of life for every Marine infantryman. I didn't particularly enjoy the course, as we were basically crewmen on larger boats like the Landing Craft Utility (LCU). These were barge-like craft, designed to ferry soldiers ashore on to beachheads, had the Marine performance of a floating log and were just about as exciting. We never even got to use the speedy Raiders, or even the chance to drive one.

Once I had passed, with flying colours, I was thrilled to learn that there was a vacancy in 1st Raiding Squadron, which was my dream assignment. I had heard all about Raiders in Hong Kong and was dying to get my hands on one. I knew that this was the kind of unit I'd sweat blood to be part of. I applied, only to be told that the vacancy was reserved for those with the rank of corporal. I knew the lad that was earmarked for the slot, but heard that he wasn't too keen because he was about to get engaged; his girlfriend didn't want him first in line for every overseas deployment, and that's what being part of 1st Raiding Squadron meant. No one else volunteered for the slot and eventually, after I hounded them about the vacancy, they relaxed the rank rule and allowed me in.

Raiding Squadron was always at the heart of the action – from reconnaissance to beach insertions, and from maritime interceptions to rescue missions. If the Royal Marine Commandos were Britain's premier military strike force, Raiding Squadron was the sharpest edge of that blade. If there was excitement going, Raiding Squadron were inevitably a part of it – and that's where I was desperate to be.

My assignment to 1st Raiding Squadron came just a few months before the word came that I was bound for Northern Ireland for a six-month tour of duty. Given the horror of recent events in Ulster, we couldn't have picked a worse time to arrive. I felt myself experiencing a strange rollercoaster of emotion – on the one hand I was delighted to be heading to Belfast to 'prove my mettle' but, at the same time, I knew that a lot of young soldiers came home from their Ulster tour in a body bag. This wasn't warfare – it was sectarian carnage of the most despicable kind. And I began a lifelong hatred of terrorists who are willing to wage vicious, dirty campaigns in a sea of civilian blood.

As 1981 dawned, Northern Ireland was spiralling towards the worst savagery of its sectarian conflict. The year had dawned with the nationalist campaigner, Bernadette Devlin McAliskey and her husband, Michael, almost being killed in a gun attack in January at their home. Later that month the former Speaker at Stormont Parliament, Sir Norman Stronge, was gunned down, along with his son. The violence was reaching such an horrific spiral that even a British Leyland executive, arriving to speak at a trade conference at Trinity College, Dublin, in the Irish Republic, was shot and wounded by paramilitary sympathisers. The poor bastard was targeted simply because he was viewed as part of the 'British establishment', whatever that might be. The same month, the first phase of the infamous H-Block hunger strikes erupted and, by 5 May, when Bobby Sands died, Ulster was in flames. British Prime Minister Margaret Thatcher had refused to concede to the Republican demands over the political status of prisoners, and it was we British troops on the ground who were now going to have to deal with the inevitable backlash.

It was decided that 1st Raiding Squadron would supply individual personnel for Marine patrols in Northern Ireland; we weren't deploying as an entire unit. It would not be like a normal overseas duty where we shipped out and arrived as a self-contained military outfit. We went to Ireland effectively as individuals and were met at Aldergrove airbase by one of our own lads, but in civilian clothing. He then took us to our base station at Moscow Camp from where you could see the giant cranes of the Harland & Wolff shipyards. We were immediately briefed on our duties and assignments, and privately warned that the sectarian violence was now in one of its most virulent cycles. Every individual then had to go on a one-week Northern Ireland Revision Training (NIRT) course, which aimed to bring individually deployed troops up to scratch on the personal security threat now facing them. The NI rain was endless for the week and the instructors just shook their heads when the men took breaks from the lessons on IED making and the only ones stood in the rain smoking were myself and a Para. Mostly because we laughed and joked and seemed oblivious to the inclement weather making the rest of the course hide under cover.

We arrived in Belfast at a time when the IRA was re-arming with modern and more sophisticated weaponry. The Lee-Enfields, Thompson machine guns and Carl-Gustafs that marked the opening phase of the Northern Ireland conflict were now a thing of the past. The modern terrorists operated with Armalites or M-16s and, in just a few short years, with Soviet Bloc weaponry, including Kalashnikov AK-47s, RPG-7s and, most ominously of all, the deadly Czech-made explosive, Semtex.

Semtex was the stuff of nightmares for us ordinary soldiers. It was five to six times more powerful than the same quantity of older explosives in the IRA arsenal – and could be used in a vast range of bombs and booby-trap devices. Put simply, the arrival of Semtex in Northern Ireland was like pouring petrol on an already blazing fire. The streets of Belfast had become a sophisticated killing zone where all the rules of civilised human behaviour seemed to be suspended.

Before we shipped out from England, we were briefed up on the security threat facing us. We were left in no doubt that the IRA were clever, efficient and posed a lethal threat to Crown forces. The worrying part was that their capabilities would only increase as they got access to modern, higher-powered weaponry and became proficient in its use. And that essentially was our job in Raiding Squadron – to sever the supply lines. Our officers were constantly lecturing us about how clever the IRA were: how they learned from their mistakes, adapted to our tactics and tried to use as many local factors as possible to stack the odds in their favour. We were warned never to lose sight of the fact that we would be operating on 'their' turf.

There were already painful examples of the IRA's brutal capability. Just two years before, on 27 August 1979, at Warrenpoint in County Down, and at Mullaghmore, County Sligo, the IRA had horrified Britain with two huge bomb attacks. The first – at Sligo – killed Lord Louis Mountbatten and fatally injured the Dowager Lady Brabourne (who died the next day) when a timed bomb was placed on their boat. A local teenager and Mountbatten's grandson were also killed in the massive blast. Just a few hours later, the IRA used a bomb hidden under hay on the rear of a flat-bed lorry to destroy a passing truck carrying members of the 2nd Battalion, the Parachute Regiment. Six soldiers died in the initial blast, with the bomb estimated to have contained up to half-a-tonne of explosives.

Two army trucks not damaged in the Warrenpoint attack immediately deployed their Parachute Regiment soldiers to secure the area, and members of the Queen's Own Highlanders were flown to the scene by helicopter to help with the security mission. Twenty minutes after the first explosion, just as the injured were being airlifted to hospital, a second huge bomb was detonated. This killed a further twelve soldiers – two Highlanders and ten Paras. The attack also claimed the highest-ranking British officer to have died in the Troubles to that point – Lieutenant-Colonel David Blair. The attack marked a lethal twist in the already vicious relationship between the IRA and the Paras.

In later years I would work in Iraq alongside a former Queen's Own Highlander called Jimmy McI. who was at Warrenpoint, and he spoke in horrified awe of the savage power of that blast. To listen to Jimmy talk about it would send chills down your spine. That day the IRA had created the perfect killing zone. When the second explosion went off, it lifted Jimmy off his feet and tossed him to the ground like a ragdoll, even though he was almost a hundred metres away. One of the lads he was with had taken up position behind a low stone wall and was standing there when the second blast went off. The trooper was virtually cut in half by the blast, with his upper torso, exposed above the wall, reduced to a liquid mass of blood, flesh and shattered bone. His legs were later found, directly behind the wall where he had died, still encased in combat boots and the shredded remains of his combat trousers.

These memories were still fresh in all our minds as we arrived in Belfast for our deployment. It may sound strange but, in the end, I was glad to finally arrive in Northern Ireland. Every British soldier in the 1970s, 1980s and 1990s knew that a Northern Ireland tour was going to be part of their career, and I felt it was high time that I was 'in country'. I had spent almost four years in the Royal Marines now and I wanted to get my Northern Ireland tour over and done with. Every single British soldier arrived in Northern Ireland with trepidation – anyone who denies it today is a liar. The truth was that you weren't quite sure whether you'd make it back home alive. That is how dangerous Northern Ireland was at that particular time. Yet, incredibly, some troopers were lucky enough to go through an entire tour without any major incidents. As you arrived in Northern Ireland, you just prayed you would be one of the lucky ones.

We had heard first-hand from veterans of previous tours just how bad it could be – from street riots to sectarian murders, from bomb attacks to sniper fire. We found it hard to believe that British troops had initially been welcomed into Northern Ireland with open arms to stop the sectarian street riots that threatened to tear Ulster society asunder. I even heard stories about troops being offered tea and sandwiches while on patrol in the Bogside in Derry and on the Falls Road in Belfast – and then getting spat at by the same people just a few weeks later. From Bloody Sunday onwards, we seemed to be in the crosshairs of an ever-deepening sectarian maelstrom where sympathy, humanity and understanding were the first victims. I even heard that one woman was shot by the IRA because she had comforted a young British soldier who was shot by a sniper and dying outside her front door.

Infantry patrols were now regularly 'dicked' by paramilitaries and their sympathisers in parts of Derry and Belfast. This basically involved one or two people monitoring the unit, shadowing their progress, noting their operating routine and trying to identify any of the individual soldiers. Being 'dicked' meant that you were being sized up as a potential or future target. Other stories were equally ominous. One rumour we heard was that IRA snipers operating along the border were being trained by an American mercenary. He was alleged to have given first-hand demonstrations of how to use heavy sniping rifles to shoot British soldiers from vantage points across the border.

If there was one weapon that all of us soldiers in Northern Ireland feared it was the heavy sniping rifle. Weapons like the McMillan M87 and the Barrett Light 50 were originally designed for destroying equipment – a sniper could shoot up a radio antenna or a radar dish. They fire a heavy calibre round – like a .50 calibre Browning (12.7mm) – which is even capable of cracking the engine block of a truck or an aircraft. The bullet is heavier and thicker than your index finger – and the result of being hit by one is a truly horrific sight.

The weapon was effective from 1,500m, but could actually strike a target from 2,500m, almost a mile and a half. The grim reality is that, when used by an expert, it was virtually impossible to completely defend yourself against that kind of firepower and massive range. There was even a debate within the US military over whether such rifles should be illegal for anti-personnel use. The IRA didn't care about that, of course, and the heavy sniping rifle became one of the most feared killers around the border. To maximise the fear factor, the IRA even erected mock road signs with the black silhouette of a sniper and the warning, 'Sniper At Work'.

It all contributed to a dark mood which wasn't helped by the fact that most troopers hadn't a clue what the hell was going on in Northern Ireland in the first place. I was typical, and I didn't hate the Irish – most people in Britain either knew Irish people, had Irish relatives or had worked alongside Irish people. But I made no apologies for saying I hated the terrorist bastards who were killing my mates and turning parts of Northern Ireland into a charnel house. Belfast looked no different to Manchester, York, Birmingham, Plymouth or any other British city. It probably looked little different to any other Irish city, for that matter, whether Dublin, Cork or Galway. Yet people here seemed to have a visceral hatred of each other simply because they went to a different church at the weekend.

It just didn't make any sense to me, especially since Britain had seen a huge influx of Muslims, Hindus, Sikhs, Afro-Caribbeans and Africans over the previous three decades. I'm not saying it was all rosy in the garden – there were riots and ethnic tensions. But, for the most part, we learned to get along and try and build a better Britain. Most of us Marines simply went to Ireland to do our job. I think none of us would have given a damn if there had been a majority democratic vote for Northern Ireland to join the Republic. That would be democracy in action. But if the majority of people wanted to remain British, then so be it. And there was no way we were going to be bombed out of Northern Ireland. We felt we were there legitimately – after all, we'd been sent there. That was as much justification as we needed. And it was a lesson we were determined to ram down the IRA's throat.

Unlike a lot of the other infantry units, who were going to have to undertake street patrols and searches of the so-called 'bandit country' around the border between Northern Ireland and the Republic, I was going to be water-borne for most of my tour. Members of 1st Raiding Squadron were assigned as coxswains to Moscow barracks in Belfast, and Carlingford Lough was going to be our playground for the next six months as part of a duty called Operation InterNit. The border itself ran right through Carlingford Lough, so we were on vital border duty on the water, our very own bandit country. We were equipped with Raiders and would be patrolling all parts of the maritime approaches to Belfast and Warren point. We would cox the Raiders – and members of the deployed Commando unit would be attached to us as the boarding party for a four-month period.

Our primary task was to intercept any attempt to smuggle weapons and explosives into Belfast via Carlingford Lough. The senior British commanders were desperate to stem the flow of weapons to the IRA and any ship carrying guns that slipped through the security net represented a bonanza for the terror machine. The IRA were desperate for modern weaponry, as the seizure of ships packed with US and Libyan-sourced Soviet ordnance would prove in the years to come. Our job was to ensure that Carlingford Lough was not the entry point.

The other major issue was trying to staunch the flow of funds to the IRA. The kind of terror campaigns they waged cost a lot of money. Weapons and explosives had to be paid for in cash, and the families of paramilitaries serving lengthy prison sentences had to be financially supported. Above all, the publicity machine of the IRA had to be oiled with funds – losing the PR war was almost as serious as losing an active service unit. A substantial portion of the IRA's cash came from smuggling goods over the border between Northern Ireland and the Republic. Not all the smuggling was conducted via road and we were ordered to pay particular attention to the movement of all small craft on the lough. While the Provos had a 'zero tolerance' policy to drugs, pretty much everything else was regarded as fair game, from laundered diesel to pirated video tapes, jewellery and antiques. If it could generate a profit, the IRA was willing to smuggle it.

I was now twenty and, funnily enough, was no longer treated as one of the 'young 'uns', or sprogs. It would be a few years yet before I got my corporal's promotion but, on arrival in the North, I wasn't one of the young Marines who was deemed to need 'mothering'. The older lads were incredible. The corporals and sergeants, who had already got several tours under their belts, were a fount of knowledge about what to do and what not to do. I saw at first-hand how experienced corporals and sergeants helped ensure units worked seamlessly – and that young soldiers got the training and advice they needed to avoid potentially tragic mistakes. Some of these guys had tours dating back to the early 1970s when British forces had to learn the hard way, by paying a price in blood. If you were apprehensive about any aspect of Belfast, they were there to help. And you looked at them and thought: Jesus, if they got through this a couple of times before, I can get through this now.

We were the only unit in Northern Ireland equipped with Raiders and we used them in virtually all weather conditions on Carlingford Lough. Within a month, we knew the lough like the back of our hand – from the shallow-water markers to virtually every single bay and inlet. Norway and our Arctic warfare training came in handy because conditions in Carlingford were sometimes little better than atrocious. Sea conditions could be truly horrendous, yet we were still expected to maintain patrols and vigilance. The bulk of our tour was spent out on the water between January and May, the worst months for storms and gales roaring down into the Irish Sea. For safety, we always operated in teams of two Raiders; one would approach a boat to make an inspection while the other Raider would stand off in support. Very often the biggest danger we faced was hypothermia – particularly if you were on a long patrol in heavy seas. The Raiders were made of fibreglass, and they would get hammered by the combination of stormy seas and having to come up alongside steel-hulled trawlers, freighters and ferries.

At times, you could see the impact of your job on ordinary people in Northern Ireland. One Saturday morning, we were skimming across the waves in Carlingford Lough and intercepted a small yacht for an inspection. We followed the usual routine of one Raider providing a boarding party while the other slowly circled in support. But it was just a father taking his young sons out for a day's sailing. You could see the apprehension on all their faces – they knew we were armed and God only knows what was going through their minds. None of us trained our weapons on them – but it was clear we were prepared for any eventuality. Northern Ireland was such a surreal world that even something as simple as taking your children out for a weekend sail could result in a security drama. You felt in your gut that people just desperately wanted to be able to get on with their lives and bring up their kids in a normal way, but that dream was still several years away. From our viewpoint, you tried to be as polite as you could while doing your job. In later years I often wondered what my reaction would be if I was stopped sailing with my sons off Flamborough Head by the navy and police and searched in this way. Most people understood and returned our friendly waves as we sped off after the inspection – others just bluntly told you to 'Fuck off, Brit fucks'.

There were times when you saw at first-hand the visceral hatred that was there towards you. Once we stopped a small fishing boat with about five guys on board, and it was very soon clear they were on a social outing rather than a commercial fishing expedition. They had had a few beers and, as we sped up alongside, I could tell, even from a distance, how their mood changed. There was silence as we came alongside and muttering as we checked the boat, its cargo and destination. There was nothing on board except fishing gear, beer and some food. But, as we wished them 'Good fishing' and got ready to leave, one of the group said, 'British Cunts' to our back. I froze and turned around; no one spoke like that to me. Another of the group smirked at me as he gave me the finger. I made a half-step forwards when the corporal put his hand on my arm and said, 'Relax'. He looked me in the eye and said firmly, 'Leave it – there's nothing more to do here. They're clean.' We sped away to a cacophony of jeers and V-signs. In hindsight, leaving was the wise course of action – I had an SLR assault rifle at my side and going back on board to challenge the drunken louts would only have escalated the situation beyond what was wise. But I was really tempted, I can tell you.

The other thing that 1st Raiding Squadron was expected to do as part of Operation InterNit was support land-based security operations by dropping off small units of Commandos for impromptu vehicle checkpoints (VCPs) in coastal areas around Warrenpoint and, sometimes, in rural areas farther afield. The advantage of using the Raiders for these deployments was that they gave no advance warning to any paramilitary sentries on road junctions. A paramilitary unit could be given the all-clear to move from sentries at two separate crossroads and then, suddenly, be greeted by a Commando patrol conducting a security check in the middle of nowhere. Such patrols could be deployed by helicopters but the choppers made a lot of noise and broadcast the fact that a security operation was about to get underway in the area. In contrast, the Raiders could silently deploy a patrol who could then run from the beach to the nearby road to conduct their snap checkpoint. The first thing a driver knew about the patrol was when he drove up to the checkpoint. More than a few weapons were seized from vehicles this way, and several arrests were made. The other huge advantage was that, by being able to exit the area by sea, we made it impossible for any paramilitary unit to ambush the patrol along the roadway back to their base. From the very beginning of the Troubles to the very end, the Royal Marines and the Royal Navy owned the waters around Northern Ireland.

For the most part, 1st Raiding Squadron and the various Commando patrols operated in close liaison with Military Intelligence and the RUC. We had a list of people, 'players' in security parlance, who were being kept under close observation because of their suspected links to terrorist groups. If they ever strayed into our patch, we were expected to either monitor them or else mount snap checkpoints to try and catch them with either arms or explosives. It was a never-ending game of cat-and-mouse – only these mice had very sharp teeth!

When we weren't operating on the water, we generally drove around in unmarked white Ford Transit vans or Land Rovers. To a casual observer, we were just ordinary tradesmen going about our daily work. The only difference was that, tucked just underneath our feet, was a Heckler-Koch MP5 submachine gun which could discharge 800 rounds of

9mm ammunition in less than a minute. We also had a couple of smoke grenades just for good measure – and we never stuck to the same route, always trying to vary our movements.

The subterfuge was aided by the fact that, unlike army squaddies, we grew our hair long while on Commando assignment. It made us look very un-military in appearance and made moving around that much safer. For the most part, we looked like we were on our way back from a rock concert. We revelled in it, to be honest, because when you returned to Stonehouse Barracks in Plymouth you didn't have to advertise where you had just been – one look from awed new recruits and they knew you were just back from Northern Ireland.

We generally operated from two ships, *HMS Vigilant* and *HMS Alert*, while on the lough. When they returned to port, we would rotate back to Moscow barracks in Belfast while another team took up inspection duties on the lough. The trip back was taken on board either ship and the routine for the journey became two seasick tablets and a crate of beer (the seasick tablets were needed because the motion of the ship is different to that of the Raider, and there was no time for adjustment). The fortnight back in base was then spent repairing the damage to the Raiders, checking the engines, assessing the gear and enjoying a bit of down time.

Incredibly, we were allowed into Belfast if we wanted. It's hard to believe that, at the worst killing phase of the Troubles, with H-Block protests still taking place in the North, we were allowed into town to go shopping, watch a match or have a few pints on a Friday night. The threat-assessment guys believed that, at that time, there was no need to restrict off-duty Marines to barracks. Mind you, no one had to tell us to be careful – we certainly wouldn't opt for a piss-up on the Falls Road. If we went into Belfast city centre, we kept a low-profile, did what business we had to and generally kept to ourselves. The alternative was to stay in Moscow barracks where there was a social club. The beer was cheap here and female members of the UDR, RUC and Royal Navy were allowed to attend. The base commander also directed that a dance be organised every so often, which proved pretty good for morale.

What I was most conscious of was my accent. I didn't have the famous Yorkshire drawl so beloved of British sitcoms, but the minute I opened my mouth you'd know I wasn't from Belfast. There were so many British firms operating in Northern Ireland that my accent didn't necessarily mean I was a squaddie. But it was an indicator – and, with my build, even the long hair wouldn't protect my identity for long. So I was careful where I went, who I was with, how I spoke, who was listening and what was going on around me. It was great to escape the barracks and head into the city centre, but you could never fully relax. That was Belfast in the 1980s.

On a Sunday, the routine was to go to *HMS Caroline*, an old RN ship tied up alongside the far side of Belfast Lough where a lot of the Women Royal Navy Reserve (WRNS) operated from. We used to call it the 'Caroline Bop', and, not surprisingly, quite a few Royal Marines ended up with Belfast-born wives thanks to *HMS Caroline*'s disco. One of my mates struck up a romance with a girl here and, eventually, used to call around to her house in Belfast! At the time, no one thought it was any kind of security risk. One of my favourite forms of relaxation was driving out to Bangor for a few pints – it's a lovely area and there was a great selection of pubs and restaurants. Amazing as it may sound, even the Paras used to go there in civvies for a few drinks, off-duty from Palace barracks.

But, I suppose, there was always a danger, given the way the political temperatures were being stoked. The Abercorn, one of the private Belfast city-centre clubs that we Royal Marines used to frequent, was later blown up by the IRA, and, by the time of my second Northern Ireland tour in 1992, off-duty soldiers were not allowed into town, on strict orders. There had been attempted shootings and kidnappings, and commanders now assessed the risk as too high. Yet the main danger always was patrolling in 'hot spot' areas – either the Falls Road, the Shankill or areas along the border. Most of the casualties that British troops suffered were through patrols suffering set-piece ambushes or roadside and culvert bombs. For example, five soldiers died when a huge landmine was detonated just as they were passing in their armoured car at Bessbrook in County Armagh. The landmine was so big the poor bastards never had a chance despite the armour around them. The level of fatalities involved shocked all of us. And, over the course of the H-Block hunger strikes a total of 61 people died – 30 of whom were members of either the RUC, British Army or Royal Navy.

I left Northern Ireland as the hunger strikes and the resultant carnage were slowly drawing to a close and the province seemed to be drawing its breath for another orgy of violence. It was typical of my luck, of course, that the weather began to improve just when my Northern Ireland tour came to an end. I have to say I wasn't sad to go home. To this day, I struggle to understand how such a beautiful place and, generally, such decent people could spawn such depths of hatred. I went home with a lot of pride in having done the job I was trained to do – and I believe it is satisfying to most soldiers to use their training in the most dangerous places.

A lot of the other lads in our section were also relieved to be heading home. The problem was you just never knew what was coming next in Northern Ireland. And, crucially, I was heading back to Britain just as the so-called 'marching season' was opening in the North, traditionally the time when Protestant groups stage street parades which, in turn, are used to fuel sectarian passions. Christ, I thought, things are bad enough with the hunger strikes without the marching season thrown into the mix. It's no coincidence that some of the darkest days of the Troubles all came in the weeks after the marching season. As I shipped home, I thought the situation was so bleak in Northern Ireland that we would be back on another tour within eighteen months to two years. But, as it transpired, it would be eleven years before I patrolled the waters of Carlingford Lough again.

6

THE CRUEL SOUTH SEA

My biggest fear in the entire Falklands campaign came at the very beginning – basically, that I would miss the whole fight. For a young Royal Marine Commando – I was just twenty years old – that was unthinkable, to the point of being a nightmare. Like most young men, I thought I was bullet-proof, and that fate wouldn't be cruel enough to allow a war to happen without me being part of it. For a start, I would never live down the slagging for the rest of my career in the military. What the fuck would I tell my mates? Oh, sorry about that, I missed the Falklands because I was owed some leave – but Benidorm was really good? Sod that for a story.

The problem was that I had just finished another three-month deployment to Norway with the 1st Raiding Squadron and the bulk of the lads headed back to Britain in March, leaving a small group of us behind as the 'rear party'. Our job was to tidy up billets, store equipment and generally have the entire place shipshape to hand back to the Norwegians. It also meant going on the piss for two weeks and not having to fight off so many other guys for the attentions of the girls. From the very beginning, I loved being assigned to rear party and regularly volunteered.

But, by the time I got back to Britain, the shit had well and truly hit the fan. The Argentine generals had obviously got tired of killing their own people in the 'secret war' and decided to try and capture the Falkland Islands – or Las Malvinas, as they're known in Buenos Aires.

It might have made sense in some Argentine war-study report, but it was total bollocks for anyone who knew anything about Britain. The Argentine generals would get an immediate PR boost and their own people might, for two successive days, actually support them. But did they really think that after facing down the best the Germans could throw at us in two world wars, and then going through thirty years of a terror campaign by the IRA in Northern Ireland, we were going to sit on our arses, do nothing and let the Argentine flag fly over the Falklands?

When news of the invasion broke, a Marine turned to me and asked, in all seriousness, why the fuck anyone, least of all the Argentines, would want to invade an island off Scotland? No one we knew had ever heard of them and presumed they were off the west coast of Scotland.

After the campaign, most of us would quite happily have sold those miserable, damp, godforsaken islands to the Argentines – but no one was going to take them by force.

I was due to go on leave and arrived home after every single task-force slot had already been assigned. In Plymouth, every ship the Royal Navy had was being placed on a war footing, and reserve ships, including cruise liners, were being commandeered as transports. It was an incredible sight. These reserve ships were jokingly referred to as STUFTs (Ships Taken Up From Trade). There were huge liners, like *Canberra* and the *QE II*, as well as large trawlers, such as MV (Marine vessel) *Northella* and MV *Cordella*, large, converted stern trawlers. These deep-sea trawlers, which operated from Kingston-Upon-Hull in peacetime, were capable of holding around a hundred men and a good deal of equipment; however, their precise role was to act in support of mine-sweeping operations around the Falklands and the British fleet, so, in effect, they usually carried between twenty and fifty personnel.

The minute people realised we were sailing to take back the islands, a wave of patriotic fervour erupted all over the country. Every street seemed to have a Union Jack flying over it, and soldiers found total strangers buying them drinks in pubs and shaking their hand on the street. There were crowds by the quaysides, waving to friends and relatives in uniform embarking on the ships.

In one way, the British government had well and truly contributed to the mess in the South Atlantic. To save money, various Royal Navy ships had been retired or mothballed over the previous five years. They had even withdrawn a vessel normally detailed to remain in waters around the Falklands, and the Argentines immediately misread the tea leaves and guessed that Britain could not care less about the islands. When the Thatcher government didn't react strongly to the landing of Argentine scrap dealers on one of the outer Falkland Islands, Buenos Aires thought it smelt a victory that could be won without bloodshed.

But the British government did care about their PR image and the public backlash if any Westminster administration did not fight to protect British territory and British citizens. The point was, it could be the Falkland Islands today, but Gibraltar tomorrow. Margaret Thatcher – mired in bad polls because of industrial lay-offs, clashes with the miners and the ongoing closure of heavy industries, particularly in the north of England – knew that if she let the Falklands go without a fight, her administration was finished.

When I arrived with the rear party from Norway, I was horrified to find that I was deemed surplus to requirements. The rest of 1st Raiding Squadron were already kitted, booted and ready to rock 'n' roll. I was told I would have to stay in Britain. One sergeant smiled and told me to head to Spain on my holidays. I panicked. My unit was going on war service for the first time in decades and I wasn't going to be part of it? It was NOT on.

I pleaded my case with Sergeant-Major Cliff D. I went individually to all my mates – especially the older guys – and offered to swap with any of them who might want to stay at home. One mate who was due to get married the next month was very interested, but was bluntly told by the sergeant-major that he was going, whether it suited him romantically or not. Eventually, I think the sergeant-major heard about my desperate efforts to join the fleet; he took pity on me and did in fact swap me with the lad due to get married. I was given the nod to join LSL *Sir Galahad*, the landing ship logistics vessel that was taking 1st Raiding Squadron to the South Atlantic. And the very ship I had just got off on my return from Norway. *Sir Galahad* would enter military history for the most tragic of reasons in a few short weeks, but by then I had been assigned elsewhere.

The bulk of the logistic ships were named after knights of the Round Table from Arthurian legend, and most of us already knew *Sir Galahad* from our regular deployments to Norway. The others included LSL *Sir Percival, Sir Geraint, Sir Tristram, Sir Lancelot* and *Bedivere*. We'd get to know *Sir Galahad* very well indeed over the journey south, which took all of eight stomach-churning weeks. Today, I never laugh when I see sailors grimace about the vagaries of the South Atlantic. I'm a pretty good sailor – most Royal Marines are – but there were days when I reckoned the seas were a bigger threat to us than any Argentine missiles. Such was the force of the swells we were lumping through that you could easily be knocked off your feet. For a laugh, we'd take off our boots and then skid on our arses straight across the deck on spilled tea from the large urns in the galley and then back again when the ship rolled in the opposite direction. The movement made everything – eating, sleeping and even working – a major trial of patience.

All the LSLs had giant Mexeflotes strapped to the side of the hull – these were floating platforms that, with an engine attached, would be used to ferry heavy equipment ashore. But, in the height of a South Atlantic storm, these Mexeflotes would loosen from their lashings and batter against the hull with a huge bang, like a missile impact. For soldiers trying to sleep just inside those bulkheads, the bangs sounded like the death-knell for the entire ship. Once the banging started, crews would have to be assigned – irrespective of the weather – to re-lash the Mexeflote to the hull.

Whatever the conditions, our Officers and Warrant Officers were determined to have us ready for action when needed. There were constant exercises, fire drills, embarkation drills and small-squad meetings. To be honest, we were all so pissed off with the routine and desperate to get off the bloody boat that we almost welcomed the chance to be shot at in the Falklands. Some lads did their best to lighten the mood: Page 3 girl, Linda Lusardi, had her image pinned up on virtually every

77

bulkhead door and newspapers were greedily passed around for news of home. Some took their minds off the marathon journey by endlessly talking football.

There were moments of humour too. One Royal Marine officer on *Sir Galahad* was determined that our time should be usefully occupied so he decided to offer Spanish lessons over the ship's tannoy. Captain Bell started with useful phrases like 'Hands Up', 'Drop Your Weapon' and 'Surrender Now'. But a few of the wits in our company offered our own key Spanish phrases like: 'Two beers please ('dos servethas')' and 'My friend, 'e has thi monee.'

When we finally arrived in the Ascension Islands, the generals and admirals decided we had to re-organise to better fit into their invasion plans. These islands had already been used as a base for 'Black Buck' raids in which RAF Vulcan bombers, with tanker support, had flown in and bombed the Falkland Islands' main runway to prevent it being used by strike aircraft to attack our fleet as it neared the islands. The raids had only limited impact, but they did put the Argentines on notice that the British were ready to fight for the Falklands. Together with the rest of 1st Raiding Squadron, I was cross-decked from *Sir Galahad* to her sister ship, *Sir Percival*, during our week-long stay in the Ascension Islands. It made little difference to us, except that it involved a painful amount of work in removing stores, repacking equipment and testing all our kit. We were joined on *Sir Percival* by other elements of 3rd Commando Brigade: Signal Squadron, Air Defence Troop and 3 Brigade Air Squadron.

Beneath decks, it was still impossible to keep things tidy, with personal possessions rolling around. There was also the all-pervading smell of puke from some poor bastard still suffering from seasickness. Some guys were so bad they had to be given special injections by the medics. But by the time we resumed our journey from the Ascension Islands, most had adjusted finally to the dreadful seas, and the number of mal-de-mer sufferers dropped dramatically. What made it all partially bearable was the general sense of mischief. We were allowed a few cans of beer at night – we are very different to the 'dry' military insisted upon by the USA on operational deployments. Needless to say, we managed to wangle a few cans more than our official quota, thanks largely to the fact that a few of the lads didn't actually drink, which I found amazing. We'd often start a sing-song on the open storage deck. On one occasion Raiding Squadron were roaring a song about 'body bags' to the 3 Brigade Air Squadron, and vice-versa. At the time we thought it was the height of hilarity, but, looking back, it's heartbreaking to realise that a few of those Air Brigade Squadron lads actually did go home in body bags just a few weeks later.

To me, it all seemed like a great adventure. I had joined the Royal Marine Commandos for adventure and to see the world. My dreams were now being fulfilled by the bucketful. My biggest concern was to stay alive to avoid causing hurt to my family, especially my mum. Mind you, I didn't advertise that to the other lads! I think every single one of us prayed that we wouldn't let ourselves down in a firefight with the Argies. I'd bled sweat and tears to become a Commando – and I wanted to live up to the Royal Marine's proud three-hundred-year-old tradition in combat. For almost all of us, this would be our first time under fire in a war situation – and every soldier worries about how he will react. In the end, most of us were relieved when we finally approached the Falklands. It meant an end to the soul-destroying cycle of training and endless waiting. We were finally about to see some action – and a soldier never wants too much time on his hands before the shooting starts.

Our mood darkened when, during one daily news briefing over the tannoy on *Sir Percival*, we were informed that HMS *Sheffield* had just been sunk by the Argentines. I was shocked. This was the first Royal Navy vessel sunk in anger since World War II. It hammered home the fact that while many of us thought this journey was a great adventure, we were actually going to war, and body bags were going to be filled. Then, as the news briefing finished, we were informed that the on-board film of the day was to be *The Cruel Sea*! One of my mates looked at me in horror and said, 'They are taking the piss, aren't they?' Unfortunately they weren't – and the troops on board watched Jack Hawkins and Stanley Baker fight for their lives, while thinking privately about the poor bastards on the *Sheffield*.

Just over two weeks earlier we had heard about the sinking of the Argentine Navy's cruiser, *General Belgrano*. The ship, an ancient United States Brooklyn-class World War II vintage cruiser, that should have been reduced to razorblades years before, was torpedoed and sunk by the Royal Navy nuclear submarine, HMS *Conqueror*, while steaming south of the Falkland Islands. Two Mark 8 torpedoes hit the cruiser, one in the bow and the other in the stern, instantly dooming the ship. None of us knew it at the time, but the stern torpedo either killed or trapped two hundred men in the *Belgrano*'s hull.

The *Belgrano*, like every large warship, had escorts – smaller ships in attendance, usually frigates or destroyers – tasked with anti-submarine patrols and mine-defence duties. Immediately after the cruiser was hit by the torpedoes, the escorts apparently attacked the place where they thought the *Conqueror* was located. But the escorts then left the area at high speed, instead of attending to the stricken boat. This had happened several times in World War I and World War II because of the fear that warships stopping or slowing to rescue survivors are themselves then a prime target for the attacking submarine. The *Belgrano* survivors were only picked up from the sea, after a gale, some thirty hours after the sinking.

Our initial reaction was jubilation and relief that the cruiser wouldn't now pose a threat to landing craft loaded with Commandos and Paras. But the news later emerged that 368 *Belgrano* sailors had drowned or been burned to death, and that was sobering enough for all of us. It was a ferocious loss of life – and we all knew now that blood would be spilled on the Falkland Islands. Every soldier looks at such combat deaths and, in quiet moments, thinks: it could have been me. I was glad it was an Argie cruiser and not one of our ships, but at the same time I knew just what a horrible death it must have been for the sailors involved. There isn't a lot of nobility in drowning in the freezing waters of the South Atlantic, or being trapped inside the hull of a rusting relic as it plunges to the seabed. Some armchair idiots might describe this as a nineteenth-century war fought over colonies and national pride, but for us soldiers, sailors and pilots who were going to pay the butcher's bill, there was nothing historic or jingoistic about it.

Dawn was just breaking as we steamed into a bay backed by a grey-green land mass, partially hidden by cloud and mist. It was 20 May, and we had just travelled 10,700km to reach the South Atlantic. I hadn't a clue where we were, bar the fact that this was one of the Falkland Islands, and what shocked me was that it looked exactly like Scotland or Ireland. It was only later in the day that I learned this was the long inlet called San Carlos Water.

I got a pretty good indication of what was to come on my first operational sortie. I was one of the first off the ship because my Raider was needed to power around the bay to support the urgent establishment of listening posts and advanced specialist positions. My first run was to bring Colour Sergeant Roy P., a Mountain Leader, and his team of three signallers ashore so they could establish a broadcast communications centre high on one of the nearby hills. We weren't even halfway ashore when, directly over our heads, an Argentine Skyhawk screamed past. It was so low we all involuntarily ducked – and then watched in awe as the pilot launched a rocket attack on a hill in front of us. He then broke away and was way out over the sea before the anti-aircraft batteries could zero in on him.

My God, I thought, is it going to be like this all the way through? I dropped the lads in the surf and zoomed back out to *Sir Percival* for my next load. Roy and his team began their long, hard trek up the side of the mountain. Poor bastards, I thought; if the Argies figure there's a communications centre on that hill, it won't be the last rocket attack. But communications were going to be vital if the landings were to be a success, both to co-ordinate land operations and to detect any raids the Argentine Air Force would mount against our ships. I was grateful I could stay mobile, and I realised that the speed of my Raider was going to be its best defence.

The frigates and destroyers escorting the fleet had already taken up picket positions, determined to protect the troop ships and carriers at all costs. Royal Navy commanders were now working round the clock to rush the troops ashore, and plans were being co-ordinated for air defence. It was a desperate race against time – and all of us knew it. Most of our warships were equipped with modern surface-to-air missile systems, but no one knew precisely how good those systems would be in action, as they had never been tested in combat. Bombing runs by Argentine aircraft were one thing, but stand-off raids by missile-armed strike aircraft were entirely a different proposition. Plus, everyone knew that the Argentines had purchased a small quantity of AM 30 Exocet missiles, whose capabilities were unknown.

The attacks weren't long in coming. An Argentine strike aircraft, an Italian-built Aermacchi MBB-339, swept over the fleet and launched a cannon and rocket attack. The fighter, flown by Lieutenant Guillermo Crippa, resulted in damage to the frigate HMS *Argonaut*, and its SeaCat missile deck was temporarily put out of action. Crippa managed to escape the area, despite being chased by a steel hail of heavy machine-gun fire, two separate missile launches and even repeated rounds from the 120mm gun on HMS *Plymouth*. Amazingly, Crippa's aircraft sustained only minor damage and he was able to limp back to base. He was later awarded Argentina's highest medal for valour.

A few of us Royal Marine Commandos suspected that units of both the Special Boat Service (SBS) and Special Air Service (SAS) were already ashore. We were right, and, over the course of the next few weeks, they would prove precisely the impact that Special Forces can have way above their actual numbers – a handful of SAS and SBS soldiers faced more than eight thousand Argentine soldiers. And they knew it. There was one story of one of the first Para and Commando units ashore being welcomed by an SBS unit; the SF lads took malicious pleasure in 'innocently' exclaiming: 'But we thought you weren't coming until the 24th!'

The Argentines were always wrong-footed by these raiders, and even the landing took them by surprise. Initially, the only response our lads had was from one Argentine scouting unit which used a 105mm recoilless gun to fire speculatively out towards Fanning Head which, with Chancho Point, marks the entry to the San Carlos Water inlet. The fire was totally inaccurate, never came near any of the fleet vessels and soon stopped once the twin 120mm guns on one warship, HMS *Antrim*, were brought to bear.

I may have been young, but even I knew that the air threat to the task force was probably what would determine the war. If the Argies could sink or damage our ships before we could get the troops and weapons ashore, they had a realistic chance of winning – or at least forcing an advantageous settlement. Our Raider unit would be fairly important in this situation, I realised. A few of us reckoned it was going to be our own 'Battle of Britain' moment – a period of days that would decide the outcome of the conflict.

On my second trip in with the Raider, towards Port San Carlos, I was grateful I was not overly superstitious by nature. As I approached the shore I stared in disbelief at the water. It was blood-red in colour; I was sure it was actually comprised of blood. For a moment I thought I was imagining things, then I spotted offal and sheep's heads bobbing past on the tide. I suddenly realised that, directly ahead, was an abattoir and our invasion parties were coming ashore through a sea of sheep's blood and guts. Sheep farming was one of the major occupations on the Falkland Islands, and most of the sheep were slaughtered at this plant. More than a few of us prayed it wasn't an omen of things to come.

That first morning was little more than organised chaos. We knew we were in a race against time and against the Argentine Air Force. We were a professional volunteer army and we were up against a largely conscript force, though we weren't sure what that might amount to. Still, this is what we'd trained for and, bravery aside, I didn't know a single guy in that task force who was not absolutely convinced that, if we could get ashore with all our gear, we would get the job done. The question was, would the Argentines allow it?

Even a humble 'grunt' like me knew the Argies were counting on sinking our ships. If they could hit one of the carriers, with the aircraft on board, the task force would be rightly fucked. If they hit one of the transports, with the soldiers, equipment and munitions on board, I knew it wouldn't be just sheep's blood that would be colouring the San Carlos Waters red. I was part of a frantic, massive, round-the-clock stampede to get the troops, equipment and logistics ashore so that the Argie pilots would only be able to target empty ships. Sleep was a luxury that none of us could afford until the ships were emptied of their crucial cargoes of men and materiel.

Even now, after a period of almost thirty years, I'm still astounded by the courage of those Argentine pilots. I hated the bastards because they were trying to kill us – but I still recognised courage when I saw it. Those guys must have had balls made of forged tungsten steel. They ignored distance and our Sea Harriers, missile defences and anti-aircraft batteries to launch their attacks, sometimes flying so low that one time they actually struck the communications antenna on one of our ships. I heard later that when they arrived back at their bases the Skyhawks had streaks of sea salt along their wings – that is how low they were flying over the waves. We learned later, too, that these low-level attack tactics were designed to avoid our missile defences; we didn't have an airborne early-warning system, so these tactics were hard to combat. None of us questioned the bravery of these pilots, and none of us questioned what would happen if they got through our defences. If I had not seen for myself just how low and fast these planes flew as they made their attacks I would not have believed it possible.

For us, the first forty-eight hours in the Falklands were a non-stop stream of Raiders and landing craft scurrying to the shore and then racing back out to the fleet for another detachment of troops and equipment. The German Field Marshal Erwin Rommel had predicted in 1944 that the first twenty-four hours would decide the success of the Allied D-Day landings. He was right, and the first twenty-four hours in the Falklands were also decisive. We got a huge amount of equipment, munitions and, most crucially of all, troops ashore in that first day.

But it wasn't all plain sailing. I recall sweeping past a good friend, Taff O., racing towards the fleet on a mission in his Raider. Taff was ferrying a helicopter pilot, who had been shot down, out to the hospital ship. That morning, two Gazelle helicopters from C Flight, 3 Commando Brigade, had launched from *Sir Galahad* to survey potential locations for Rapier anti-aircraft missiles. One of the Gazelles – with Sergeant

Andrew Evans and Sergeant Edward Chandlish aboard – went to ride 'shotgun' for a Sea King helicopter, which was using its sling to bring the missile equipment ashore. The Sea King pilot, realising that he was flying into a heavily defended position, aborted his flight path and warned the other choppers away. Evans and Chandlish decided to launch six unguided missiles at the Argentine position as part of a fire-suppression mission. But, as the Gazelle banked away following its attack, it was struck in the rotor and gearbox. The chopper crash-landed in the sea some 50m from a jetty. Evans had been mortally wounded. As the helicopter began to sink, Chandlish dragged the dying Evans from the wreckage and tried to swim ashore. An Argentine officer ashore, seeing that the men were wounded and defenceless, ordered his troops to cease fire. However, either some troops didn't get the message or chose to ignore it, because they opened fire on the aircrew with assault rifles as they struggled in the water.

Incredibly, Chandlish made it ashore without letting go of his friend. Some islanders found the men on the beach and took them to the relative safety of a local house, but Evans died a short time later of his wounds. Chandlish had shown amazing bravery in refusing to abandon his dying comrade, but the word quickly spread that injured and defenceless aircrew had been targeted by the Argentines. More than a few Paras and Commandos were mightily pissed off. When I passed Taff in the Raider, he was actually bringing Evans to the hospital ship in a body bag.

Within hours of Forty Commando and some of 2 Para getting on to the beaches, I learned later, our side were taking Argentine prisoners. Some put up a fight, but others, mostly conscripts, just seemed happy that it was all over. Being outdoors in the Falklands for any length of time was a miserable experience, particularly for troops not trained for it. The combination of SAS and SBS raids behind their lines and heavy gunfire from helicopters and Navy warships had persuaded them that resistance was pretty futile. Unfortunately, there was still a long way to go to Stanley, the capital of the Falkland Islands.

I worked with a really tight-knit unit: myself, Taff O., Bill K., Barry G., Sergeant Ginge S. and Sergeant Plym B. Plym was a godsend – superb under pressure, a natural leader and he knew exactly who was pulling their weight and doing their best. I had actually dreaded the thought of working under him because he had made my life a misery when I first arrived in the squadron – I reckon he thought I was a little cocky and needed to be shown, the hard way, how things operate in a Commando unit. But in the Falklands, he was the best sergeant anyone could ask for, and a lot of the success of our operations was down to him. We needed every bit of leadership and luck that we could get in these awful conditions.

Occasionally, the battle had a surreal edge to it. One evening we were operating near Estancia, in support of an SAS unit raiding deep behind enemy lines. There were four of us, led by Sergeant Ginge S., who had previously been stationed in the Falklands and knew a few of the locals, and was married to an Argentinian now living back in Plymouth. He kept telling us he had great connections around the island, and this particular night he finally got the chance to prove it. The tides in and around San Carlos Water could be treacherous and, sure enough, we got stranded up an isolated estuary called Estancia creek. Our Sergeant took his bearings and said, 'Not to worry, lads, I have a few friends around here.' We were in shock as he led us cross-country to a 1930s-style farmhouse. We kept lookout while he cautiously approached the house. Eventually, he signalled us to come inside and we were stunned to find a local couple merrily chatting away with him. Within minutes, they had ushered us over to the blazing fire of their Kelpers' cottage and served us plates of steaming hot mutton stew and cups of tea. It was the first decent food we'd had in months and I swear it tasted better than anything from the Ritz kitchens!

Unfortunately, our peaceful sojourn didn't last long. In the distance, I could hear the crackle of small-arms fire. Then, with a boom, we heard the distinctive sound of bombs being dropped. By the force of the explosions, I guessed they were 500kg bombs – and weren't that far from our location. The Falklands couple were terrified and sprinted for the hastily dug air-raid shelter in their garden. We were reluctant to leave the warmth of the fire and, when one round fell worryingly close to the house, dived under the kitchen table as a shelter! It slowly dawned on us that the bombs being dropped were probably British – and were meant to destroy an Argentine helicopter base not far from our location. Under the table, we kept saying, 'It's a game of numbers', counting down our chances of survival, though I don't think we actually believed our own logic. I started to giggle at the thought of our ridiculous predicament and, soon enough, we were all in tears of laughter at the hilarity of our plight. Here we were, three highly trained Commandos lying under a kitchen table for shelter from a bombing raid! We looked at each other for support. Before we knew it, the raid was over and the night once again descended into calm.

The next morning, as we sped back towards the fleet on a rising tide, I was amazed to see one of our LCVP's from HMS *Fearless* sitting 3m high in the air on top of a giant rock in the middle of the creek, just like a cherry on an ice-cream sundae. It was Barry G., who was driving Scouse K.'s Landing Craft Vehicle Personnel boat, and had apparently driven on to the rock which, at high tide, was totally invisible, though less than 10cm below the surface. Barry didn't want to abandon his stranded boat and was now desperately waiting for the tide to reach its maximum level so he could re-float it. I don't think I have ever seen anything funnier than the look on his face as we roared by – he was rightly pissed off as we rolled around in gales of laughter. We didn't improve his mood much by banking our Raiders at high speed around him, shooting waves of cold creek water all over him. Anyone watching wouldn't have thought we were in the middle of a war zone.

Sometimes, though, we knew that the laughter was merely a mask for our fear of what might happen next. I already mentioned the demise of the HMS *Sheffield* even before we arrived: on 4 May, she was on radar picket duty when a sea-skimming missile was detected. It had been presumed that even *Sheffield's* ancient radar system would pick up the launch aircraft and give sufficient time for counter-measures to be mounted. But a French-built Dassault Super Étendard aircraft, with a 1,200kph top speed, a range of 650km and maximum weapons payload of 2,100kg, launched a missile without being detected, and

Sheffield's crew had only seconds to react when the faint smoke trail from the French-built Exocet was spotted. The Argentine missile struck eight feet above the waterline and tore a huge gash in *Sheffield*'s hull and inner decks. Twenty crewmen, mostly in the galley area, died, while dozens suffered horrific burns. The rest were evacuated to a sister ship while the *Sheffield*'s burned-out hulk later sank under tow in heavy seas. The fires on board *Sheffield* burned for six whole days, and post-war studies showed the dangers of having too much light aluminium in a ship's structure. Good old-fashioned steel and armour was always hard to beat when it came to a firefight. The word went around the infantry units that as the *Sheffield*'s crew patiently awaited rescue they sang 'Always Look on the Bright Side of Life' from *The Life of Brian*; this was typical of the spirit of the time.

The seventeen days from 21 May would painfully underline to the Royal Navy the lethal new shape of marine warfare. On 21 May, the Argentine Air Force struck and sank HMS *Ardent* and HMS *Antelope*. On 24 May, Skyhawks struck San Carlos Water and a 500kg bomb hit *Sir Galahad*, the ship on which I'd just crossed most of the Atlantic. Incredibly, the bomb failed to detonate, but *Sir Galahad*'s luck had just run out. On 8 June, at Bluff Cove, she was hit by three more aerial bombs, which caused massive damage. The ship was unloading members of the 1st Welsh Guards at the time and a total of forty-eight personnel were killed. Dozens of others suffered terrible shrapnel and burn injuries. Fires wrecked what was left of *Sir Galahad* and the hulk was sunk at sea off the Falklands by HMS *Onyx*. Had I not been transferred to *Sir Percival* I could have been aboard.

On 25 May, the Argentine air force raided once more and claimed two more victims, HMS *Coventry* and MV *Atlantic Conveyor*. Coventry was a sister ship to *Sheffield* and she was hit while trying to deflect air attacks away from the troop ships in the fleet. While her loss was grievous, it was the sinking of the *Atlantic Conveyor* that caused mayhem. The merchant vessel was hit by two Exocets and the 19,500-tonne vessel was engulfed in an uncontrollable fireball as a result. When the inferno was finally brought under control, all that was left was a smoke-blackened, scarred hulk. She had been carrying a huge load of heavy-lift Chinook helicopters, runway construction material and even extreme-weather tents for the logistic and support units. With the loss of this shipment, transport would now become a major headache for the remainder of the Falklands mission. However, in the weeks before the attack, *Atlantic Conveyor* had managed to unload her priceless consignment of fourteen Harrier jets, which ultimately did enough to win the skies over the Falkland Islands.

I was particularly shocked by *Sheffield* getting hit. I mean, this was a major warship, one of the most powerful vessels in the Royal Navy. I remember thinking: Jesus, this is for real. How could a tin-pot army manage to sink *Sheffield*? What's next?' Even though *Sheffield* sank out at sea, we all knew she had been lost. And I'd be a liar if I didn't admit that the loss of a warship like this did not affect morale.

As I worked in my Raider around San Carlos Water, I could see the consequences of the air raids all around me. The bay was packed with ships and hulks, several still smouldering. We could all see for ourselves what happened when an Argentine missile or bomb got through the defensive shield. We all knew that the telltale plume of smoke on the horizon meant that body bags were going to be filled.

One of my mates, a lad called 'Knocker' W., was on *Sir Galahad* when it got hit. He reacted in true Commando fashion, defying the flames and explosions to throw fuel tanks from his Raider over the side so they didn't add to the inferno. It took real guts to do what he did – one gust of flame and he would have been incinerated in an instant. But it wasn't the fire or explosions that hurt Knocker most. I later heard that it would be years before he could manage to banish the image from his mind of the Welsh Guardsmen trapped on a burning *Sir Galahad*. Some of those who survived – like Simon Weston – would live the rest of their lives with horrific scars from the burns they suffered – proof, if ever anyone needed it, of the true horrors of modern warfare.

The landings were a close-run thing. The reality is that had either of the fleet's two carriers – HMS *Hermes* or HMS *Invincible* – been destroyed, we would have been without proper air cover and horribly vulnerable. The Argentine Super Étendards and their stand-off Exocet missiles were a lethal danger, but, as it transpired, there were too few of them to pose a decisive threat. Still, without our Harrier fighter cover, we would have been sitting ducks for bombing runs by Skyhawks and Mirage jets which now, to avoid the Harriers and our defensive missile cover, attacked almost at wave-top height, though with limited results.

I believe the difference was made by the Harriers and the American-made AIM9-L Sidewinder air-to-air missile. The Harrier was lethal at the low-to-medium altitude at which all the battles in the Falklands were being fought. The Argentine's best fighter, the Dassault Mirage, was deadly at higher altitudes – but the battle wasn't being fought up there. As we established land bases for the Harrier to refuel, its additional endurance made the Combat Air Patrol (CAP) over the Royal Navy fleet massively more effective. And the latest model AIM9-L Sidewinder missile that the Harrier carried – nicknamed the 'Lima' (for radio control purposes) – took a terrible toll of Argentine aircraft. After the war, I read in Max Hastings' book on the conflict that of the twenty-seven Lima Sidewinders fired by British pilots, twenty-four hit their targets.

The Argies knew they had to come in at low altitude and that the Harriers couldn't be everywhere at once. A further benefit of their tactic was that the 'ground clutter', or the misleading radar signals from such altitude, made some of our anti-aircraft missiles less than effective. The Sea Dart – our primary defence weapon – found it hard to achieve a 'lock' on an attacking aircraft at such low altitudes. The Blowpipe missile, in which many of us foot soldiers had such faith – was discovered to be virtually useless for anything but a target approaching directly upon the firing point. It all added up to giving the Argentine pilots a thin window through which to press home their attacks. And they attacked with no small measure of success.

In fact, for a time, the Argentines thought they had hit a carrier when they confused *Atlantic Conveyor* with either *Hermes* or *Invincible*. I heard after the war that the Argentines had hit our ships a number of times but, because of their low-level attack tactics, the bombs didn't detonate. Apparently, they were released at too low an altitude and simply didn't have time for the detonators to arm themselves prior to impact. Sixteen bombs in total had hit fleet ships in this manner and failed to explode. I cringe to think what the consequences would have been if those sixteen bombs had actually detonated. After the war, Lord Craig, a former marshal of the RAF, is said to have remarked that, 'Six better fuses and we might have lost.' As the war reached its climax, the Argentines realised what was happening and tried a temporary 'fix' of the fuses on their bombs. This is apparently what did for *Sir Galahad*.

Maybe it was the knowledge of the damage that they had inflicted on the British fleet that made the Argentine Skyhawk pilot fight with such desperation when I tried to cut him free of his lines after his plane was shot down that day in San Carlos Water. I've no doubt the pilot was convinced that I was going to cut his throat when I drew my combat knife to release him from his parachute lines so I could haul him aboard my Raider.

The poor bastard had just gone through every soldier's worst nightmare. One minute he was flying a multi-million-pound aircraft, trying to sink British ships and feeling bullet-proof, and the next he was being fished out of the frigid waters of San Carlos Water and staring at the combat knife of a bloody big Commando.

I wondered whether the Argie officers had told their pilots that the British didn't take prisoners. Part of me felt sorry for him as he struggled feebly to fend me off, looking more like a drowned rat than a proud fighter jock. I could tell the pilot was brave because of the way he tried to ignore his wounds and the numbing cold to fight me off, but his eyes betrayed the fact that he was afraid. I'd been a Commando long enough to know that you studied a person's eyes because they gave the clue as to a person's intentions. And this soaked, flailing pilot was scared.

It dawned on me, as I struggled with the tangled parachute lines, that sometimes the difference between life and death is a matter of mere seconds. If this Argie pilot had waited just two or three seconds longer to punch his eject button, he'd now be little more than a red stain on the cockpit of his fighter as it settled on the seabed below San

Carlos Water. But, because he'd reacted precisely the way his training had taught him, he would live to see another day, albeit safely under lock-and-key in a British warship.

Shit, he might actually get to know what it feels like to be under air attack, I thought. Mind you, it would be really tough luck to survive being shot down, only to die in a British warship from a bomb dropped by one of your Argie mates.

The only thing left of the fighter aircraft now were a few bits of flotsam on the sea surface and an oil slick from the aviation fuel, spilled by the ruptured tanks as the plane cartwheeled into the sea. I could smell the acrid stench of burned fuel still wafting over the sea surface despite the stiff breeze that whipped around San Carlos Water. There was now no trace of the other Skyhawks in the flight, and no sound of another incoming raid.

I also knew it was the courage of bastards like this that had sunk so many Royal Navy ships. On the long journey over I'd heard so many of the lads talk about how they hated the Argentinians for what they'd done and how they had humiliated the Falkland Islands garrison when their invasion took place. But when I looked at this guy – shivering from the combination of cold, fear, pain and adrenalin release – I just saw another young man, like myself, trying to do his duty. Deep down, it reminded me of my greatest hope in the Falklands: that I would do my job properly, support my mates and not fuck up. I didn't particularly hate the pilot, even though a few minutes earlier he had been trying to sink our ships and kill my mates. In hindsight, it would have been very easy to just circle the boat around him while he either drowned or got hypothermia. But the thought never entered my head.

In those situations, your training simply takes over. I was ordered to rescue the guy and that's precisely what I was going to do. I didn't hate the pilot enough to kill him just for being Argentinian and an enemy of my country. I actually respected his bravery because it took guts to attack our ships, given the shit-load of fire we were sending up into the air to protect ourselves. Those Argentine pilots were courageous – and they too paid a price in blood for that bravery. But my training and my orders told me that a prisoner like this was possibly worth his weight in gold, given the intelligence that could be gleaned from him. Ultimately, rescuing him could end up saving British lives. Mind you, if he had tried to pull a pistol on me I'd have taken him with my knife or drilled him with my submachine gun without a second thought.

When I finally got the pilot free of his parachute lines and dragged him on board, I could see he was close to the limits of his endurance. He was pale as a ghost, his knee looked wrecked, he was moaning in pain, and shivering so much from the freezing water that it looked like he was connected to a live electrical wire. This was the part of warfare that no one tells you about – the fear, the injuries, the horror and how brave men can be pushed beyond the limits of all endurance.

I doubted if the poor bastard had a clue what was going on around him by now. He just lay there, shivering and moaning, while an assault rifle was pointed at his head. But, as he was transferred to the boat that would bring him to the British hospital ship, he gazed around him and muttered something through chattering teeth. I didn't catch precisely what he'd said, but it sounded like 'Gracias'. It was a moment of humanity that I would never forget.

7

STERN TRAWLER TO COCHON ISLAND

The second phase of the Falklands operation involved breaking out from the bridgehead we had just established and fighting our way to the capital, Stanley, some 70km away. Our task force had landed in San Carlos Water by Port San Carlos, which was in the north-west of East Falkland Island. However, Stanley was to the south-east, on the eastern side of the island – and that's where the major Argentine garrison was. Until Stanley was taken, the war wouldn't be over. I knew we had two options: to starve the Argies out with a sea blockade, which would take time, or force them to surrender by smashing through their lines. Being young and probably a bit stupid, I was all in favour of the latter strategy.

But to get to Stanley overland, we would have to negotiate mountains, bogs, windblown scrubland and some freezing rivers and streams. Before Stanley could even be assaulted, strategic points en route would have to be taken, including Darwin, Goose Green and Teal Inlet – though there were some who felt the Argie garrisons there could have been bypassed and isolated. Goose Green and Darwin sat astride the southern approach route to Stanley – and dominated a thin strip of land which connected East Falkland Island to Lafonia in the south – it was an isthmus, with Darwin to the north and Goose Green to the south. Both settlements were ringed with forbidding mountains, shrouded in fog and freezing mist. The problem with ignoring Darwin and Goose Green was that they both contained sizeable Argentine forces – and I knew none of us liked the prospect of armed Argies to our rear. Teal Inlet was the biggest bay in East Falkland, and with it the sea cut a jagged gash into the northern coast, almost extending to the heart of the island. There were some small settlements there, but its strategic importance was that it extended close to Stanley – and offered us a chance to get troops by sea to the northern approaches to Mount Kent and Mount Longdon, which dominated the landward side of the capital.

Ultimately, Goose Green and Darwin were assigned to 2 Para and 5th Brigade. The mid-island approach to Stanley was assigned to 42 Commando and would be supported by the SAS. However, seaborne units of 42 Commando, including my unit, 1st Raiding Squadron, were being kept in reserve for special duties. The northern approach route was given to 3 Para and 45 Commando, unlike the other two routes, which would be massively supported by ship and helicopter transport if necessary; the northern approach would have to be undertaken largely on foot, with only minimal support by sea. This was partly because some of the heavy transport helicopters were now sitting on the bottom of the South Atlantic, thanks to the bombs and missiles of the Argentine Air Force.

'Yomping' was the term given to the overland march by the Marines and I felt it was very suitable, as it really expressed the feeling of trudging through this boggy terrain. It became one of the phrases synonymous with the Falklands War. In fact, a photo of a soldier trudging across country with a heavy pack and a radio antenna topped with a Union Jack flag became one of the most iconic images of the Falklands, and the picture was simply called: 'Yomping to Stanley.'

The idea was also for Stanley to be cut off by sea to the south by the Royal Navy, and to be approached by three different 'pincers' from San Carlos Water – to the north, north-west and west of the capital. The Argentine garrison would be forced to spread their defences around the entire perimeter at Stanley, rather than concentrating in strength at any one location. And the Argie garrison would also be constantly forced to look over their shoulder for a possible invasion from the sea by Commandos. There was nothing worse for the morale of defenders than the fear of being attacked from behind. But the Falklands Islands capital was ringed by small mountains including Mount Kent, Mount Longdon, Mount Tumbledown, Wireless Ridge and the Two Sisters, all of which were ideal defensive positions for the Argentines if they wanted to make a serious fight of it. And the indications were that the Argies weren't finished fighting quite yet.

As the infantry units marched off to join with their various 'pincer' groups, I discovered I wouldn't be going with them. Much as I wanted to be part of the assault spearhead, I was going to remain on reconnaissance, logistic and special mission duties with the rest of 1st Raiding Squadron. We would remain with our fast boats, and we hoped the fleet bosses had special plans for them. I was praying that we'd see some action – though that wasn't perhaps the smartest thing in the world to be praying for.

As the emphasis switched to the break-out from the beachhead, I eventually found myself at the centre of my most exciting operation of the entire Falklands tour.

My prayer for action had been answered – and beyond my wildest dreams. I was ordered, with the other members of our section of four men, to report to our commanding officer who told us we were being assigned to support a joint SAS/SBS Special Forces mission. It was precisely the kind of thing we had trained for – covert insertion of Special Forces troops behind enemy lines. It was all part of the 'fuck with their minds and morale' effort. While the Argies would be trying to fight off three separate British assaults on their lines in front of Stanley, we would be giving them something to worry about behind their lines.

Two SAS lads, Ray and Geordie, came in to brief us. Both were ex-Paras and were hugely experienced. They outlined the mission, which was to carry out a pre-emptive strike at facilities in the Port Stanley area. The SAS and SBS were tasked with ensuring the Argentines couldn't call upon local logistical support, even if that meant blowing up the islands' main oil storage depot. Ray told us that we would load our

Raiders on to the stern of the trawler, *Cordella*, in San Carlos Water and then slip quietly out to sea. The 1st Raiding Squadron would be the transport and escort team for an SAS/SBS detachment who would then sabotage the oil tanks. There would be twenty-four personnel in total, roughly six per Raider.

The *Cordella* would steam out to sea and, when out of sight from land, would swing south and skirt around Lafonia island. Then, while still out at sea, we would unload our Raiders from *Cordella* under cover of darkness and transfer to a small island called Cochon, where we would lie low until the following night. Cochon Island was located to the north of Stanley, but was fewer than sixty minutes from the capital by Raider. Though Cochon was little more than an uninhabited lump of rock, it offered us a chance to shelter and prepare for the oil-farm assault which would occur at night and in blanket darkness.

We would then bring the Raiders to an agreed rendezvous point where we would link up with the rest of the Special Forces team. Once everything was locked and cocked, we would ferry the SAS and SBS guys across the channel to a landing point a short distance from Port Stanley's oil storage depots. As well as denying the Argentinians the use of the oil, the idea was that such an enormous explosion would make them suspect we were attacking the capital from that side. Senior British commanders hoped that we'd cause enough havoc to force the Argentine commander to divert troops away from his inland defence lines – thereby making the job of the Commandos, Paras and other troops converging on Stanley that bit easier.

The concept of the raid was that we would get in and out fast – and avoid getting engaged by heavier forces. I couldn't wait to go. At last I was going to see some action and not just act as a glorified water-borne taxi driver for the fleet. I tried hard to stop myself grinning like an idiot and desperately tried to look as serious as the two SAS lads. But I hadn't yet fired my SLR in anger – and I wouldn't get any better chance than a Special Forces mission in support of the SAS and SBS.

The SAS lads paused and looked around at us – as if sizing us up and judging whether we were ready for the mission. I glanced at Sergeant

Plym, and knew without asking that he was gung-ho for this kind of thing. A sergeant wouldn't normally be running a small section of Raiding craft on a mission, but our section commander, Corporal Taff B., had been flown back from Ascension Island with a trapped nerve in his back and Plym had taken over. Ray stressed that we weren't going to go toe-to-toe with entrenched Argentine forces. We were there to do two things: get in and out as fast as we could and, just as importantly, inflict as much damage on the oil-tank farm as possible. It was the old infantryman's fondest dream. I would finally get the chance to blow shit up.

The rest of 1st Raiding Squadron were as elated as I was and were determined to show the SAS lads that we were up to the task. I looked around and realised that the mood was one of relief that we were finally seeing some action. No one was worried about going into harm's way. I reckoned Commandos were more than equal to anything the Paras could do – and the SAS, after all, were Paras with attitude. I made eye contact with the SAS lads, and I hoped they read the enthusiasm on my face. One of them smiled a little. 'Pack light,' Geordie added, which I took to mean: bring as much ammunition as possible.

Meanwhile, the three inland 'pincers' were now closing remorselessly on Stanley. The Argentinians had fought stubbornly and bravely at Goose Green and Darwin, but had been forced to yield the field on each occasion. Goose Green had been the first major target of the land war. It didn't pose a particular threat to the march on Stanley, but, because it had a strong garrison and a partially damaged airstrip, it was felt it had to be taken. Goose Green was located due south of San Carlos Water beyond the freezing Sussex mountains and, with Darwin, controlled the southern approaches of East Falkland. From talking with other Commandos on fleet duties in San Carlos Water, I knew the Paras had been stuck in the Sussex mountains since the initial landing and were now bulling for action. To their dismay, they hadn't been allowed to probe the defences around Darwin or Goose Green up until now because the SAS were operating in that area and had been causing havoc in the Argentine rear areas. It didn't help the Paras that conditions in the mountains were pretty miserable.

Prestige was now at stake because the Argentine gunners at Goose Green had already shot down one of the priceless Harrier jets – though, of course, I didn't know this at the time. The eventual assault on Goose Green was led by the Paras who, in the fighting, lost the Commander of 2 Para, Colonel H. Jones, who was shot and killed as he led his men against entrenched Argentine positions. Jones was immediately lionised by the press back in England, who loved his tough leadership style and his battle motto: 'Hit them really hard and they will fold.' He was killed when the battle was already virtually won.

The Paras and Commandos had taken serious losses, but the best Argentine forces had been unable to keep well-prepared and well-defended positions from their attacks. Goose Green cost 2 Para sixteen men killed and thirty-four wounded, a small number compared to almost a hundred Argentine fatalities and more than a thousand personnel captured. The Argentine conscripts saw what was happening, and their morale, little by little, began to collapse; their Task Force Mercedes units at Goose Green had been among the best on the island. Their commander, Lieutenant-Colonel Italo Piaggi, knew his job and was respected as one of the best fighting soldiers they had. He and his troops had fought bravely and stubbornly, but still couldn't defend Goose Green. The question the young conscripts now asked was: if these crack units could not hold out, then who the hell could?

The weather conditions didn't help and everyone, on both sides, was now feeling miserable because of the constant rain, snow and bone-chilling cold that swirled around the islands. Some soldiers were spending so much time in waterlogged fox holes and shelters that trench foot became a problem. The conditions were testing both men and materiel to the limit. I was still operating from San Carlos Water and, to lighten the mood, a few of us had decorated our camp with sheep skulls mounted on poles. Looking back, I don't know what we were at, but it seemed a good idea at the time. The reality was that life in the open in the Falklands was tough, miserable and stamina-sapping. As some Argentine positions were taken around Goose Green, Darwin and further inland, British troops marvelled at how some artillery pieces had sunk almost above their wheels in muck and sludge.

In fact, the weather was now as big a danger to the Argentine Air Force as the rapidly improving British air defences. Two Pucará ground-attack aircraft flew a last-ditch fire-support mission to Goose Green from Stanley, but the pilots became separated in dense mist. The Pucará was a twin-turboprop aircraft that had originally been built for a counter-insurgency role in South America. Although it had very heavy firepower, it was slow and extremely vulnerable to ground fire. It was never suited to the kind of war being fought in the Falklands, but it was all the Argies had on the island. We all knew the concrete runway at Stanley had been damaged in the long-range 'Black Buck' raids by the RAF's Vulcan bombers, and the Pucará, with its short take-off run, could still be used. I heard later that the Argie pilots had attacked Goose Green from the south-east, hoping to avoid overflying British land positions and British warships which had taken up position offshore. But the danger was that the centre of East Falkland Island was studded with major mountain ranges – and was notorious for the way fog, mist and treacherous winds swirled around the steep slopes. Even experienced pilots shuddered at the thought of going from reasonable visibility to zero visibility in a matter of seconds, all the while surrounded by major mountain ranges.

One of the Pucarás vanished without trace and the pilot was not found until 1986, four years later, when the wreckage of his plane was identified on a mountainside. He had apparently become totally disoriented in the thick mist and had flown straight into the hillside. While it was one less Argentine pilot to worry about, I couldn't help thinking that it was a dreadful way for any warrior to die.

Yet, Goose Green was a lesson for all. The German general, von Moltke, once remarked that even the best-laid battle plans don't survive their first contact with the enemy. It was a theory I would also learn well that night as we finally launched our own assault on the oil depot. The *Cordella* slipped quietly out to sea from San Carlos Water and, in a matter of hours, had swung south to bring us into position to the north of Stanley. I had helped load my Raider on to *Cordella* in a feeling of pure exhilaration – but now, as we neared our launch point, I felt an icy knot tightening in my stomach. Whatever happens, don't let me fuck up, I prayed. I just wanted to prove myself a good Commando – I wanted to show I was worthy of that Green Beret and that I didn't let my mates or my unit down.

We left *Cordella* without incident and the crew gave us a cheery 'thumbs up' salute; one whispered, 'Give 'em hell for us, lads.' We headed as quietly as we could towards land. We were on silent operations so any communication was by hand signal or in a hushed whisper. There were no lights to give away our position and everyone had their faces blackened. I focused on my job of getting the Raider safely to our hiding place on Cochon Island. I wondered whether the SAS troops in my boat could hear the 'thump, thump, thump' of my heart, I was so pumped up in anticipation of combat.

We reached Cochon Island without incident, under the cover of a mercifully dark night with absolutely no moonlight. But the rest-up period that followed seemed to drag by. This place wasn't so much an island as a two-hundred-metre-long lump of rock. It had only two saving graces for us: there was deep water to the north, which was out of sight of the mainland on East Falkland, and it was covered in kelp. Our Raiders were covered in camouflage paint which, combined with netting and thick layers of dark-green kelp, made us virtually invisible to any Argentinian, even to a spotter aircraft overflying us. We were ordered to keep low and avoid being silhouetted against the skyline. We were north of Stanley, so I knew we would be taking our Raiders south in the darkness. In the distance, I could make out the mountains of East Falklands, and one of the SAS lads told me that the mountain nearest us was Mount Low.

The other guys and the SAS lads tried to get a little sleep, but I knew it was a wasted effort for me because I was so flush with adrenalin. I grabbed a little food and checked my kit and weapon for about the thousandth time. I had brought a little extra ammunition 'just in case', though I knew that the mission would be deemed a real success if we could blow the oil-tank farm sky-high without having to fire a shot. Finally, when darkness fell again, we prepared for the final leg of the mission. We re-checked our kit one last time; I had brought along a spare outboard motor, and checked and re-checked my SLR assault rifle to the point almost of obsession. I had stowed my extra ammunition clips within easy reach, though the fighting was supposed to be left to the SAS and SBS. We boarded our four Raiders and silently began the crossing from Cochon Island. After a time, the Raiders switched from a course due south to a westerly route – this would bring us right up the inlet towards Stanley. The Raiders crept slowly up the channel, all four coxswains, including myself, keeping the engine revs as low as possible to avoid being heard. One of the things we'd been taught was that noise carries for some distance over water, and even farther in the cold, frigid conditions of the Falklands.

Unfortunately, as we approached Stanley, we realised that an Argentine hospital ship was steaming down the same channel, almost parallel to us, obviously heading to berth off Stanley. The ship was lit up like a Buenos Aires disco, and the lights from the vessel carried for a hundred metres or more out into the gloom and darkness of the channel. The chances of our Raiders being highlighted against the illuminated hospital ship were quite high, but we had no other way of making it to the beachhead in time for the rendezvous with the rest of the strike force. 'Christ, that's bloody bad timing,' I cursed. We couldn't afford to wait and let the ship pass up the channel because every minute of darkness was vital to our mission. We had no option but to keep going.

I cringed as I realised we had to pass within a hundred metres or so of the hospital ship. I figured that the lights were so bright they were sure to illuminate our Raiders as we crept past. The only saving grace was that the Argentinians had enforced a strict curfew on Stanley and the farmhouses scattered around the inlet. They had also ordered all householders to 'black out' their windows so that the lights of Stanley wouldn't act as a reconnaissance beacon to British forces. This meant that there were no lights behind us on land that could betray our presence to suspicious eyes on the hospital ship. 'I hope the Argies are trying to get laid with those nurses on board', I thought silently, almost willing my Raider to leave the hospital ship behind and return to the safety of the enveloping darkness.

We could also hear noises from the hospital ship and voices in Spanish from the ship's tannoy system carrying over the water surface on the frozen air. We hadn't a clue what was being said or whether we had been spotted. But it was too late to change route now. I glanced around and marvelled at the two SAS lads on the Raiders. They were alert, focused and ready for action – but they seemed no more concerned about the threat of the hospital ship than the choice of menu in the brigade canteen. 'Jesus, these are cool customers', I thought.

We crept on, as silently as we could, ready to accelerate to maximum throttle at the first sign of trouble. Plym was constantly checking the route ahead with his night sight for any obvious navigation references and any enemy patrols that might be about.

In the distance, I could make out the shale beach that was our destination. I gestured with my hand to the SAS troopers and gave the ready signal. I carefully brought my Raider up to the surf line and, soundlessly, I slipped into the sea and began dragging the boat up on to the beach. We rendezvoused with the rest of the assault party and began to disembark silently with the weapons and explosive charges. We had landed on the northern side of the channel – and directly to the south, across about 150m of water, lay the oil-tank farm which was our target. The tank farm was to the north of Stanley itself, but on the southern side of the inlet channel. I strained my eyes to see through the darkness and gloom and thought I could make out the looming shapes of the oil tanks in the distance.

After checking their gear and loading all the assault team, three of the Raiders set off for the small beach opposite us where the oil tanks were located. My orders were to stay with the fourth Raider and secure the return point on the beach opposite the tank farm and directly across the channel. The withdrawal after the attack would be co-ordinated from here with the two SAS troopers, Ray and Geordie. If necessary, we would provide covering fire for the other Raiders after the attack as the assault force re-crossed the channel, hopefully against the backdrop of thousands of litres of burning oil. Ray, Geordie and I would then ensure that everyone got away, even if one boat was damaged. Initially, I was deflated to be left behind – I wanted to be in the thick of the action. But then it dawned on me that I was just as likely to see action as the assault teams if something went wrong. Very clever, I mused. We'll be covering the retreat and protecting against the Argies trying to cut us off from behind.

My thoughts were cut off suddenly when the dunes ahead of the attack party erupted in a hail of smoke and gunfire. I was still in the relative safety of the beachhead opposite, but even I physically cringed at how the silence had been so completely shattered. It was as if the gates of Hell itself had been torn open. The three Raiders were clearly highlighted, such was the flare of gunfire now being directed at us. Special Forces missions depend to an enormous degree on surprise and stealth – and we had lost both in a matter of seconds. What the fuck had gone wrong? Had the Argentinians known we were coming or had they spotted the Raiders against the lights of the hospital ship? Either way, it didn't matter now. The Special Forces team immediately ordered a 'hot' extraction. Given our numbers and our light weapons, we couldn't hope to engage dug in and heavily armed Argie forces. If the assault team persisted with their attack, they'd be cut down before they could even cross the beach to the oil-tank farm. It was suicide to try and take entrenched positions which were covered by squad machine guns.

I knew this was our nightmare scenario. We were miles behind enemy lines and, between us and British lines in the distant mountains, we had learned earlier from newspaper accounts, there were close on eight thousand Argentinians. I knew that the SAS and SBS lads had been making life hell for the Argies for weeks, so they would face a particularly rough time if captured. Our main withdrawal option was to get back down the coast – and bloody fast before every Argie with a rifle decided to take a potshot at us. But trying to flee down the channel in daylight, close to the Argentine lines, was pretty much a suicide mission.

Plym was desperately trying to ensure that the three Raiders and the assault force got back to the RV beach. It was Plym who had ordered me to beach my Raider and support Ray and Geordie, who would now act as rearguard to allow the rest of the Special Forces team to extract safely. Christ, that spare engine is going to slow us down, I thought desperately to myself. It must weight 300kg or more – I'll have to dump the fucking thing as soon as I can. However, because we weren't part of the main raiding force, we became separated from them as they made their way back to our beach. Owing to the intense volume of Argie fire, they landed to the east of our position, some distance down the shoreline. The combination of the darkness and the confusion of the firefight resulted in all the Special Forces lads and the coxswains making their way to a section of beach 300m from where the Raiders had originally landed. Lucky for them, they were closer to the sea and the route down the coast to British lines. The assault party came ashore, checked their gear and immediately began an emergency evacuation.

Ray and Geordie were flashing the coded signal as a guide to the returning assault party, but the Argentinians, who must have spotted the signal on the opposite beach by the oil tanks, immediately opened fire on us. I hit the dirt as all hell broke loose and assault-rifle rounds peppered around us – but Ray and Geordie stood upright, kept the signal flashing, and faced the incoming fire as if they were bullet-proof. I still don't know why they did that as bullets hammered around them, but the two lucky bastards escaped without a scratch. In that one instant, I realised what made the SAS man so special. No matter how much training you do, there is nothing like the 'zing' of 7.62mm rounds flashing past your head to teach you what combat is all about. All it would have taken was one lucky round and the Argies would have been scraping bits of Yorkshireman off this godforsaken beach.

It was my job now to get these guys out. I knew that we were way behind enemy lines, miles from friendly forces and hopelessly outnum-bered, but I wasn't going to leave Ray and Geordie's side. I didn't think what I was doing was particularly courageous – I was simply being a Royal Marine Commando. You don't run from a fight – you run towards it. To be honest, it never even entered my head to abandon them, nor did I worry that by sticking with them I could be signing my own death warrant. I was fucked if I was going to leave them to their fate. Simple as that. Whatever happened to them was going to happen to me as well.

The weight of Argentine fire we were now attracting was pretty serious. Bullets were whistling all around us, but I noted instantly that the defenders thankfully didn't have mortars, which would have made things very tricky indeed for us. The Argies were clearly dug in around the tank farm and were firing at us not only with assault rifles, but with heavy machine guns. Within seconds, incoming rounds were kicking up sand and pebbles from around my beached Raider, which the Argies had clearly spotted. All the Raiders had their engines damaged by rifle rounds, but miraculously they kept working.

Ray and Geordie, having confirmed that the rest of the Special Forces team had finally extracted, decided that we should get away overland. And fast. Because we had become separated from the main assault party during the extraction, I could see their point about abandoning my Raider. Such was the volume of Argie fire that we probably wouldn't make it 50m from shore without being hit. As a Commando and a member of 1st Raiding Squadron, it totally ran against my training to abandon my boat. I thought to argue with the SAS lads, but decided they had extensive combat experience and I didn't. If they said to leave the Raider and head inland, that's what I'd do. I trusted them and their operational experience and this wasn't the time for an argument with all hell breaking loose around us.

I suddenly realised that, even if we had got the Raider off the beach and headed out to the channel, where would we have gone? We would be a sitting target in the channel for every Argie with a rifle. We had successfully covered the extraction of the main assault party, which was our primary job, but we had lost vital minutes as a result for our own withdrawal. If the Argies had flares, we would serve as little more than shooting practice as we struggled to rejoin the main group whose Raider engines were now little more than a fading noise in the distance. I guessed that the three other Raiders would now head far up the coast beyond the Argentine perimeter, beach their craft and then go inland to rejoin British lines.

But that option was clearly now beyond Geordie, Ray and me. There was also the small problem that we had no more operational intelligence on precisely where either the Argentine or friendly forces were around Stanley. The only choice we had now was to head inland towards positions we knew for certain were in British hands. With Ray and Geordie already ready for a combat-march inland, I knew I hadn't a second to lose.

I stripped off my waterproof suit, put on my combats and got ready to trudge off with them. I had combat gear, my SLR rifle, a good stock of ammunition and just for good measure, a light anti-tank weapon, called a LAW 66. I strapped this to the top of my pack and, despite the extra weight, I felt a lot more comfortable with the extra firepower it offered. We weren't likely to come across any Argentine light tanks or armoured patrol cars in these conditions, but I wasn't about to take any bloody chances. Ray and Geordie were waiting for me, ready to combat-march inland.

Neither of the SAS lads was injured, though we later discovered that a few of the guys in the main assault party had taken serious hits in the firefight. All three of us knew the importance of putting as much distance as possible between ourselves and the beach before dawn broke. I silently blessed the fact that we had launched our assault just after midnight – and that we still had several hours of darkness left as we made our escape. We skirted widely around the dunes to get behind the flank of the Argentine defenders and then made a beeline for the brooding mountains in the distance. Ray and Geordie told me that G and D Squadrons of 22 SAS had established base positions around Mount Low, and that was now our best hope of safety.

We tried to make speed, but also had to be as silent as we possibly could. Our nightmare scenario was to unwittingly stumble upon an Argentine sentry in the dark. I kept a firm grip on my SLR in case I heard the faintest sound or a Spanish voice. But Ray and Geordie were real pros; they halted every so often, listened carefully and gauged our progress by compass. I also reckon that their night vision must have been radically better than mine because they seemed able to make out features of the countryside that were familiar to them. I realised, with a jolt, that Ray and Geordie either had the entire topography of Stanley memorised, or else they had been roaming around here with other SAS units while the rest of the British forces were landing on the other side of the island. All I knew was that we were heading to Mount Low, about 15km to 20km away.

But, despite doing our best to put distance between us and the oil-tank farm, we were not able to make it to the foothills of the mountains by the time dawn was breaking, and a bleak light began to illuminate the dreary landscape. In horror, I realised that there was fuck-all cover – the entire bloody place seemed to be bog, moor, open scrubland and only a few pathetic windblown trees. If we kept moving in daylight, we were going to stick out like sore thumbs and would be easy pickings for even a short-sighted Argie sniper. I couldn't see any houses, though I reckon there had to be a few farms around here somewhere. But I knew it would be a risk approaching anyone for shelter – you never knew who would give you shelter and who would discreetly call the Argentinians just to protect themselves and their family. I cringed as I realised I was bound for a day-long sojourn in a freezing, water-filled ditch.

It was no surprise when Ray ordered that we lie up, so we rolled out our sleeping kit in a shallow ditch, partially covered in snow. We had to eat cold rations, as it was far too dangerous to attempt to light any kind of fire. Needless to say, the food tasted like shit, but it was better than nothing. The other major fear of moving in the daylight was the risk of attracting sniper fire from the Argentine positions. I knew from the briefings we'd had that the Argies were dug in all around Stanley – and that their best hope now was that we'd suffer such heavy losses in assaulting heavily defended positions that the British commanders might call off the pincer attack. I also knew that three men in military gear crossing moorland would be taken as target practice for any Argie infantryman worth his salt.

I lay in the ditch and listened carefully for any sounds around us. A conscript army was hard to keep disciplined, and raw recruits often broke the boredom of duty by chatting, smoking or eating – all of which gave us the chance to have some warning of what was going on around us if the Argies were close by. Every so often, Ray or Geordie would carefully scan the countryside around us for signs of movement or Argie patrols. If we're caught out here in the open we're totally bollocks'ed, I thought. Not even the bloody anti-tank rifle will be much good. But I ensured that my SLR was kept as dry as possible, and that the extra ammunition clips were easy to hand.

The combination of tension and cold, wet and miserable conditions made it impossible to sleep. The best we could hope for was to be able to rest our legs for the remaining trudge to the mountains. We needed food to keep our energy levels up and to avoid hypothermia as best we could. I carefully stuck my head up and glanced over to the mountains, trying to judge the distance. Maybe 10 clicks (km) more? I wondered. Just then, I heard Geordie hiss in my direction, 'Get under cover, chopper coming.'

We tried to bury ourselves deeper into the slimy ditch as the rotor blades of the helicopter got louder and closer. In the end, I couldn't help but twist on to my back and gaze upwards as the helicopter swept directly over our position. In shock, I realised that it was a British scout helicopter – maybe a Gazelle – and it was flying a huge white flag draped beneath its landing skids, weighted down by a large metal disc. Oh Jesus, don't tell me we've surrendered, I thought to myself in panic. I wondered whether the Argentinians had hit the carriers and the sound of the explosions hadn't reached us. I actually thought I recognised one of the occupants of the chopper as Major General Jeremy Moore, the British ground forces commander.

'Was that Major General Moore?' I whispered to Ray. 'Don't be daft – that's probably Maggie Thatcher come to tell the Argies that Buenos Aires is next if they don't fuck off home soon,' the SAS trooper snorted. 'Get some bloody sleep,' he grunted, as he rolled over and followed his own advice. I lay on my back and wondered what the hell was going on. I wasn't so much worried now about making it to the mountains in darkness as finding out what was happening with the war. Had any more ships been sunk? And why was a British helicopter flying into Stanley when fighting was still going on?

On the ground, Ray, Geordie and I did the only thing we could – we waited, and when dusk finally fell many hours later, we got ready to move on. There was less likelihood of coming across heavy Argentine positions as we got farther away from Stanley, but snipers were still a major concern. I knew we only had to be unlucky once for our escape to end in tragedy. Our trek had also become much more difficult as we neared the foothills of Mount Low – we had to be careful not to fall over gullies and crevices – and I suddenly thought with dread about being accidentally shot by an alert British sentry. But, throughout it all, Ray and Geordie focused on the job at hand – getting us near enough to the lines and then establishing careful contact with the SAS positions to allow for our safe approach.

It was an exhausting march, but, in the early hours of the morning, almost thirty-six hours after we had set off, we finally reached British positions. We approached with great care, but the SAS lads established contact and we were cleared to approach British lines. There were few comforts on offer – 22 SAS were operating from a clearing on the Mount Low mountainside. The major advantage was that the height offered a panoramic view of the approaches to Stanley. I was simply told to bed down in any snow-filled nook or crevice I could find. This was 1982 and waterproof Gortex was very much a future dream for all British forces, and even Special Forces – who traditionally got the best equipment first – were only just benefiting from waterproof equipment that didn't make you sweat on the inside. So, most of my kit was either soaking wet or pretty damp. One of the SAS lads at the base gave me a semi-dry sleeping bag cover and told me to try and keep warm. What they didn't know was that to me this was still like a holiday camp compared to Lympstone! And the Falklands had the added benefit of the fact that, miserable as you might be, the NCOs and officers were actually trying to help you rather than deliberately make your life more painful. And working alongside the SAS lads was an incredible experience because the confidence and training of these guys was like nothing I had ever seen before. But that night in the open was like exercise Compass Rose all over again. I spent the night wiggling my toes to prevent frost 'nip' or, even worse, frostbite, from setting in. I wasn't helped by the fact I was wearing thin Northern Ireland boots designed for the streets of Belfast and not the extremes of the Falkland Islands tundra.

The next day, a Sea King rendezvoused with the Special Forces and I was shipped back to *Sir Percival* in San Carlos Water. I never met Ray and Geordie again, not even to say good luck or goodbye. They both reported to the commanding officer at the Mount Low position and then went to rejoin their SAS unit. I arrived back on ship to be told that Plym and the other lads in 1st Raiding Squadron thought I'd been killed when there was no sign of me or the guys I was with. After weeks of praying to get off the logistics ship, I was now glad to be back on board, dry and away from the muck and snow. After a hot meal and a warm drink, I began to feel human again and I was assigned a cabin to rest up. I opened the berth door and stood open-mouthed at the sight in front of me: Plym was there. 'Thought you were dead,' he said. 'Take a seat. Get yourself ashore and go to Ajax bay for some war reserve clothing.'

It was at this time that I met Bill Kavanagh who was doing the same as me. It coincided with the mass burial of Colonel H Jones and the Paras who were lost in action at Goose Green.

A Royal Navy sailor nonchalantly told me that a 500kg bomb from a Skyhawk had hit the ship two days beforehand, slashing from one side of the hull to the other. But it had failed to explode and *Sir Percival* escaped with merely a gash in her hull. It was defused as we slept safely in our beds.

I heard later that the chopper that had flown over Ray, Geordie and me contained a parlay team from Major General Moore to his Argentine counterpart, Colonel Menéndez. Major General Moore – famed for wearing a desert hat no matter what the weather conditions – had been sending out peace feelers to the Argentinians since Goose Green and Mount Tumbledown. From a military point of view, the matter had already been decided – in our favour – it was just a question of ending the fighting before more lives were needlessly lost. When the talks

111

hammered out a ceasefire agreement, which was subsequently endorsed by General Galtieri in Buenos Aires, the white flag was slowly hoisted over Stanley. Unfortunately, I wasn't there to see any of it because it had all happened while I was marching to Mount Low and then being transferred back to *Sir Percival*.

We later learned that some of the senior Argentine commanders were worried about the consequences for the civilian population if the fighting degenerated into a house-by-house fight for Stanley. To date, the war had been fought according to the rules and with an absolute minimum loss of life to civilians. Some newspapermen later wrote that it was the last colonial war. Sadly, it would also be the last war in modern times that would be fought according to such civilised rules.

General Menéndez knew that his position was hopeless from the point when Mount Longdon, Wireless Ridge and Mount Tumbledown had fallen. He knew that once his forces had lost the necklace of mountains that surrounded Stanley, the capital couldn't be defended. The fighting had been savage and the Argentinians had thrown their best troops into holding those positions, but the loss of the high ground meant that, from a military point of view, it was now virtually impossible to hold Stanley without massive reinforcements. And the Argentine commander knew that there was no hope of fresh troops from Buenos Aires making it through the maritime exclusion zone that the Royal Navy had erected around the Falklands. The sea approaches to Stanley were now firmly closed. The air attacks had failed to cripple the British fleet, and losses to Argentina's irreplaceable pilots and air crew were now at catastrophic levels. The senior Argentine commanders knew the battle had been fought – and lost.

When I was on *Sir Percival* I heard that one of the first units to spot the white flag over Stanley and confirm the Argentine surrender was 1/7th Gurkha Rifles, which was probably quite apt because the Argentine conscripts, for whatever reason, had come to believe that the Gurkhas were cannibals and traditionally ate their slain enemies as a ritual of warfare! Like a lot of other British troops, I found this hilarious, but it served its purpose in terms of black propaganda that sapped Argentine morale. Argentine prisoners were visibly terrified of the Gurkhas, often a full head smaller than themselves. I always had enormous regard for the Gurkhas – they were incredible soldiers and never seemed to complain, no matter what the conditions or the orders. It was also pretty inspiring to see these little guys marching with kit bags almost as big as themselves and weighing close to their own body weight.

The Argentine surrender was confirmed the next day – and it was cheers and beers all round. I was at sea but would have given anything to be in Stanley when the actual surrender occurred. Word later spread throughout the units that the British commander arrived at the West Store in Stanley with the immortal words: 'Hello, I'm Jeremy Moore. Sorry it has taken such a rather long time to get here.' A lot of the islanders still seemed to be in a bit of a daze – I reckon a lot of them were still trying to figure out why two major powers would think these cold, miserable, windswept islands were actually worth fighting over. Years later, I heard that the South American author, Jorge Luis Borges, described Britain and Argentina's decision to start a war over the Falklands as akin to two bald men starting a punch-up over a comb. Having shivered and trudged across the islands, I bloody well know what he meant.

Within twenty-four hours of the surrender, a huge storm swept over the Falklands from the South Atlantic. When our section went to recover my Raider by the oil depot, all we were able to find were scattered scraps of fibreglass and a single engine flywheel. Mother Nature had done in one swoop what the Argentinians couldn't do in several weeks. For the next week, we were based ashore in an old Argentine barracks with 3 Para. We later moved to a local vicarage with another of our sections. The priority now was finding some decent food and some booze. Trust me when I say that women were simply not an option. One enterprising mate, called Phil V. from Barry Island, eventually managed to get his hands on some altar wine and, with some fried tinned beef and chopped onions, we savoured a true Commando feast, complete with altar candles; he even acted as waiter, with a small towel over his arm.

One night, the section that had been on the Stanley raid was invited out on to the ship, MV *Cordella*, for a few beers. The *Cordella* was at anchor in the middle of the bay and we took one of our Raiders out to it to have our party. The beer on ships is notoriously strong and, after three months with none at all, I was very confused after tearing into a few pints. When we left, they even gave us a crate for the journey home. I had it tucked under my arm as I left. The Raider was tied up at the bottom of the stern trawler ramp and we had a rope to get down into the boat. I was that drunk that I imagined I had hold of the rope and stepped forwards, only to proceed to fall straight down, head first, into the black cold water of Stanley harbour below. It was absolutely freezing – so cold it nearly took my breath away. When I popped back up, the beer tins were bobbing all over the place. One of the lads saw what had happened and shouted: 'Get his hand quick, we don't want to lose him in this dark.' But one of the others bluntly replied: 'Fuck him, get the beer before the cans sink.' It was taken in good spirit and we all had a good laugh at my expense. I was in denims and normal shirt and jumper this night, so the trip back to shore was particularly cold with a wind chill of 30 knots. They were in a hurry to get me back and in the warm, or so they reckoned.

Most of the units and regiments had shipped back to the UK within a week of the Argentine garrison being fully disarmed. We were in the middle transfer group and shipped back on board *Sir Tristram*. All the troops on the liners, like the *Canberra*, would have to sail home but, for others, there was the prospect of being flown back with RAF transport planes. Our priority was to get a little extra booze for the long journey home, so my mates Bill K. and little Griff were discreetly sent out in a Raider to try and buy some stocks from other ships. When they arrived back four hours later, we saw the Raider was riding low in the water and thought they'd got enough booze for a transatlantic party. The two lads had indeed got a few cases of beer – but had also filled themselves up in the mess of every ship they'd visited. The two were pissed out of their skulls and didn't realise that the self-bailing mechanism wasn't working and their Raider was slowly filling with water. Not that they gave a shit and just stood in the boats up to their shins in water, laughing like schoolgirls. If they'd lost the beer I think we would have seriously considered letting them drown.

We stowed the beer in every nook and cranny we could find on board and, eventually, had enough to get us back to Ascension Island. I was thrilled to learn that we wouldn't have to travel on *Sir Tristram* all the way across the Atlantic. We were being flown from Ascension straight to Brize Norton in Oxfordshire on a VC-10. We had no idea that there was a very special welcome home waiting for us. However, two of the lads took the partying a little bit too far with a bottle of gin that a RAF movements guy gave them and one of them arrived in Brize Norton having pissed himself while in a drunken stupor; Bill, sat behind him, couldn't understand why his feet were wet when he woke up – until he realised his legs were located directly underneath the previous lad's seat. I never found out what their parents thought of the state they were in when they arrived.

Brize Norton was very special. Our families had been notified we were coming home and were there at the base to greet us. I was particularly thrilled because I'd been told that, because of my actions during the oil depot raid, I was being honoured with a 'Mention in Dispatches'. For any Commando, this is quite a big deal. It involves getting a written acknowledgement of your actions from the Secretary of Defence, the Royal Marines Commandant General, your own unit leader and eventually, from the commander of the Falklands task force. It stays on your record and is taken into consideration for future promotions and duty assignments. I was really chuffed for my family because they were very much 'old school', and my dad, as a Royal Navy veteran himself, was really proud of it.

After Brize Norton, we arrived home in time to watch the celebrations on TV, as the *Canberra* and others were welcomed home. As long as I live, I will never forget the crowds that day, or the mood of the entire country. Back in Flamborough, my parents had erected a special 'Welcome Home Geoff' banner outside our home, and everyone, from relatives to neighbours and old school friends, had gathered for a party. The Mayor of nearby Bridlington called to our house with his wife to pay tribute and one British Legion veteran presented me with a bottle of whisky as a token of respect. Once the crowds had left, I just wanted to watch the ongoing Falklands homecoming on TV – and get to sleep in a warm bed. The blessing was that we had been given seven weeks' leave, and, smack in the middle of my leave, came my twenty-first birthday.

My parents insisted on hiring the village hall for the birthday bash, and the village authorities wouldn't accept payment when they heard who it was for! The Mayor called to wish me a happy birthday and I was even photographed for the local paper in Bridlington. My twenty-first was attended by virtually every living relative I had in England and, by the time my leave was over, it was almost a relief to head back to Plymouth.

The only other major event on the horizon was a very special invitation we had received from 22 Special Air Service. In light of our support for their operations in the Falklands, we were formally invited to a party in their legendary 'Paladrin' Club in Stirling Lines, Hereford, as a 'thank you'. It was a big deal. All the ships' captains brought oil paintings of their vessels to present to the SAS, while our Royal Marines section, from 1st Raiding Squadron, had a special token made up of a Commando dagger mounted on a mahogany plinth. Needless to say, the SAS loved the dagger presentation and it got a place of honour on one of their mantelpieces as a memento of another overseas action.

The evening, as expected, turned into a bit of a boozing session. I had other things on my mind too and struck up with a young nurse who had been invited along to the celebration. Her friend took a fancy to my mate, Bill, and so we both skipped the end of the party to escort them back to their caravan, wherever it was. By the time we left to return to the Hereford base, the Paladrin Club party was well and truly over. We were able to get past the civilian and then the MP patrols with our written party invites, but still had to climb a barbed-wire fence around the officers' mess, where our accommodation was located. The next evening, we made up for lost time at the bar – and were shocked when we were handed a massive bill at the end of the session.

Apparently, the bar had only been free on the previous night. One of the lads came up with the idea of signing our CO's name to the bar

116

chit, and we thought it was the least we deserved after our Falklands exploits. Unfortunately, he didn't agree and gave us a ferocious lecture on honesty and loyalty back at base. Then he promised to take the cash out of our hides in training. Some things never change.

8

FEARLESS TIMES

Six years after I joined the Royal Marines I finally landed the assignment that, I discovered, most young recruits dread because of cramped conditions and often restricted port leave, plus the prospect of working alongside Jolly Jack Tar (RN) – duty on board a Royal Navy warship.

In early 1983 I was assigned to HMS *Fearless* as part of the 4th Assault Squadron RM. *Fearless* was due to undertake a series of exercises in the Baltic and the Mediterranean as part of general NATO commitments. But I was looking forward to it because the stories that arose from the port leave granted during these operations were legendary. I couldn't wait.

Fearless was part of the dreadfully named 'Landing Platform Dock' or LPD class of ships. *Fearless* had one sister ship, HMS *Intrepid*, and they were vessels I was to become intimately acquainted with over my eighteen years in the Commandos. I had also been on both ships a year or so before in the Falklands.

Fearless was commissioned in November 1965 when, for a time, it appeared that the only aviation assets required by the Royal Navy (and thereby the Royal Marines) would be helicopters. All the defence assessments stressed that the days of manned aircraft were effectively over – the future belonged to the guided missile and the guided missile cruiser. The only problem with that assessment was that it was utter crap – as the Gulf War would shortly prove. So, within a decade, while helicopter support was vital for Commando landings, the Royal Navy

118

wisely insisted on maintaining a carrier force, though, to ease ruffled political feathers, these were conveniently referred to as 'through-deck cruisers' rather than as proper aircraft carriers.

Fearless was built by Harland & Wolff in Belfast and, like *Intrepid*, built by John Brown & Co in Clydebank in Scotland, she was the first dedicated landing asset purpose-designed for Royal Navy/Royal Marine operations. As well as handling the usual roster of landing craft, she also had a substantial landing deck and could use her small fleet of helicopters to get assault parties ashore and priority-lift any crucial equipment. *Fearless* could carry up to five Sea King helicopters, a Scout helicopter, four Landing Craft Utilities, four Landing Craft Vehicle Personnel, a Land Rover, a Bedford four-tonne truck, two tractors and a Centurion BARV (basically a Centurion main battle tank with its gun removed and adapted to work as an engineering vehicle). Crucially, the BARV had the power to deal with any Commando landing craft that got stranded on the beach. There were two 20mm weapons in single mounts and two Phalanx CIWS (Close-in Weapons System). The latter were basically radar-guided, computer-controlled Gatling guns whose job was to explode incoming missiles in a hail of bullets. Mind you, I was grateful I was never aboard for that theory to be fully tested out.

In Operation Corporate (the recapture of the Falkland Islands) *Fearless* had been an integral part of the fleet and I had refuelled my Raider from her bowsers on numerous occasions. At that phase of her career she didn't even have the more up-to-date air-defence suite and depended entirely on a pair of ancient 40mm Bofors cannons and a SeaCat system not designed to tackle missiles. I shudder to think what would have happened if *Fearless* or *Intrepid* had been targeted by an Exocet. They ranked alongside the carriers as the vital strategic elements of the task force.

This LPD class of ship was designed to support Commando landings, and exploited to the full the lessons of both World War II and the Korean War. In the Italian Campaign at Anzio during World War II and at Inchon in Korea, the value of a marine landing was fully underlined. In Italy, the German commander, Albert Kesselring, was forced to continually look over his shoulder as his forces retreated up the leg of Italy amid the constant fear of an Allied landing behind him. Anzio didn't work out as planned for the Allies but it showed the potential of what could be done. At Inchon in Korea, a landing behind the lines of communist North Korean troops proved decisive and quickly won back freedom for South Korea. There is nothing quite so morale-sapping to an enemy as knowing that troops have landed behind their positions and stand between them and safety.

The LPDs were capable of carrying a full assault squadron of Royal Marines (about ninety men) and the vast amount of logistical equipment required first to capture and then retain a beachhead. The LPD also provided a platform with full communications equipment for a Royal Marine headquarters team to 'manage' the landings. But it was their vast storage capacity that made the LPDs so supremely useful.

What few people realise is that this vast cache of equipment is stored on board in very precise order so that when an operation is launched, everything runs like clockwork. The success of a landing is determined by how quickly the Commandos can get ashore and how quickly they can get strategic logistical equipment on to the beach. Throughout their deployment, every single member of an assault squadron knows their precise role – where their equipment is stored, when it is deployed and how long it should take to get it ashore and operating.

Both LPDs could also carry a vast supply of munitions to support the assault squadron ashore. The squadron's job was to seize, consolidate and then defend the beachhead pending the arrival of the main landing force or the extraction of the elements they had arrived to protect. Such operations were among the most specialised in any Western army and had to be practised relentlessly as a result. Given ongoing issues in the Far East, Africa and the Middle East, we knew it wasn't beyond the realm of possibility that another Marine landing could be required.

Fearless and *Intrepid* gave Britain a significant amount of muscle to flex in any overseas crisis. Without them it would have been virtually impossible to retake the Falklands. Their flexibility is also borne out by the fact they were even able to operate as detention ships for Argentine

POWS before their repatriation to Buenos Aires. Because of their value, they were always at the forefront of training exercises and regularly operated around the Baltic, the Mediterranean, the Caribbean, the Gulf and even the Far East. The reality is that if Britain was ever involved in an overseas deployment, these ships would be at the very heart of it. Joining *Fearless* was a great thrill – and it was a dream come true to see, first, the Med and then the Baltic from her deck.

Our LPDs were slightly smaller than the Marine assault ships operated by the US Navy and US Marine Corps. For instance, *Intrepid* and *Fearless* had a displacement of about 18,000 tonnes, whereas US ships were all around 20,000 tonnes. In fact, the new USS *San Antonio*, which is the current class of US Navy Marine assault ship, has a displacement of 25,000 tonnes and can deliver eight hundred fully armed and equipped Marines around the world. But, as we regularly told US Marines in bar and navy messes around the world, it was far better to be the best than the biggest. Mind you, they were a decent bunch to work alongside. They regarded themselves as elite troops and their training was very similar to our own. In places like Norway, Malta and the Gulf, co-operation and co-ordination between us Commandos and the US Marines, or 'Jarheads' as they liked to refer to themselves, was absolutely crucial.

My first deployment with *Fearless* in 1983 was to the Med and Cyprus. Someone had decided to break up the Raiding Squadron old boys, despite the fact that our tight-knit group had performed so magnificently in the Falklands the year before. Several of us were drafted to *Fearless*, including myself, Bill K., Spit N., who was in Ireland when the Falklands broke out and had to spend an extra six months there., Jerry D., Taff B. and Litte G. Not to mention the lad who had pissed himself on the VC-10; he was the Squadron signaller.

Fearless had a lot of young Royal Navy trainee officers on board as well. For the most part, the trip was a goodwill cruise, effectively flying the flag in various ports of allied or neutral countries, while training the young officer cadets in basic seamanship.

Our next trip, however, was more serious. Once we were past Gibraltar we discovered we were bound for Cyprus, but our ultimate destination

121

was to resupply various allied factions in the Lebanon. Every single week for three months we were patrolling at sea off Lebanon, using our large LCUs and some of the plant equipment on board the ship to deliver munitions ashore. Our officers were constantly aware of the possibility of attack from a range of potential sources – various militias, Israeli or Syrian forces – and, together with the other boat operators, I had to paint a large Union Jack on the roof of the craft to ease identification for aircraft.

Every weekend we went back to the Sovereign Base in Akrotiri in Cyprus for leave where our small VPs were used as liberty boats for both sailors and Marines. It was a stark contrast. In Cyprus, it was beach, sun, booze and girls for anyone lucky enough to have shore leave. Back in the Lebanon, the country was in an orgy of violence unleashed by the Israeli decision the previous year to invade Southern Lebanon. It was slowly descending into a chaos of militias, assassinations and kidnappings of Western politicians, journalists and even Church statesmen, like Terry Waite. Beirut, once known as the Paris of the Mediterranean, was now one of the most dangerous places on earth. Much as we would have liked to have been able to do something to help, we were effectively powerless when faced by the maelstrom of Middle Eastern politics. We had only a limited armed detachment on board HMS *Fearless*, nothing like enough men and firepower to seriously intervene in Beirut and its militia battles. As the US discovered, the danger in the Lebanon was that an entry by a foreign power tended to unify the militias that had previously been butchering each other; they united and then proceeded to attack the foreign soldiers. As the horrors of the US Marine Corps barracks bombing in the Lebanon proved, getting safely out of Lebanese politics was the hard part – getting dragged in was the easy part.

Ultimately, the only thing we could do with our limited resources on HMS *Fearless* was to provide support for limited Special Forces operations. But they depended crucially on local intelligence that we just didn't have – so Special Forces missions were never actually ordered. It was very frustrating for us because we were all shocked at how a developed, civilised country was slowly tearing itself apart. And, throughout it all, there was the constant reminder that Israel kept a wary eye on all developments in Lebanon – and were perfectly willing to intervene hard and fast to protect their interests.

On one particular occasion in Cyprus, one of the VPs had gone ashore and had just discharged its passengers. We turned the engines off and suddenly heard a strange noise, like a tap running. When we lifted the engine lids we discovered that someone had left out the seawater bungs and seawater was flooding over both engines. The corporal coxswain, Steve P., in a panic, dived into the engine compartment to try to put the bung back in, but forgot he had a self-inflating life-jacket on. It inflated the minute it got wet and he was instantly trapped inside the compartment. He had to get his knife out, pop the life-jacket, get to the bottom of the compartment to replace the bungs and we then had to make our way back to the ship, pumping out water as we went. Once we got back, it was a major problem for the navy engineers to replace the two marine diesel engines in the VP.

One of the worst jobs going was to operate the return liberty trips – bringing drunk and obstreperous officers and ratings back to *Fearless*. Some of the officers wanted to treat the VP like their own personal transport – and you had to tread warily between doing your job and not pissing off an officer who could later make your life hell.

Another time, in Naples, a lot of us took off in a four-tonne truck and headed to a navy base where we had been invited for a few beers, called NavSouth. On the way back, the driver of our truck had had a beer and unfortunately hit a car side-on. It caused absolute mayhem on the Italian street and we were ordered to stay in the back of the truck for safety reasons. A large crowd gathered to debate the cause of the accident – and, because we had all been drinking, suddenly the need arose for us to take a piss. We all decided to get off the truck and go at once – by which time hundreds of Italians had gathered from the local side streets and surrounded us. A good few were armed with flick-knives and were clearly spoiling for trouble. Luckily, our Military Police shore patrol arrived and, totally ignoring the crowd, pushed us back into the truck and ordered it to drive away. One of the only times you relished their presence when you had been drinking.

The funniest incident came in Helsinki where we had sailed on a goodwill visit. A few of the young lads had gone on the piss in town – and, when we woke up the next morning, were stunned to discover a huge flag draped around 2C2 mess on *Fearless*. We had no idea where it came from, but discovered later in the day that a few of the lads, drunk as skunks, had spotted the flag on the top of a local government office complex and decided to take it as booty. They'd climbed the building, scaled out on to the roof and stolen the flag – and, in the process, caused a massive diplomatic row when the theft was discovered by the Finnish authorities. They still had no idea how they had successfully removed it and the local authorities we impressed with their clandestine skills, if nothing else.

Sometimes, though, it was your own sister services you had to worry about. Taking leave while in a port overseas was something every young Commando dreamed about, but it came with its own share of dangers and risks. If you were having a few beers and generally going 'on the piss', you had to ensure you stayed in reasonably tight groups. Going drinking alone – particularly if you were identifiable as a Commando – was an invitation for trouble. There was always some arsehole who wanted to prove himself tougher than you were, usually by waiting in a dark alley with a bottle or a club to attack you from behind. And ever since the Greeks and Romans fought in oar-driven galleys in the Med, sailors were regarded as an 'easy touch' for robbers and thugs in every port.

If several warships were in port at the same time – particularly after a major NATO operation – there would almost certainly be trouble. All US Navy warships were 'dry' – it was a serious offence to get caught on board with alcohol. Hence, the US lads usually went bananas on booze when they hit port. It was even worse if a British Army unit was in town because they seemed to regard it as their right and duty to brawl with the Royal Navy. We nicknamed soldiers 'Pongos' and took pride in never shirking from a fight. It was supposed to be all fists and boots, and using a bottle or a knife was frowned upon as much by your mates as by the Military Police (MP) who tried to keep some semblance of order. It wasn't easy, but what else could they expect when a couple of hundred young men, cramped on board a ship at sea for weeks on end, were unleashed on a foreign port?

Eighteen months soon passed. By the time my first tour on HMS *Fearless* ended, I was glad to resume more normal duties back in the UK. Such overseas cruises were great if you got to see decent foreign places and had the time to enjoy the wonderful climate (which we generally didn't). But the conditions on board were cramped, the social outlets were very restricted and we all missed our normal routines back home in a Commando unit, away from uptight matelots. I was glad I had undertaken such a tour, but I preferred the normal rota of training and waiting for a Norwegian/Irish assignment.

Six years later, I was again assigned to 4th Assault Squadron and was supposed to rejoin HMS *Fearless*. However, in 1989 the ship was still in dry dock as part of a long-planned overhaul. There simply wasn't room for a full detachment of ninety Commandos and their combat kit. So we were instead sent to Poole, where we were used as a 'top-up' unit, being sent wherever we were needed. We spent some time helping train the part-time Territorial Army (TA) units in assault drills and fitness instruction. Most of us took a malicious pleasure in it – some of these TA officers thought they were the modern equivalent of Wellington or Marlborough.

One scene reminded me of something from Bernard Cornwell's *Sharpe's Rifles*. We were training TA recruits on Raider operations and most of them were what we called 'weekend warriors'; others, who were clearly gung-ho, were referred to as SAS, 'Saturday and Sunday' soldiers. From Monday to Friday they were bankers, accountants, civil servants, builders and businessmen. They had lovely homes, wives and, more often than not, drove a Mercedes or BMW sports car. But, come the weekend, they transformed into part-time Rambos, and loved nothing better than combat operations, as long as they finished in time to make it to the pub or the golf club.

On one particular day, a group of TA guys were messing around by the lakeside. They clearly didn't want to get splashed or get their clean combat fatigues dirty. So I ordered them into the frozen water up to their chests. 'When you're that wet, you won't have to worry about getting splashed,' I stated, smiling. The guys stood in shock and didn't move, until their officer, who was leaning on his cane, swirled it over his head and ordered his men into the water. He was a short, heavy-set man, who, I heard later, was a banker in civilian life. I turned to him, smiled, and said politely: 'You too, Sir. Officers lead from the front.' The man went purple, but had no other alternative except to follow his men into the frigid, murky water. In the Commandos, he would have failed his training course for not leading from the front in the very first instance. I was later chastised for sending them into the water. Apparently rats loved nothing better than to piss in this particular lake and I had unwittingly exposed these guys and their officer to the potential threat of lockjaw – to this day, I will never forget the name 'Leptospirosis', or Weil's Disease.

The 'top-up' duties continued unabated and while officially we were an Assault Squadron, in practice we were everything else. Once, we were even dispatched as a colour party, parading in full-dress blues through the streets of Worcester as part of a formal escort for a bicentenary charter celebration. It delighted the crowds but, to be honest, I'd much rather have been in the Baltic or Med on *Fearless*. Finally, I think the brigade got tired of us being fall-guys for every type of fill-in duty that arose. Several of us were transferred to HMS *Intrepid* which was heading on a NATO training exercise. I was glad to go but slightly fazed by the fact that, in 1989, I was now undertaking an operational deployment on a ship that had been retired before the Falklands War and had, way back then, been taken out of mothballs to support the invasion task force.

The only major sign of her age, however, came from an unwelcome boarding party. *Intrepid* was infested with cockroaches, the biggest I'd ever laid eyes on. We lost count of the number of scurrying bugs crushed by combat boots in cabins, hallways and mess areas. They seemed to be everywhere and in everything. Other than that, *Intrepid* was a pretty solid lady, though I suspected there were parts of her being held together by little more than Royal Navy military-issue grey paint, applied over the decades, and the famous 'Harry Black', which was slang for black masking tape.

This was a fairly fallow period for me. The only major danger I encountered was, somewhat ironically, a brawl in Portsmouth between an army unit, some Royal Navy sailors and the Royal Marines. The army unit had just returned from a six-month tour of duty in Northern Ireland and, I suspect, wanted to take out a few of their frustrations. The word had gone around the town that they were looking for trouble. I was one of the older Commandos by this time and was simply out that night for a few beers. A few of the younger guys were bulling for action, but the army unit was nowhere to be found. Then, just as I left a club with my mate, I spotted six of the army lads outside. They were lined up across the street, blatantly issuing a challenge. A few of our lads were facing them and, with more balls than brains, I decided to take my place in the line.

One of our Commandos started it all off by ripping into one of the army lads with his fists. In seconds, the entire street was a mass of swearing, punching and kicking men. The guy I was facing was smaller than me and, in no time, I'd caught him a few times with my fist and he was struggling just to stay on his feet. Then, behind me, I heard someone call my name. I glanced around to spot my mate caught in a headlock by a giant army private. The guy must have stood six-foot five-inches in his stockinged feet. My mate was just five foot nine and was clearly in the process of being strangled. I abandoned my guy, caught the giant by the hair and dragged him off my mate. He lost his footing and fell heavily backwards on the pavement. As I turned to check my back, the entire world suddenly went black. All I can remember is feeling an almighty smack in my jaw and then falling to my knees on the roadway. It took me several seconds to recover and, when I did, I thought I spotted two lads running away when they saw my face.

The fight was over almost as quickly as it had begun. No one wanted to be around when the Portsmouth constabulary or the Military Police arrived to investigate what was going on. As I stumbled away, it felt like half my face was numb. The next day, I could hardly move my neck, and I had two chipped teeth, a deep gash under my nose and one of my eyes had virtually closed. It wasn't much comfort when I heard that the two lads who hit me as I tried to help my friend were sailors from *Intrepid*. They had presumed I was army and, having hit me, suddenly realised their mistake and decided to flee the scene of the crime. I may have been getting older – I was 29 now – but at least honour had been served and the army lads reminded of just who really ran Portsmouth.

Not all port visits ended that way. I did see my fair share of port bars and clubs, but I also got to see some amazing parts of the world. Approached from the sea, Gibraltar is a truly magnificent sight, while the fjords of Norway must rank among nature's greatest glories. The attraction of the Med over the Baltic is that you have glorious heat – though scant time to enjoy it, unlike the bronzed sun-worshippers on speedboats, yachts and jet skis who zoom around every warship when it comes into port.

In the end, not even thick coats of paint could save *Fearless* or *Intrepid* from being turned into razorblades. *Fearless* was decommissioned in March 2002 and remained in mothballs for six years before finally being sold for scrap to a Belgian ship-breaking yard. *Intrepid* – her sister ship – had been decommissioned three years earlier and for the latter part of her life, had suffered the ignominy of being cannibalised for spares for *Fearless*. In 1999 she was fully decommissioned and, in September 2008, was transferred to Liverpool for what was termed 'environmental recycling'.

HMS *Albion* and HMS *Bulwark* replaced *Fearless* and *Intrepid*, with support from the helicopter assault ship HMS *Ocean*. *Ocean* was the first ship of her type in the world, and a hint of her capability comes from the fact she was effectively converted from a light-aircraft-carrier. *Albion* was commissioned in 2003 and now ranks as one of the most high-tech vessels afloat. Displacing almost 21,000 tonnes, her major advantage over the older ships is her defence systems and her range, which can extend to 7,000 nautical miles (13,000km). She is the lead ship in her class, with *Bulwark* a near-identical copy.

As I got older I realised that the amount of action I had seen in the early part of my Royal Marines career was totally contrary to the norm. A few of the older salts I knew had years and years of training and courses interspaced only with tours of duty in Northern Ireland and maybe Norway. But that was it. I was barely in my twenties and I had already undertaken tours in Norway, the Falklands, Northern Ireland and Hong Kong. Serving on HMS *Fearless* had taken me all over the Baltic and Mediterranean.

Having experienced the tough life in barracks and during routine overseas ship duties, I could understand what a friend had once told me about the French Foreign Legion. Apparently, the Foreign Legion reckons that British and Irish recruits make the best fighting soldiers – but the very worst troops when confined to barracks duties. This is largely because the British and Irish troops revel in action and excitement and cannot stand the drudgery and boredom of life in barracks. It wasn't that bad in my case in the Royal Marines because there was always the hope of another serious deployment in one of the world's 'hot spots'. But sometimes the drudgery of barrack life (or ship-board life, for that matter) could test your Commando resolve.

As for me, I decided to hang in there and hope that things would get better. There are a lot of ups and downs in military life – it isn't all action, despite what the stereotypes might lead you to believe. Our aim was to try and drink and party a lot when we weren't kicking butt.

9

HALLS OF MONTEZUMA – SHORES OF TRIPOLI

In 1985 I was just twenty-four years old, but I already felt like a Commando veteran. In the blink of an eye I'd gone from the youngster being looked after by the older Commandos to the veteran who was now 'mothering' the new lads. And just when I thought I couldn't be surprised by another overseas deployment, I learned that I was to return to Hong Kong with 3rd Raiding Squadron. It was like Christmas come early. Only this time, instead of sweltering in an observation post overlooking the Yellow River, I'd be zooming around Hong Kong harbour in a powerful SeaRider, a small, rigid inflatable boat.

The emphasis of our work had shifted pretty dramatically from my earlier tour. Illegal immigration was still a problem, though nothing on the scale of 1979. This time, the problem was the feared Chinese gangs, the Triads. The gangs – notorious for their violence and brutality – were making a fortune around Hong Kong on everything from smuggling to gambling, prostitution to drugs. Tackling any aspect of the Triads was a serious challenge, and, even in China, with its draconian judicial system and widespread use of the death penalty, the Triads remained in operation.

The Chinese gangs realised there was money to be made from illegal immigration – firstly they would fleece the immigrants and their families of virtually everything they owned and then they would smuggle them into Hong Kong, Europe, North America or the Far East and effectively sell them as slave labourers. The Hong Kong police, 3rd Raiding Squadron and the Royal Navy were up against gangs with access to enormous resources. From detecting illegal immigrants on rafts or homemade boats we were now faced with hundreds of immigrants being piled on to flat-bottomed aluminium craft powered by huge outboard engines. Some of these craft were powered by four 700 horse-power engines and were capable of racing into Hong Kong with huge loads. They were unstable and highly dangerous, but they had the speed of a water-borne missile and were extremely difficult to intercept. And they almost always attempted their smuggling runs at night, which made the interception even more difficult and dangerous.

The SeaRiders we used were capable of 30 knots and more, and they still couldn't catch these craft. So what we had to do was hunt them, and try to drive them towards a zone where they could be trapped by the shoreline or shallow water and detained. To do this we had to use three or even four boats, with the entire operation usually co-ordinated from a Royal Navy minesweeper. Once a radar contact was picked up, two or three SeaRiders would surge towards the area. Sometimes they would be supported by a Fast Pursuit Craft (FPC) which had twin 200 horse-power outboard engines and was easily capable of 50 knots. The initial response to an alert usually required a SeaRider or FPC to race towards a distant radar contact, usually in pitch-black conditions with zero visibility. It was often a hair-raising experience – trusting completely to radar guidance while the boat reached maximum speed.

One SeaRider would then begin firing Shamoolies, a parachute flare which, after being fired, slowly descends towards the ground in slow time. It burns brightly and lights up a substantial area below. It was the job of one Commando to keep firing the Shamoolies so that the area being searched remained lit at all times. If you couldn't light the area, you'd probably lose the contact. Each SeaRider carried up to a hundred Shamoolies, and sometimes even this wasn't enough, because once the first flare was fired, the smugglers knew they'd been detected and the chase was on. If you ran out of Shamoolies, you then became night-blind from being plunged into darkness after being exposed to such brightness.

We worked very closely with the Royal Navy and the Hong Kong Maritime Police, and they knew the local waters like the back of their hand. The Royal Navy had for decades been recruiting locals for security patrols in Hong Kong – known as Locally Employed People (LEPs) – and they always remained on station in Hong Kong. Needless to say, they were quickly dubbed 'Leppers' by the Commandos and Navy ranks. After a while, we also learned the smugglers' favourite routes and channels, and these earned special attention.

Most patrols operated from Victoria Basin where HMS *Tamar*, our base, was located. If you were assigned to night patrols, the SeaRider was usually patrolling the various channels from 8pm until 3 or 4am. Once launched, we stayed on patrol, often eating our meals against the stunning backdrop of Hong Kong's neon skyline. When it was quiet, and particularly during a summer night, it could be a truly magical experience. I remember one particular night coming back down the narrow passages between cargo terminals on the shoreline with streaks of lightning bouncing off each bank around us. It was a very exhilarating experience and, knowing that our antennae were 5m in the air, we were transmitting to each other for fun saying: 'Wow, did you see that?'

Sometimes the system worked very well. To avoid the combined forces of the SeaRiders, the minesweeper and the FPC, the smuggler would be forced to constantly change course, all the time bleeding speed and getting himself closer to either shipping or shallow water, where he could be trapped. Sometimes the smugglers managed to get away – having such enormous power and speed at their disposal was a major asset. Unlike in 1979, we also knew that the Triads wouldn't lose any sleep over shooting their way out of an arrest. So we always carried weapons and were always ready to use them. We often had warning shots fired at us from a distance, but luckily we never had a major shoot-out where anyone was injured.

Unfortunately, the combination of high speed, aggression and panic did occasionally result in tragedy. Once, a smuggler was identified on radar trying to make a night-time run into Hong Kong. His position was illuminated by multiple flares, and the man panicked. He tried to make a run for it, but the FPC was on the scene within minutes. Despite repeated warnings to stop, the man kept going, with his outboards screaming at full throttle. Eventually, he realised that he couldn't outrun the FPC, so he tried to evade it by weaving directly across its path, and fatally misjudged this manoeuvre.

The smuggler cut directly across the bow of the FPC and the Commando coxswain hadn't a chance to avoid the craft. The FPC ploughed directly over the smuggler's boat, damaging the FPC, and sinking the smuggler. Unfortunately, the smuggler had been paid to bring a family into Hong Kong and, having been thrown into the water, they all drowned. The smuggler was later convicted and jailed for his part in the tragedy.

There were other nights when tragedy was narrowly averted. One particular night, as an FPC was being vectored by a Navy Radar, we came across a coxswain and his corporal who were as white as a sheet and pretty shaken up. It turns out that they were told to investigate a ship out at sea in the pitch-dark. They followed a course that took them between two other marks on their radar screen. But it turned out that the two radar blips were actually one ship towing another, and they hit the tow hawser while they were going at almost 50 knots. The heavy steel tow line flipped the FPC clean into the air and the two guys narrowly avoided being decapitated by the hawser cable.

I was enjoying this assignment immensely. But one event almost brought my entire career to a premature end. Inevitably, copious amounts of drink were involved, coupled with a rather tasteless T-shirt. Unlike the Fleet Club brawl six years earlier, this time I didn't escape so lightly.

The trouble all started when the US Seventh Fleet arrived into Hong Kong for their formal birthday ball, to mark the 1775 foundation of the US Marine Corps. Admirals the world over love formality – it's a wonderful excuse for wearing dress-whites, polishing up their medals and basically showing off their warships to the great and good of the local community. One of the features of these visits is always a dinner bash, which ranks as the must-have invitation in town. It is usually hosted in the swankiest hotel available, in this case the Hong Kong Hilton on Hong Kong Island. Every local dignitary from the military, political and business worlds is invited. Sometimes a few dignitaries are flown in just for the occasion. But in my case, it would have been better if I'd come down with man flu.

The US Seventh Fleet dinner proved to be a who's who of Hong Kong society. Those in attendance included the Governor of Hong Kong, the Commander of Hong Kong military forces, the US ambassador, as well as various business and political leaders. The First Sea Lord (titular head of the Royal Navy and Royal Marines) had even flown over to Hong Kong from the London admiralty for the occasion. All the senior Royal Marine commanders in Hong Kong were in attendance, including my sergeant-major and that of the Branch back in Poole, the captain who led 3rd Raiding Squadron, not to mention the commanding officer of the landing-craft wing from the UK.

That Friday, I had been undertaking a special combat driving course on Land Rovers and was surprised to be told that the invitation to the Hilton hotel party extended to me. The Royal Marines were invited at the behest of the US Marine Corps. Like us, US Marines also serve aboard major warships and the invitation was seen as a good inter-service gesture.

By now I had been in Hong Kong a few months and had struck up a friendship with a very pretty WREN, who was working in a Navy dental surgery as a hygienist. I'd had plenty of relationships over the years, but this was the first time I'd actually felt something special for someone.

Needless to say, all the Commandos' wives and girlfriends (WAGs – also known as FADs, 'Families and Dependants', or PADs in the Army) were thrilled at the idea of such a formal dinner – it was an excuse to buy a new ball gown, get their hair done and their nails manicured.

For us, unfortunately, it was an excuse to drink free booze by the bucketful, courtesy of US President Ronald Reagan. In all, about twenty Royal Marines and their partners attended the bash, and we all opted to wear No. 1 dress uniforms, largely because it saved money on hiring a dress suit, although it meant we were easily identifiable if anything went wrong.

So we arrived in full-dress Blues. One of the lads thought it would be hilarious if he wore an 'Adolf Hitler – European Tour 1939–45' T-shirt underneath. As the night wore on, and the more he drank, the more he insisted on unbuttoning his dress jacket and showing off his T-shirt. Grinning inanely, he failed to spot that our commanding officer, who was sitting at a table right beside us, was throwing him dagger looks. But it was too late. To make matters worse, a few of the WAGs had followed the bad example set by their partners and consumed enough cocktails to power one of our Raiding craft.

It didn't help that the Americans' love of pomp and ceremony made them easy targets for our rude and obnoxious behaviour. As the US Marine Corps colour party marched into the ballroom, carrying the Stars and Stripes and US Navy flags, the drunken women started to shout abuse. The famous US Marine Corps battle song, 'From the Halls of Montezuma to the Shores of Tripoli', was booed by the girls in the opening address and then one of the wives decided it would be quite appropriate to use her cigarette lighter to set fire to the miniature 'Stars and Stripes' flags decorating the dinner table. Other guests were horrified, but decided it was unwise to intervene. The problem was that having listened for years on end to us running down the US Marines and extolling the virtues of our beloved Royal Marines, they saw no problem in letting their feelings be known. Unfortunately, it was the wrong time and the wrong place. We were embarrassed by their antics.

But it set the tone for the entire evening which, by the strict codes and standards of the Royal Marines, was little more than total anarchy. The Americans were apparently disgusted by our behaviour, and probably by our rampant ingratitude. After all, it was their party, they paid the bill and we insisted on insulting them. The nuclear button was well and truly pressed when the senior British commanders – and particularly the Royal Marine officers in attendance – felt our behaviour reflected badly on them.

I didn't help matters by breaking a golden Royal Marine rule and unbuttoning my dress jacket and loosening my shirt. Despite the air-conditioning, it was stiflingly hot in the ballroom and the combination of booze, dancing and the amorous attentions of my WREN date were beginning to tell. However, the tradition was that no matter how hot it was, no matter the occasion, dress blues were always to be worn properly. I was out on the dance floor doing my best John Travolta impression when suddenly the crowd parted and I found myself staring directly across the ballroom at the officer commanding 3rd Raiding Squadron. Coincidentally, it was the same officer who'd been my boss in the Falklands three years earlier. Drunk as I was, I instantly knew I was in deep shit. I began to sober up there and then. The wisest thing I did all night was leave the party with my date and head down to a bar in Wan Chai for a few private beers. But the damage was already done.

The captain took the behaviour of our table as a personal insult, a direct challenge to him and his authority, and felt that when I was out dancing with my dress jacket undone, I was basically taunting him in public. He was powerless to do anything about the rude shouts and flag-burning antics of the British wives and girlfriends, but it was a very different story when it came to me. He had me by the short and curlies, and I was now the obvious scapegoat for the embarrassment at the dinner. Either way, I knew the following morning wouldn't bring happy tidings.

As it turned out, it was even worse than I had feared. My sergeant-major told me, in a comically understated way, 'Things aren't looking too good for you.' I had reported for the next stage of my Land Rover training course at Kowloon, only to be told to report immediately back to headquarters on Hong Kong Island. I tried to comfort myself by saying they could hardly sack me for dancing with my jacket undone. I had been Mentioned in Dispatches in the Falklands and had a pristine record over the previous seven years. Surely, I thought, that counted for something.

When I was eventually ordered into the boss's office, I got both barrels. He told me I was a disgrace to the Royal Marines, I had let him down and I was entirely responsible for the Hilton debacle. I felt this was very unfair, but the captain just did not want to hear any excuses. 'Marine Nordass, get your kit packed up, you're being sent back to Poole,' he said, dismissing me with a contemptuous wave of his hand.

I couldn't believe it. I still had four months of my Hong Kong tour to complete. Worse still, I had applied for a training course that was entirely dependent on my commanding officer's approval – the free-fall parachute display team in which the Royal Marines were the current world record holders. I was bluntly told that my application had been shredded, so I could forget all about it. I was worried that having been refused the training courses I could have a problem with future promotions. I was also disgusted that my time with 3rd Raiding Squadron was being cut short. The happiest times I had in the Marines were with both Raiding Squadrons and I was heartbroken to leave.

There was also the fact that, by being sent home, my relationship with my girlfriend was also being destroyed. I really fancied her, but I knew if I went back to England the relationship would pretty much be over because, as a WREN, she had to stay in Hong Kong to finish her tour. I didn't know what to do, so I talked it over with my mates who were horrified for me and a little bit ashamed that their own behaviour might have contributed to my problem. Another corporal, a good friend of mine, took me aside and advised me to return to my commanding officer immediately and offer a full personal apology.

By now I was desperate, so I went back to the captain's office, waited to be called and then proceeded to eat humble pie. I apologised for my behaviour and any offence I had caused. I took responsibility for what happened and promised it would never happen again. Royal Marines don't beg, but I came as close to it that day as my honour would allow. 'Please,' I asked, 'let me finish out my tour.' But I was wasting my time. 'Sorry, Marine Nordass, you had the chance to apologise earlier. It's too late for all this now,' he said.

I also went to the Officer Commanding Landing Craft, who was still in Hong Kong, and apologised. I was hoping he might agree to have a word with the captain and maybe I'd be allowed to stay on in

Hong Kong. But he told me bluntly that the final say was with my commanding officer. The dinner had been an embarrassment and it was felt that an example had to be made. And that was me.

So I was shipped home just five days later. I lost 3rd Raiding Squadron, I lost my training courses, I lost the remainder of my tour and I lost my girl. The only little bit of good news from the whole sorry episode was that, a few days after arriving back at Poole, I heard via the grapevine that I needn't worry about future promotion prospects as my punishment was deemed more than sufficient for what had happened. So at least my corporal's stripes were still on the horizon if I wanted them.

Yet, bad as it was, it could have been an awful lot worse. One Commando came back from Hong Kong in a body bag that year after falling from the sixteenth floor of the building we were based in. To this day, no one knows precisely what happened, bar the fact that he had been drinking in the pub just a few hours before. I had been on patrol that night and was returning to base when I was ordered to another location and told to remain there with my section until HQ were ready for us. I felt an icy ball form in the pit of my stomach, not least because a few of us had been selling off excess petrol fuel to the local fishermen and farmers who were only too delighted to buy it at knock-down prices – and SeaRiders were so notoriously heavy on fuel that it was difficult for anyone except the boat crew to accurately assess what they were burning. The whole black-market enterprise kept us in beer money and was also a very handy boost to our Christmas fund. Unfortunately, it was also a potential court-martial offence. But, we reckoned, it was worth it – anyway, they'd have to catch us first!

As we waited to be called to base, we pondered over our fate and how the sergeant-major could possibly have discovered our little private enterprise. Then, when we arrived back, we were told that this poor lad had fallen from close to the top of the building and that the circumstances of the tragedy were being investigated. I still feel a little guilty when I recall that my first feeling was one of utmost relief. It was only later that we spared a thought for the poor bastard who was being scraped up from the concrete outside.

10

ROMAN CANDLES

From the time when cavemen first shaped tree branches into clubs and went to war with the neighbouring tribe over the best women or most food, every soldier has wanted to be part of the elite. Military history is, in many ways, a succession of stories of the achievements of great units – the Persian Immortals, Alexander's Companion Cavalry, the Roman Ninth Legion, the Knights of St John in the Crusades, the Turkish Sultan's Janissaries and even Robert E. Lee's Virginians in the American Civil War.

I first settled on joining the Royal Marines because I wanted to be a Commando, a special kind of soldier. The Paras are special, and so are the Special Air Service (SAS) and the Special Boat Service (SBS). It is no surprise that most of the members of the SAS and SBS are drawn from the Commandos and the Parachute Regiment.

It all started, funnily enough, with the blow-out in Hong Kong. When I arrived back in Poole, I feared for my future. I had ambitions to become a corporal and, if possible, to transfer to Operation ORCADES, an SBS support unit, or to the SBS itself, or even go on a two-year exchange with the US Marine Corps. But, a few days after arriving back in Dorset in ignominy, I was taken aside and told not to worry – the punishment I had received in Hong Kong was deemed quite harsh and, I suspected, a lot of people knew that I wasn't the one responsible for what had happened. Sometimes, being unfairly made the scapegoat has its advantages.

My new commanding officer, who I think felt a little sorry for me, asked me what assignments or courses I was interested in. I thought for a moment and then asked for ORCADES, a special small-boat group trained in the techniques required by the SBS. They used seven-metre Arctic RIBs (Rigid Inflatable Boats) and specialised in maritime anti-terrorism work. I already had small-boat operational training, which was a major asset, but the ORCADES assignment required specialised training so that Raider or SeaRider drivers could bring their craft right up alongside huge freighters, tankers or even military vessels to allow the insertion of a small SBS team. It also involved being able to parachute from a plane out at sea to operate with these boats. My boss smiled at my answer and immediately approved the move.

I was told that I needed parachute training and was being dispatched on a course immediately to RAF Brize Norton. The huge airbase in Oxfordshire is home to a major RAF training establishment and is used for all types of assignments – strikes, bombing and logistical. It was also used for parachute training for Paras and non-Parachute Regiment units. I couldn't wait! I arrived to find about a hundred Royal Marines from other units waiting for the same training cycle. A substantial portion were from Comacchio Company, who were the specialist nuclear protection unit based at Rosyth and Holy Loch. I felt a bit like a boy scout who knew that a major merit badge was on offer, and the chance to wear Para wings is something most soldiers dream about. The first morning, we were mustered in a huge hangar and given some basic rules: no drinking, no fighting, no wandering to the Women's Air Force (WAF) quarters – and no going out dressed as women. I thought the guy was bonkers, but he took out a large plastic bag and emptied the contents onto the stage; it consisted of dresses, wigs and false breasts. We all roared with laughter. Marines do like to push the mark when letting off steam and anything that shocks is regarded as an extra bonus. But it was hammered home that any breach of the rules would involve an immediate RTU (return to unit).

Like all such training programmes, it wasn't all fun and games. The first three weeks were spent inside a huge hangar learning everything about parachute procedures – safety checks, how to jump, how to land, how to untangle your lines. It was repetitive, it was meticulous, but you paid attention because you knew these checks were designed to save your life and prevent you turning yourself into a splat on some foreign battlefield –this was known to the jump instructors, in a suitable understatement, as being 'a Roman candle' because an unopened parachute resembles a flaming Roman candle flame as it hurtles to the ground. As the safety drills were being delivered, I noted that all the 'baby' Paras were very well behaved for a change – probably because there were just four or five of them on the course and they were surrounded by about a hundred combined army and Royal Marine Commandos.

The fourth week brought us outdoors to begin our practical training and to introduce us to the dreaded first 'jump' at Weston-on-the-Green's balloon. When I first heard we were jumping from a blimp, I thought it was to prepare us for the harder step of jumping from an aeroplane. But most Paras will tell you that a still-air jump from a balloon can be much more intimidating than a jump from a speeding aircraft at altitude. For a start, there is complete silence – there is no wind, no engine noise and nothing to blot out the thumping sound of your own heart in your ears.

The parachute jump instructor (PJI) revels in his role and, I reckon, foams at the mouth with excitement at the thought of another crop of green Paras arriving at his balloon, which is moored to the ground with a heavy cable. You're welcomed to the two-hundred-and-fifty-metre-high basket platform four at a time by the PJI, who dares anyone to tell a joke, and then proceeds to offer to buy a pint for anyone who can get an erection. From my experience, it's a bet the PJI has never lost. The worst part is if you're at the rear of the jumping queue; by the time it is your turn, your knees are literally knocking with the adrenalin rush of what you know is in front of you.

It was my turn to go first, so I was ushered to the front of the balloon basket gate. The PJI tells you to place both your hands on the vertical bars by the gap. He will shout 'red on', which means you take one hand off the bar and place it across the reserve 'chute strapped to your chest. He will then shout 'green on', and you take your remaining hand off the bar and place it across your other hand on the reserve 'chute. At the shout of 'go' you step into space. Almost every single trainee puts both hands back on the vertical bars at the shout of 'green on', a fact that sends the PJI into spasms of laughter. It usually takes two or three goes for the trainee to finally follow procedures and defy every single rational thought in his brain, and step into thin air.

Once you step clear of the basket, you start counting upwards from 1001, and by 1005 you look upwards to check that your canopy has properly opened. The biggest danger is that trainees are so terrified of a malfunction, they race through the count much too quickly to allow their 'chute to properly deploy, and then panic when they don't see it fully open. I landed with all the grace and skill of a falling sack of potatoes – but I had done it. Even the dodgy ankle that I had injured playing football in school had stood up to the challenge. The next seven jumps were all from a C-130 Hercules, which I found a lot easier than the balloon. Not everyone agreed, and I struggled to keep a straight face during one morning jump when the nervous farting from soldiers behind me in the queue sounded like distant mortar rounds. Most of the boys had just finished a full fry for breakfast and it obviously didn't sit well with pre-jump nerves. For obvious reasons, I was never so glad to jump from the plane into clean, fresh air. The truth was that guys handled the pressure in different ways – some joked and giggled before the jump, others just went quiet. Others were content to let their bowels – or stomach contents – do the talking.

Having successfully completed the course, I was stunned to learn that I was being sent on a 2nd Class Landing Craft Course. I thought that it wrecked my ORCADES chances, but I also knew that an LC2 qualification would boost my promotion chances in the long run. I never really fancied full-time landing-craft operations because the boats were simply too big, too awkward and too slow for my liking. I knew that they were essential to Royal Marine operations and that without them, we could never undertake a proper beach landing. But I still preferred the exhilaration of Raider and SeaRider operations. Immediately after this course, which lasted for twelve weeks, I was told that I was now one of forty of the most senior Marines in the corps and was on the next Junior Command course or corporals' course. So it was back to Lympstone for another ten weeks. I didn't fancy my leadership skills and lecturing abilities. It could be very embarrassing to stand out in front of an entire training cadre and give a full forty-five-minute lecture on a military subject they chose for you. I managed to pass this also and was, by now, sick of courses, having spent a total of four consecutive months in a training cycle.

Not long afterwards I was offered the chance to rotate to the giant US Navy base in Diego Garcia in the Indian Ocean as an acting sergeant as soon as I had my two stripes on my arm. I knew it was a great opportunity, but I was rowing with my girlfriend of the time and turned it down so that I could patch things up. I decided to wait my chance at Poole in the hope of landing an SBS assignment. In 1987, my wait finally ended and I was attached to the SDV (Swimmer Delivery Vehicle) section of the SBS which required a short stint in the USA. We were deployed to Little Creek in Virginia, one of the biggest naval bases in the world. It was my first time in the US and I loved every single minute of it. What was great was that we had enough downtime to be able to do a little touring – seeing the nearby Williamsburg battlefield museum was one of the highlights of my stay.

Working alongside the SBS was an absolute thrill. They were soldiers at the very top of their profession. They were supremely fit, all had major experience in the units they were drawn from and had fought and trained their way to make it into the SBS. They were the cutting edge of Her Majesty's water-borne forces – and they knew it. The SAS, largely drawn from the Parachute Regiment, may be better known because of their exploits, including the embassy siege in London, but the SBS are equally talented. Most SBS members are drawn from the Royal Marines, though, since my time working alongside them, they have been getting closer to the SAS; there were signals that the two units were going to work in much closer harmony, effectively becoming one Special Forces operation while retaining the SAS and SBS titles.

The lines of demarcation were pretty clear. The SAS dealt with land-based threats and the SBS dealt with water-borne risks. My job was basically to ensure that the SBS teams reached their target. We practised 'hot' insertions at night, in daytime, in all kinds of weather conditions, through both speed and stealth. Because of the propellers and the busy nature of the shipping channels we trained in, a single mistake could easily cost someone their life.

The craft they used was basically a mini-sub. It was exposed to the sea and was designed to get frogmen closer to targets undetected – a speciality put to good use by the Italians in World War II. I was on the surface in an eight-metre RIB and acted as safety for the lads who were mostly in training to be navigators and pilots of the subs.

At the end of my eighteen months with the SBS, the whole world of special operations suddenly began to appeal to me. I was as fit and experienced as any of these SBS lads – why wouldn't I have a go at it myself? The problem was that I had just met Julia, my future wife, in Poole and we were getting on famously. The subject of moving in together had already cropped up in conversation and we were even talking about buying our own house. But if I went into special operations I could be away for months at a time and often unable to return even for brief periods of leave. When I mentioned the prospect, Julia didn't like the idea. Not to put too fine a point on it, she hated it. I wondered whether it would be the end of the relationship. This factor, and a few others, caused us to split for a few months and it was during this time that I volunteered for a special operation.

Working alongside the SBS you get a taste for proving to yourself precisely what your limitations are. Most of the SBS lads didn't think they had any limitations – well, not of a physical or capability kind. I think a little of that rubbed off on me and, almost like being seventeen all over again, I thought I was bullet-proof. I signed up for a special course for Northern Ireland operations, but I had to do an 'Acquaint' programme first, which was designed to see if you were made of the right stuff. It was being run by the army. This ongoing course was training soldiers for special operations, and many of those selected were then likely to transfer into units called DET or 14 Int (Intelligence). I also knew, without having to be told, that undercover special operations meant only one thing: Northern Ireland.

I decided to give it a try. The Acquaint programme was operating from a base outside Liverpool called Altcar. The course can be run anywhere and, for security reasons, moves around quite a bit. When I arrived I realised that a lot of the lads who had signed up were from the Royal Marines, though there were lads from a few other regiments as well. The tone was set from the first day when we were each assigned a number and told that that was our only personal reference. We were not to refer to each other by name, we were not to talk about our personal lives or service histories. We had been ordered to remove all insignia and all signs of rank from our combat fatigues. Any attempt to question or simply converse with another soldier about their personal details was regarded as an immediate RTU (return to unit) offence. We were also warned that we were not to talk about any mutual friends or service connections. If you knew anyone else on the course, you forgot about that immediately. The message was well and truly hammered home when one of the instructors produced copies of Her Majesty's Official Secrets Act and we were required to sign immediately.

The training was brutal and demanding. Huge emphasis was placed on individual initiative and on how to respond in a crisis. We were also expected to be able to put up with enormous levels of hardship and still perform to a ferocious degree as infantrymen. Every aspect of our skills was tested – hand-to-hand fighting, target recognition and evaluation, evasion and surveillance. I can't discuss a lot of what went on at Altcar for obvious reasons – suffice to say that it wasn't for the faint-hearted. It was about testing you to the very limits of your endurance. The aim of the course was to assess who could survive in the lethal world of special ops and undercover operations.

One example, perhaps, perfectly illustrates the situation. We were awoken one morning at four o'clock and the instructors screamed at us to get our arses into the gym. Human responses are at their lowest point at this hour and I assumed it was a simple training exercise. We were told to pair off and that we would need our tracksuits and a towel for swimming in the canal. I guessed it was a survival exercise, so I picked a six-foot three-inch Marine that I knew from a couple of years back. I can manage you in the water and you can definitely pull my weight ashore, I thought to myself. The instructors ordered us into the gym and I realised that all the gym benches were set out in a square. I knew instantly I was in trouble – whatever we were going to have to do, it would not involve swimming.

I was right. We were told that we faced three minutes of 'milling'. This is an age-old military tradition whereby recruits box each other. It teaches aggression, stamina, courage and adaptability. In the old days, it was bare-knuckle stuff; now we were issued boxing gloves, soft helmets and told to get on with it. My choice of the huge Commando now looked a little unwise. But the purpose of 'milling' was that it taught how even smaller guys can hold their own for short, concentrated bouts of fighting. When it was my turn, I let loose. If you held back or shied away, the instructors would be all over you and you'd spend five or ten minutes milling instead of just three. My 'pair' was no slouch and he caught me full in the face with a right hook. Luckily, my nose wasn't broken, but the blood was pouring as though he had switched on a fountain. For my part, I caught him straight in the eye with a left jab. When the bout ended, my singlet was soaked in blood and his eye was puffed out like a golf ball and the match was declared a draw.

Another time we were put in teams of three and given orders far too fast for us to take down or understand. Each of us was then given a piece of equipment to carry, and a bed roll, a sleeping bag and a poncho cover. If the wrong person got the wrong item it was confiscated. In the end, they took it all away from us and gave us two ponchos between three of us. We were then taken to the sand dunes at night (it was by now the depth of winter) and left there to fend for ourselves for thirty-six hours. Some of us coped with it reasonably well, but others were clearly not prepared for this type of hardship and pressure. People started dropping like flies and the course group gradually got smaller and smaller.

A few weeks later the emphasis shifted from the physical demands of operations to the classroom side of things. It was very intense and very detailed, but I think a lot of people in that room knew that by paying attention to the small details, you might end up saving your life. It was repeatedly drilled into us that one mistake, one lapse in judgement, one moment of not being able to respond correctly to the unexpected could result in you taking a bullet in the back of the head. And there were other far worse scenarios. Unfortunately, my mind was already elsewhere. I'd heard a rumour that those who successfully passed the course would go on a nineteen-month duty rotation, which would involve a lengthy period in Northern Ireland. I knew that would mean the end for my relationship with Julia. And I think I had already proved to myself that I was able to hack the course just as well as anybody else. The question now was, did I want nineteen months on special ops in Northern Ireland or would I return to my old life in the Royal Marines and the prospect of a future with Julia? The longer I thought about it, the more I realised that there wasn't a lot to consider.

Quitting wasn't so easy. I had to make a formal request, in writing, to be withdrawn from the training programme. A few of the instructors let it be known that they thought I should stay and I guessed that I'd already been earmarked for some duty or other overseas. But I knew I had other options in the Commandos – I still hadn't qualified as a diver and that was a course open to most Marines with my experience. Why not try that and work to set up home with Julia? I wished the lads the best of luck and left Altcar to catch a train back to Dorset. It was definitely the right call at the time, but I often wonder what might have been if I had finished the course.

Unfortunately, my alternative proved a little bit more problematic than I'd first thought. I started training as a diver, only to discover that I was claustrophobic. I was surprised by the feeling of panic as I first went down in a diving suit. I had got through the flooded tunnel in Lympstone without any problem and done helicopter dunking drills off Portsmouth, so why was I panicky now? I learned that time is a major factor with the condition – in Lympstone I was into the tunnel and through it in a matter of seconds. I didn't have time to get claustrophobic. But, in a diving suit, slowly descending below a ship or submarine's hull, you have all the time in the world for your mind to play tricks on you. It's very hard to escape the fact that there is an awful lot of ocean over your head, and your capacity to make it back to the surface is strictly regulated by the length and depth of your dive.

I fought it with every ounce of fibre I possessed. I learned in the Commandos that you never surrender to fear; you do your best to conquer it. You keep doing something often enough so that it becomes second nature to you, and the fear slowly evaporates. But sometimes that is easier said than done. I persevered and got through the Dive Aquaint part so that I could go on the course proper in Portsmouth at HMS *Vernon* and HMS *Nelson*. I started out by learning what the diving instructors call 'finning'. Basically, you use your fins to propel yourself towards a lake bottom while holding on to an underwater wire. This was followed by a lot of classroom theory, and physical stuff with the twin sets on your back and a dry suit. The classroom stuff included air mixtures, depths, how to properly inspect your gear, how to calculate weights, how to plan a descent and then an ascent. And what to do if something went wrong. The Royal Navy always prided itself on the quality of instruction given to divers. We were told that a Royal Navy diving cert would get us work anywhere in the world as a civilian.

We then moved onto training proper. This involved wearing a full diving suit and descending to the harbour bottom at Portsmouth to work on underwater objects. The Hollywood film, *Men of Honour*, portrays it very well – though the equipment has changed quite a bit and we never went as far as training for really deep diving. In the harbour bottom you might have to screw four bolts onto a large metal plate. That would then be hauled to the surface, checked by the instructors and then lowered to the harbour bottom again so you could undo all four bolts. You also learned how to communicate with the surface through a series of jerks and pulls on your contact line. Throughout it all, you learned the strict safety rules – basically how to operate without killing yourself or another diver.

The next phase was a little more practical. We were taught how to locate mines on the hulls of ships, an exercise that we practised till we were sick of it on the hulls of frigates tied up in Portsmouth dock. We then moved onto HMS *Rame Head*, where we had to come alongside the vessel, get on board, climb an interior staircase to the bridge wing, jump the 15m to the harbour below and then swim back to repeat the exercise. We had to do this three times without stopping. It was all about stamina, swimming ability and the capability of handling repeated dives and climbs. Diving is one of the most physically demanding of all disciplines, and there is no margin for error. Experienced divers will tell you that even having a few pints the night before a dive can play havoc with their systems if they're diving for any length at an extended depth.

But the exercise that I remember most is the one I'm sure was devised by instructors just for their own personal amusement. We were taken to an old Royal Navy ship called HMS *Kent*, which had been set aside for reservists. We had to climb up the anchor chain from the water, climb through the ship to the bridge wing and dive into the water below. Again, the exercise had to be repeated three times – part of building us up for the thirty-metre dive that we had to complete to pass the course.

I'm not sure if this was a modern variant of the ancient navy punishment of keel-hauling. That basically involved an errant sailor being tied to a rope, thrown over the stern and then hauled by men on the deck, underneath the hull of the ship from side to side. By the time he reached the other side, his back, arms and legs would be shredded by the sharp edges of the barnacles clamped to the hull. But that was if he was lucky. More often than not, there was a sharp tug on the rope and the sailor was gone – no more than a tasty treat for a passing shark attracted by the blood in the water. Our test was a little more humane, and, given the pollution around parts of Portsmouth, it would be a brave shark that would risk those waters.

Before we undertook our thirty-metre dive, we had to complete a tower jump. This was deemed an integral part of diver training and involved climbing an old tower in the Solent, dating from the Napoleonic wars. The tower was 20m high (60 feet) and it looked a long way to the sea surface below. Needless to say, because I was the only Royal Marine on a RN course, I was naturally expected to go first. I was the only Commando on the course, and I reckon it was the Royal Navy's way of hinting that I'd joined the wrong unit. From the top of the tower you had a panoramic view back towards Poole and Bournemouth on the horizon, not that I took too much notice. I was far more concerned with making it to the sea surface below me in one piece.

I put my Para training into practice, followed the dive count and stepped into the air. My recollection is that it was a long time before I hit the water, and, thanks to the flotation gear I was wearing, I shot straight back up to the sea surface within seconds. Unfortunately, the sea was quite choppy that day and I hit the surface just as a wave was slamming into the tower. I entered the sea at a bad angle and my neck took most of the resultant stress. For days afterwards, I could hardly move my neck – and, even today, if I twist at a bad angle, the neck immediately gives me grief. But I had qualified as a diver and added another qualification to my CV. Best of all, a diver qualification added a little more money to my paycheck as long as I continued to get my dive minutes in and remain deployed to a unit that supported an official dive team. The claustrophobia never quite went away – I fought the feeling every single time. I was all right once I was underwater, but getting there was always a struggle. I dived in the Marines and after for ten years before finally hanging up my fins. Sod the pretty fish!

11

SAME WAVES

I had opted out of the 14 Int Acquaint programme because I didn't fancy a lengthy undercover deployment to Northern Ireland. Yet, having completed my parachute training and then the ship's diver's course, that is precisely where I ended up. Only this time I would be in Northern Ireland as a Royal Marine Commando rather than on special operations.

I knew that a six-month tour in Northern Ireland would, with all the qualifications I had already obtained, be the precursor to my sergeant's training course. At this point in my career I wanted to be a regimental sergeant-major. With that rank I would be exempted from the mandatory retirement age of forty, and I wanted to spend my life, or as much as possible of it, in the Marines. But first I had to get through another six months in Ulster.

This was 1992 and, in the eleven years since I had last served there, a lot had changed. The febrile atmosphere of 1981 and the H-Block hunger strikes were now, thankfully, consigned to the history books, but Ulster was still an exceptionally dangerous place to be, particularly if you were wearing a British uniform. In the late 1980s the IRA had managed to get their hands on serious Soviet Bloc weaponry via Libya and had been making deadly use of it. The AK-47 had now supplanted the Armalite, but what everyone dreaded was Semtex, the Czech-designed high explosive. It was believed the IRA had also got surface-to-air (SAM) missiles but didn't have the guidance systems to operate them. More than a few Royal Navy and RAF pilots would say silent prayers of thanks for this over the coming years. There were also a few heavy sniping rifles in circulation and these, too, were weapons to be feared.

Things might have changed in Ulster, but not for us Commandos. I felt in a kind of time warp. We had bigger boats now and our base ship had changed, but, essentially, I would be doing exactly what I had been doing eleven years earlier – patrolling Carlingford Lough, checking vessels for contraband and supporting any impromptu checkpoints that the Commandos, RUC or Special Branch wanted to mount on roads around the lough.

The men for the job were now selected from the base at Poole and not 1st Raiding Squadron, as the latter was now a troop and amalgamated into a larger unit called 539 Assault Squadron. The only other major change in operational routine was that in addition we would now mount patrols of Lough Neagh. This was also done by lads from Poole, and this lough was land-locked rather than open to the sea.

However, if the work was the same, the place had definitely changed. Almost twenty years of horrific violence had taken its toll on Northern Ireland society. There was plenty of black humour and one of the things I admired most about Irish people, particularly Belfast residents, was that amid all the carnage they never lost their sense of humour or the ability to anticipate a bright new future. Unfortunately, people had learned the potential cost of not being cautious and careful in their day-to-day lives. That meant that new arrivals – particularly those with a Yorkshire accent – were treated with circumspection. In 1981 you could still have contact with ordinary people amid all the madness going on around you. But not now.

The army, too, had learned lessons. A number of soldiers had been shot or injured after being identified while off-duty so, when I arrived back, we were pretty much restricted to barracks. The old days of going into Belfast city centre for a pint were a thing of the past. It was an 'unacceptable risk', so our off-duty socialising was at the barracks or approved clubs and messes. Again, this only served to isolate us even more from the lives of daily people.

The fact we were advised to take a special course, called PPW (Personal Protection with Weapons) at Ballykinler in early 1992, further underlined the risks to our safety. It was designed by and for the Ulster Defence Regiment (UDR), who lived and fought on their own turf. The course was recommended for all personnel serving in Northern Ireland, particularly those who may have family or relatives in the area and who sometimes didn't overnight at their barracks. It was a direct response to the latest development in paramilitary violence. Soldiers and policemen had always run a risk of attack, but now the paramilitaries had taken a special interest in the movements of individual personnel: where they lived; how they socialised; whether they had a girlfriend in the area; whether they were football fans or had any personal hobbies. In one case, a few RUC personnel had gone into the Republic on a fishing trip, and either they were followed or word of their trip became known. They were ambushed on the way back and one man was taken hostage. The poor guy had a long history of depression and had been out sick from his RUC work for ages. But it didn't save him and he was still murdered in cold blood.

So, when we were advised to opt for a place on the PPW course, most of us accepted. The course was run by the UDR, a regiment created in 1970 in a bid to provide valuable support for the RUC. The aim of the UDR was to protect Northern Ireland from paramilitary attacks by guarding strategic installations and patrolling the cities, towns and countryside. The UDR – a part-time force, though under strict military rule – also carried out security checkpoints, roadblocks and supported the security forces in whatever way they could. The UDR was created to serve only in Ulster and, while strenuous efforts were made to ensure the regiment represented both sides of the Northern Ireland community, brutal targeting by both the IRA and INLA ensured that Catholics became reluctant to join or to continue serving. By 1990 there were just 160 Catholics left in a regiment originally designed for 6,000 personnel.

The PPW course drew on all the UDR's hard-won knowledge of what it took to stay alive in Ulster. They had paid a pretty steep price in blood for trying to keep Northern Ireland safe. They explained that every single aspect of your daily operations had to be carefully reviewed, and, above all, you had to be acutely aware of the dangers posed by establishing predictable daily routines. That is easier said than done – after all, there are only so many ways of driving from your home to your workplace. But varying the route or your time of departure could mean the difference between life and death. You also learned to get paranoid about what was going on around you – to notice things. Anything out of the ordinary, anything that was suspicious could prove to be the only inkling you would get about an attempt on your life.

You learned not to take anything for granted, starting with jumping into your car in the morning. You were taught that, before you did this, you had to carefully check the vehicle for bombs or booby-traps. The IRA had developed a lethal fondness for magnetic bombs slipped underneath cars. They could be detonated remotely, or wired to explode when the car's radio or cigarette lighter was engaged. These were all lessons that would stand me in good stead when I ended up in the Middle East in years to come.

Thanks to the Semtex now wielded by the IRA, even small devices hidden underneath or inside cars could prove devastating. We learned that a lot of security personnel kept a special long-handled mirror in their hallway specifically for the purpose of examining the underneath of their car before heading to work in the morning. Other tips involved putting heavy chains on all doors into your home to make it harder for paramilitaries to break in and to give yourself a few vital extra seconds to arm yourself. Any unexpected call to your door had to be treated with caution. Perhaps the madness of Ulster at this time is best underlined by the fact you were taught to open the front door with a weapon in your hand discreetly aimed at the chest or the head of the stranger standing on the other side.

How people lived full-time in that kind of atmosphere I will never know, let alone how they raised kids and tried to have normal family lives. I suppose you can get used to almost anything, but, coming from Yorkshire where the biggest danger on a Saturday night usually came from having a bad pint of ale, I found it absolutely astonishing what some families in Northern Ireland lived through. PPW even taught us how to respond if your vehicle was cut off in an ambush either in a rural area or a built-up urban zone. The course was all about giving yourself those vital few extra seconds that could end up keeping you alive, and learning, as we did in the Commandos back at Lympstone, to treat your personal firearm as an extension of your arm. You kept it by your side at all times because, in Northern Ireland, it could ultimately prove to be the difference between living and dying.

By now I was one of the 'old salt' Commandos in Ulster. I was twenty when I did my first stint in Northern Ireland but I was arriving back with my thirty-first birthday firmly on the horizon. To the young Commandos, I was like the old man of the sea, though I was only a corporal at that stage. Yet, when things went wrong, I was one of the guys they turned to for advice and support. One lad called Kenny, from 40-Commando quietly took me aside one day and asked my advice. He was nineteen, had just got engaged to his childhood sweetheart back in England and wanted to know how best to invest the £2,000 he had saved up. Christ, mate, you should be giving me advice, not the other way round, I thought. But I advised him to spend it on a holiday, changing his car or even a weekend away with his mates. My view was that, at nineteen, you had the rest of your life to scrimp and save, so it was best to do the things now that in later life you just would not be able to do. I imagine he was expecting advice about property investments or stock-market tips! In hindsight, it was undoubtedly the best possible advice I could have given him because, in 1993, he died of asphyxiation while on Arctic warfare training in Norway, as I mentioned in Chapter 4.

We started our deployment in the gales, sleet and freezing temperatures of the Northern Ireland winter that I had already learned to dread. Our boats may have been bigger, but Carlingford Lough was every bit as windblown, desolate and frigid as I remembered it from eleven years earlier. There were times when we treated the vessel inspections and patrols as pretty routine, but you got the occasional reminder that Mother Nature could be every bit as lethal an enemy as the IRA or the INLA.

One dark, stormy, rainy January night we were finishing up a patrol. There were four craft out that night, three RIBs and one Rigid Raider. One of the boats had been damaged during the patrol and was being towed back to the mother ship. Because we were concentrating on the damaged boat, no one paid too much attention to the Raider, bringing up the rear of the patrol. It was being driven by a young coxswain called Gary, and he was nonplussed when suddenly his outboard engine began to cough and splutter. Finally, the engine died and within seconds the other boats had left Gary behind. He focused on trying to restart the engine, but couldn't get it to fire, despite his best efforts.

All the while, the winds and tides were driving the Raider out of the normal entrance channel to the lough. Gary didn't have a radio to alert us and was reluctant to use a flare, for obvious security reasons. He desperately kept working on the engine until, an hour or so later, he had been driven on to the tidal shallows of the lough, far away from the main channel. In desperation, Gary gave up on the engine – which, we later discovered, had suffered from seawater contaminating its fuel lines – and jumped into the sea in a bid to pull the Raider back to shipping channels where it might be spotted.

We had arrived back at the mother ship anchored in the middle of the lough and carefully tied up the damaged craft. We were just about to shut up shop when someone asked where Gary was. We scanned the approaches to the ship, realising he should have been here ages ago. We immediately jumped back into the boats and headed back out to sea. One of the ship cooks happened to be there and he insisted on coming out with us to help in the search. I knew almost every inch of Carlingford Lough by now and guessed that, if Gary's engine had failed, the wind and tides would have driven him in a specific direction. We split up and began to comb that area for any sign of him.

I knew all the buoys and shallow markers, so proceeded to get as close to them as I could to scan the waters beyond. It was, by now, pitch-black, windy and raining, and the only light was from the flashing strobes on the buoys and shallow markers. In the distance, I could see a faint green light that I didn't recognise by its location. It wasn't one of the shallow markers and wasn't a light like those on the channel buoys. As I went closer to investigate I realised it was Gary. He had turned his waterproof torch on and hung it around his neck so its beam reflected on to his face. He was by now up to his chest in the shallows, desperately trying to drag the Raider back towards the channel. But he was having to fight against the wind, the tides, the weight of the Raider and the freezing waters of the lough.

By the time I reached him it was clear he was already suffering from hypothermia. Even though he was wearing his waterproof suit, the cold water had slowly taken its toll. We dragged Gary on to the Raider and John, our cook, lay across him in a desperate effort to keep him warm while we raced back to the ship. He was shivering so badly that it was actually hard for John to grip him. Once back on the ship, we got Gary into a warm shower and then some dry clothing. We plied him with as many hot drinks as he could take. I thought the poor guy would shake his teeth loose he was shivering so much, and his lips had turned blue. But with the warmth and hot drinks he soon rallied. If we hadn't found him for another half-an-hour, it could have been disastrous.

Mercifully, that was the closest we came to losing someone during the six-month tour, which in itself was a miracle because the IRA was by now a pretty sophisticated killing machine. The RUC, UDR and army Special Forces had their successes and certain IRA units had been very badly hit in special crackdowns. But, as the chilling IRA message after the Brighton bombings went: we had to be lucky all the time, they only had to get lucky once. It was a lethal game of cat-and-mouse, played out with assault rifles, plastic explosives and sectarian savagery that had to be seen to be believed. I met some lovely people in Northern Ireland and was really taken by the beauty of the place. There are few sights in the world as magnificent as a sea approach to Newcastle, as the mountains of Mourne suddenly appear from the mist. Even Belfast, for all its nineteenth-century industrial grittiness, has a special kind of charm. But I was still glad to go home when my six months were up.

Unfortunately, it wasn't all plain sailing for me back in Poole. Julia and I were talking about getting married when suddenly she complained of blinding headaches. At first, we thought it was little more than migraine but, as the headaches increased in regularity and severity, I began to get worried. She was then told in our nearby hospital that they planned to carry out an exhaustive series of cranial tests, including a scan for a possible tumour. She got the news just as I was called up for my senior command course. We both knew that if I didn't take the course I would drop back on the promotion roster by about two years. I decided to go on the course, but it was a disastrous decision. I was constantly worried about Julia and was doing my best to keep in contact and get updates on her tests.

The course was a head-wrecker. It aimed to match the physical intensity of basic training with a mental assault course designed to cream off the best prospects for the grade of sergeant. There was only a limited number of promotion slots available, and what I didn't bargain for was the political aspect. Almost everyone on the course had specialist backgrounds: weapons, explosives, artillery, landing craft and so on. The problem was that certain specialisations were better suited to the course involved. And certain areas of expertise, such as weapons, clearly resonated better with the instructors who were themselves specialists in the same area. It basically meant that some guys had a pretty significant head-start when it came to one of the most arduous courses operated by the Royal Marines.

I began the eight-week course just hoping to pass it, as I knew I wasn't firing on all cylinders. We were assigned various command tasks and I was aware I didn't exactly set the military world on fire with the way I handled them. There was a lot of classroom work and we also had to give lectures about various subjects to demonstrate our grasp of the material. Some of the lads had great egos and confidence in themselves, which was perfectly suited to these lectures. I just wanted to get them over and done with. In the end, I think I was struggling to convince even myself that I wanted to be at Lympstone.

I failed the course. It was like getting a kick in the testicles. I lost two years' seniority and was told I also had to wait at least two years for the next course. My pride was badly wounded and I was devastated that I had lost out on extra pay, which Julia and I badly needed for our wedding and home-purchase plans. I didn't know it in 1992, but not passing that course was catastrophic for my long-term career prospects. Had I passed, I reckon I would have made sergeant-major in time to avoid the worst fall-out from the defence cuts of the mid-1990s. But that's a story for another day. I went straight into another course, Landing Craft 1st Class. Ultimately, I made it to sergeant in 1993, finally getting my head sorted for the focus needed.

My heart belonged to Raiders and switching to the lumbering hundred-tonne Landing Craft Utilities (LCU) didn't exactly set my world on fire. But LCUs are what assault squadrons are all about and the skills I learned in handling Raiders stood me in good stead when it came to the landing craft. I was chuffed to receive a superior pass on the course, which meant that I qualified for an inter-service assignment – basically, the chance to serve for a period under a Royal Marine exchange programme with either the Royal Dutch Marines or the US Marine Corps. A US Marine Corps assignment meant being based in California for two years, something I knew I'd enjoy and Julia would probably jump at the chance of. But our Commando branch sponsor was an old comrade called Dave O., whom I had served with in both 1st and 3rd Raiding Squadrons. Dave had other plans for me – and they didn't involve a stay in the US. 'I'm not losing you for two years, Geoff,' was his blunt assessment of my exchange programme chances.

Dave was the landing craft RSM (Regimental Sergeant-Major) and told me we were to reintroduce the hovercraft into Royal Marine service. A new twelve-metre hovercraft had just been developed and defence chiefs were adamant that it offered advantages for Commando operations. I was asked to serve as Senior LC (Senior Landing Craft) for the introduction trials for the new craft and would train in Instow in Devon, working alongside the Amphibious Trials and Training Unit (ATTURM) until we were competent on it, then we would be part of 539 Assault Squadron in Turnchapel, Plymouth. It was a great honour and, if the programme worked out well, potentially very career-enhancing. But, deep down, I really would have preferred to go to California.

In the end, I had little choice. The hovercraft programme was deemed a high priority for the Royal Marines, particularly given the improvements in the new design. In the 1950s, hovercraft were big, heavy and unbelievably noisy. They also had all the fuel efficiency of a tiger tank and for all these reasons they were quietly dropped from the UK forces' operational fleet. But the new hovercraft was a very different animal. Thanks to advances in engine technology and a variable-pitch propeller, it was quieter than its predecessor and had been designed so that it could be transported in the cargo bay of a C-130 Hercules transport aircraft for rapid deployment.

At Instow, we spent a month getting to know the hovercraft and how to maximise its capabilities. In the correct conditions, it was an absolutely stunning craft to operate – capable of travelling at up to 40 knots over the sea before slowing to mount the beach and then transition overland. With the commissioning course under my belt, I returned to 539 Assault Squadron and we waited for a chance to show what the hovercraft could do in operational manoeuvres. Unfortunately, a few of the craft's failings quickly came to light. To make them air-portable, weight had to be kept to an absolute minimum, and some of the hovercraft panels were made of aluminium just 2mm thick. This meant that they bent or dented quite easily, so had to be kept on the main deck for protection and repair.

Worse, the hovercraft couldn't operate safely in heavy seas or high winds, so they spent longer in storage on the deck than more flexible craft such as the Raiders and LCUs, which could operate in everything bar storm-force seas. There is nothing worse in a Royal Marine Commando unit than a piece of equipment that cannot be deployed; storage, space and weight are always at a premium, so everything on board an assault ship has to constantly justify itself. The old adage goes that: 'If it cannot be used, it shouldn't be here.'

Slowly, the word spread that hovercraft were basically a waste of space and that the money they cost would be better spent elsewhere. I have no doubt a lot of the guys viewed them as high-tech, expensive luxuries. I don't think our senior officers were too pleased with them either. It would be in Norway and the jungles of Africa and Asia, several years later, that the hovercraft truly proved its worth. The hovercraft could go up frozen fjords far beyond the point accessible to either Raiders or LCUs, thus for Arctic deployments they offered enormous advantages and dramatically improved troop mobility, irrespective of the snow or ice. Similarly, in the tropics, they could operate over marshes, swamps, deltas and even travel up shallow jungle rivers and streams without fear of getting stranded. But the hovercraft never quite fully silenced its detractors. It also didn't help that, in the drive to save vital weight, the craft didn't carry much armour and was far less resilient to damage than the humble, lumbering LCU.

So, as 1995 dawned, I was a sergeant hoping for promotion to colour sergeant and then sergeant-major, but who was specialised in landing craft and hovercraft operations that the Commandos clearly valued less highly than weapons specialists. Suddenly, my future looked far from certain.

Julia and I married in 1993 in Chettle, Dorset. I was back in Instow, instructing the next batch of hovercraft crews to take over after a two-year attachment to the task. I wasn't ready to leave the job but I was very proud that I was the first to bring hovercraft back into service since they were disbanded from military life in the UK.

12

FROM POTATO PEELER TO BODYGUARD

'Safety, your Princess is dead.' The radio call from Captain Lacteridis was unmistakable. But I hadn't a clue what the hell he was talking about that glorious summer morning in 1997. 'Safety' was my radio call sign on board Royal Caribbean International (RCI) cruise liners where I was now working as a Safety and Security Officer. My first thought was that the vastly experienced Greek skipper, a lovely old gent, was either losing his marbles or had had just a little bit too much ouzo for lunch. We were in Port Canaveral in Florida on the ship's turn-around day. It was a couple of minutes later before another radio call came in to confirm that 'my Princess' referred to Diana, Princess of Wales, and that she had died in a crash in a Paris tunnel earlier that morning with her then boyfriend, Dodi al-Fayed.

Captain Lacteridis presumed that, being British, I would be upset by Diana's tragic death. But what he could not have known was that I had a much closer connection to the other person to die in the back of the speeding Mercedes limousine in the Alma tunnel early that August day. I had worked as bodyguard for the father of Dodi al-Fayed, and was friendly with the only person to survive the horrific crash, Dodi's long-time bodyguard, Trevor Rees-Jones. The thought crossed my mind that, given a different set of circumstances, it could easily have been me instead of Trevor in the front of that wrecked Merc.

I worked for four months for Dodi's father, Mohammed al-Fayed, the Egyptian-born billionaire, who is perhaps best known for his ownership of Harrods, the London department store, and the Ritz hotel in Paris. It was one of the strangest periods in my life. One minute I was a Royal Marine Commando on the verge of promotion, the next I was earning £60 a week peeling potatoes and then, suddenly, I was a bodyguard for the al-Fayed family and surrounded by the trappings of wealth and the jet-set lifestyle.

It all started with then British Prime Minister, John Major. The Tories were struggling with a poor economy and exchequer problems, so the decision was made in 1995 to save a few quid with a round of Ministry of Defence cutbacks. These didn't just involve mothballing a few warships and putting off an order to buy new fighters for the RAF. It meant axing some regiments, merging others and reducing the overall number of Army, Navy and RAF personnel. Their main target was the so-called middle-management – the sergeant majors, captains and majors – whose wages were higher than those of ordinary soldiers.

Initially, I thought the whole thing wouldn't affect me. I was now a sergeant 1st class, awaiting my promotion to colour sergeant and then sergeant-major. I was thirty-five years old and ranked as one of the most experienced and qualified Commando sergeants in the Royal Marines in my chosen field. I'd qualified to handle landing craft, hovercraft and Raiders. I'd got my diving qualifications and could even work with mini-submarines. I was parachute-trained, Arctic-warfare-trained, could ski and was trained in small weapon personal protection. At that point in 1995, I had been working with 539 Assault Squadron for some time, and I was probably going to be on the next promotion round. Once I was promoted to colour sergeant, then sergeant-major or warrant-officer rank, I was effectively exempted from the mandatory retirement age limit, which would hit me within the next five or six years. The initial round of voluntary early retirements didn't affect me, though we were all a bit taken aback that some of the experienced personnel being let go did not really want to leave.

Having seen what could be saved, the government suddenly wanted even more personnel savings from within the three services, and senior chiefs were basically told that high-investment projects could only be delivered on the back of manpower savings. The Royal Navy were trying to commission new nuclear submarines and through-deck cruisers, the Army were updating their Challenger tanks to the Challenger II model, while the RAF were saving every pound, shilling and penny they could to fund the horrendously expensive Eurofighter programme. The bottom line was that technology was in, manpower was out.

To my horror, I realised that the cull extended below the rank of sergeant-major and that veteran sergeants and corporals were to face the axe. I was bluntly told that there were no foreseeable vacancies for sergeant-major in my area. The only way I was going to get promotion was if a number of guys ahead of me in the list quit, or for some unanswerable reason, dropped down dead tomorrow. For the first time, the spectre of life outside the Marines appeared before my eyes.

It was suggested to me that I should think very carefully about the early retirement package on offer. There was no guarantee that the terms would be as generous in twelve months' time, and the prospect of not reaching the rank I wanted was a pretty devastating reality check. My wife, Julia, was then expecting our first child, Aaron. I knew she was keen for me to think about a life outside the military and I could see her point of view. She was not overly thrilled at the prospect of her new husband spending months at a time overseas on training manoeuvres or operational deployments. She wanted stability for her new family – and the Royal Marine Commandos didn't exactly fit the bill.

My problem was that I had been a Marine since I was seventeen and I simply didn't know any other way to live. I had spent so long – more than half my life – in the Commandos that the rigours of military life were ingrained. Only people who have served in uniform understand that a military life offers specific certainties – your life, at least in peacetime, follows a very regular, ordered pattern. Life outside is a very different prospect, fraught with uncertainty, irregularity and, in many ways, a very different value system. Sure, I could take the package and accept a lump sum, a partial pension and swap the demands of Commando life for the easy living of civvie street. But what would I do then? Who would want the specialised skills that Her Majesty's government had worked so very hard to equip me with? There aren't too many jobs available for hovercraft operators or machine-gunners on the Thames or Severn.

My biggest fear was that if I turned down the early retirement package I'd be denied promotion and then be forced to leave at the age of forty anyway. I reckoned it was better to face up to the challenges of civilian life with a few quid in my pocket now and still be relatively young at thirty-five. I was advised that if I wanted to apply for early retirement I should request a training course – as was my right – before I formally left the Royal Marines. Such courses were seen as a very useful way of helping former military personnel integrate into civilian life, and, most important of all, securing a new source of income. I was in Norway on an Arctic training deployment and returned to discover that my entire branch of the corps was now directly affected by the personnel cuts. We were told by our senior officer that they were looking for volunteers.

I agonised over the decision. One helpful factor was that I already had the offer of a job from an ex-major of the Royal Marines who had set up a contract fishing business targeting high-value species. He was in the running for a lobster contract in the Seychelles. If he got the contract, he promised that there was a job for me that would offer not only a salary, but a share in the catch. It was seasonal work, but I thought it would tide me over until something better came along.

With a heavy heart, I realised that the best decision would be to quit the Royal Marines, though I felt I was leaving part of me behind. In March 1996, my early retirement was approved. I got my EVT (Extra Vocational Training) course request, and I also received a grant to put towards a private-sector training programme. Like a lot of other Commandos, I thought my training and skills were best applied in the burgeoning private security sector, so I applied for a bodyguard course run by Task International.

The Royal Marines recommended this course as the ideal entry point for 'Close Protection' bodyguard work. Most of the instructors hired by Task were former soldiers and policemen drawn from the Special Branch. The company was founded by Jeremy Moore, who was the land force commander from the Falklands, so, in a way, I was rejoining old comrades. The course ran for a full month from Maidstone in Kent, and I found that it was ideally suited to former military personnel. I actually felt a little sorry for the civilian guys undertaking it because what came as second nature to us was clearly very hard for them. Some of these lads were nightclub bouncers who fancied the better pay of being a celebrity bodyguard, but they hadn't a clue about threat assessments or security judgements, which came naturally to us ex-soldiers.

I found the course very interesting. It went from anti-kidnapping training to vehicle protection, and from pistol-shooting to high-speed evasion in armoured limousines. We were also taught how to survey buildings for potential security threats – luxury hotels, fancy restaurants or theatres that celebrity clients might want to visit. On one occasion, this led to a comical false alarm where Royal Marine headquarters and Task received an urgent call from MI5 querying why a Commando was staking out a London hotel! I had gone to the hotel, clipboard in hand, to list all the potential security threats I could identify, but the paper I was using was embossed with the Royal Marine crest and, unfortunately, some bigwig was obviously staying in the hotel at the time. My activity was spotted first by his protection detail and then by MI5. That's how paranoid security details have to be – and this was five years before the attack on the Twin Towers and the London Tube bombings.

I got my qualification – a Special Security Class 3 Cert – but to find work I would have to go to London where most of the bodyguard work was sourced. London security work was known as 'the circuit' in the bodyguard and protection trade. When you finished one short-term contract you simply waited for another to arrive. London ranked alongside Paris, New York, Los Angeles and Rome for celebrities – it was virtually a 'must see' on any European tour for movie stars, musicians, politicians and celebrities of every ilk. It was like a conveyor belt of stars arriving every week, and they all wanted their own private security as they shuttled from five-star hotels to expensive restaurants. Hence, 'the circuit' was created, and a bodyguard who had established his reliability, discretion and ability could move seamlessly from job to job. There were guys who, in the space of a single month, had protected foreign presidents, American rap stars, dot-com millionaires and even a Hollywood starlet.

Getting a foothold in the circuit was a challenge. Most of the work was distributed on a personal-contact-and-reputation basis, and when you made a name as a professional operator, you were never short of contracts. But breaking into the industry usually depended on one ex-Royal Marine doing a favour for another. At that time, however, it simply wasn't practical for me to commute from Plymouth in Devon where Julia and I lived. So I took a month off and relaxed with my wife and new son.

After five weeks, I was beginning to climb the walls and knew I needed to get back to work fast. I'd spent eighteen years in an adrenalin-packed military career, and suddenly the biggest decision of the day was whether to have fish and chips or tandoori for supper. I had rung my friend, the retired Royal Marine major, about the lobster job, but his Seychelles contract had not materialised. Without that contract, he couldn't offer me work. I spent a small fortune printing up hundreds of CVs and mailing them to every security and bodyguard company I could find. But I didn't hear a thing back. I rang a load of ex-Marines about work, but no one had anything available. I knew it meant working from London.

In desperation, I cast about for work in Plymouth. Julia and I were living in Ivybridge, a small village outside Plymouth and a neighbour happened to mention that his employer had a few jobs available. The man ran a vegetable company and specialised in delivering prepared veg to schools and shops in Devon and Cornwall. The man, an ex-navy chief caterer, had a vacancy for a delivery driver and I gratefully accepted. My delivery work started at 3am, but I soon realised that if I were to stick solely to deliveries, my wages would be pretty terrible. To boost my earnings, I had to stay on and help with preparing and vacuum-sealing the vegetables.

I stuck it for two months and I'm still amazed I lasted that long. I was walking up my drive one evening, wet through to my socks from standing in potato juice, and smelling of spud peelings, when I stopped and laughed out loud at the silliness of it all – just four months previously I had been in charge of £8 million worth of Marine assault equipment, including four hovercraft and four LCVPs. My word was law and young Marine recruits jumped at my every command. Now, I was peeling potatoes and earning the vast sum of £60 per week. I earned more in one day in the Royal Marines than I did here in an entire week. I didn't know whether to laugh or cry.

Then, out of the blue, my luck changed. A letter arrived saying that my CV had been received and would I attend for an interview in London about a security contract for a high-profile businessman. I jumped at the chance. I had to attend an initial interview at Hyde Park Lane and was quizzed about my military career. I was then asked my opinion about various security issues before being asked to sit a graphology test. I'd never heard the word before, let alone sat such a test, but I said 'Fine'; I needed the work so I was ready to do whatever was necessary. (Later on I heard that the test was designed to identify loonies – but it obviously failed in my case!). It was only later that I discovered the businessman involved was Mohammed al-Fayed, who maintained one of the most elaborate private security operations in Britain. I was offered a job the next day. I would be in static security – that is, security maintained on key buildings owned by al-Fayed and his family.

Julia didn't like the idea of me working so far from Devon, but I felt I simply didn't have a choice. I'd already seen enough potato peelings to last me a lifetime and there was nothing else on the horizon. I accepted the job and was told I would start out on probation. If it worked out for four months or so, I would be given a longer contract with the promise of better rates; the rolling contract involved one week on, one week off. There was no question of us carrying firearms. My assignment was residential security officer at the al-Fayed Hyde Park residence and the office buildings around it, which served as the London base for Mohammed, his son Dodi and his brother Ali.

The first thing I discovered was that the job was very political and very eccentric. Every one of the senior security team leaders seemed to be looking over their shoulder and were determined to run a military-style operation to impress their boss. It really was a case of lots of chiefs, very few Indians. Almost everyone seemed more worried about the activities of paparazzi photographers than kidnappers, terrorists or armed lunatics. Another of the biggest fears was that al-Fayed's motorcade would be delayed on entry into the compound – and the boss would be kept waiting. Everything had to be timed to perfection by the security team so that the limousine could sweep straight in when it arrived. Mr al-Fayed also liked to have doors open and elevators ready for him when he arrived. All security personnel were expected to be clean-shaven, with hair combed, and wearing smart suits at all times.

For the most part, the work was pretty routine. We were constantly checking security alarms, perimeter cameras and conducting foot patrols around the three buildings. Every watch was twelve hours long, and every security staff member answered to an Ops (Operational) Commander, based in the security centre, equipped with a full bank of CCTV cameras. The static security team always liaised with the personal security guys who were with individual members of the al-Fayed family at all times. And there weren't just static security teams on Hyde Park Road; there was also one at Harrods and one at the al-Fayed country mansion in Oxted.

All the static security guys wanted to switch to the personal security detail, as much for the better money as for the higher profile and travel involved. The pay for us static security guys was pretty bad – better than peeling potatoes, though not a whole lot more, given the grief we sometimes had to put up with. At least no one ever tried to tell you that you were peeling a potato the wrong way! I didn't envy the personal security guys their work; it was tough, they always had to be on their toes and they never knew where they were going to end up from one minute of the day to the next. They also took a lot more of the in-house political grief than the rest of us. Some of the personal security guys were really decent blokes, and, like me, had a long military career behind them. In particular, Trevor Rees-Jones was a total gent. Trevor always worked with Dodi alongside a former Royal Marine military policeman.

As I was part of the static security detail, Dodi was our responsibility when he was 'in residence' in Hyde Park Road. Invariably, our tasks were more like those of a butler than a security guard. Dodi loved food from two particular restaurants – Japanese and Chinese – and would regularly phone through a take-away order, particularly if he wasn't entertaining. These places were among the most expensive restaurants in London, but they were only too happy to prepare a take-away meal once they knew it was for the al-Fayed table. It was my job to collect the orders in a Range Rover Vogue and bring them back to Hyde Park Road. On other occasions, particularly if Dodi was trying to impress a lady, we would often be dispatched to collect flowers, chocolates and speciality foods from Harrods. Any guests arriving at the residence had to be personally greeted, their cars had to be parked by security personnel and the guests then discreetly escorted inside.

If Dodi left to go out on the town with his female companion, he was no longer our responsibility – security was immediately handed over to his personal detail. But they liaised with our Ops Commander and we were always on standby to deploy in support, if required. That never happened in my time at Hyde Park Road – the only nuisance was paparazzi photographers who would regularly cruise outside in the hope of snatching a shot they could then sell to one of the Fleet Street tabloids. These press photographers were only a minor irritation during my time, compared to the serious and round-the-clock headache they became the instant Dodi was romantically linked with Diana. Once that happened, there was always a small army of them in London and Paris chasing the couple. A photograph of the duo was worth serious money from a global media industry totally besotted with Diana; in fact, the shot of the two of them on board a yacht in the Mediterranean was rumoured to have sold for a staggering £1 million.

During my time, photographers were much more interested in

Mohammed al-Fayed than Dodi. Mohammed was a figure of tremendous fascination in Britain, and he was determined to keep the omnipotent British media at arm's length. That, I suppose, was really what our job was about.

I left al-Fayed's employ in November 1996 and it was just a few months later that Dodi would begin the relationship with Princess Diana that would end so tragically in the Alma tunnel. I felt really sorry for Trevor Rees-Jones as he was just trying to do his job, and almost lost his life as a result. It did briefly cross my mind that it could have been me in the Merc. But, in the end, I was relieved to quit al-Fayed's employ. I have to say that in the few dealings I had with him I found him to be both polite and gracious. Similarly, Dodi came across as a decent enough guy, and he treated his security people really well. However, within a month or so of starting work at Hyde Park Road I realised it just was not for me. There was too much stress with too little cause, and the money on offer just didn't justify the hassle. It might have been different if I had been transferred to one of the personal security teams, but there were other guys on the static security teams several months ahead of me who were biding their time for that transfer.

Another part of the problem was that I was never one for honouring life's little vanities. I'm a straight operator and a straight talker. If I think something is wrong, I say so. If I don't understand something, I ask questions. If I think security priorities are not correct, I won't be politically correct and sit silently by. Being from Yorkshire, I suppose it is part and parcel of my DNA. So, when my probation was up, it was pretty much a mutual decision to part company. I think they knew very well my opinion of the operation, so my leaving was definitely the best for both sides.

13

FLIM STAR OR MARR

Once again I was on a journey to nowhere career-wise, headed back home with another tale of woe for Julia and having to tell her that I was unable to provide any wages from that point on. The future was bleak and my self-esteem was at rock bottom again.

I had picked up a *GQ magazine* from the office on Park Lane for the journey home and hoped the editorial bollocks could ease my troubled mind. Inside one advert grabbed my attention, and for an out-of-work, former Park Lane bodyguard/Royal Marine, it was right up my street.

The advert said that they were looking for former service personnel to act as extras in various TV projects. The extras had to be genuine veterans so they could handle weapons properly and the projects would not get criticised by Joe Public for inauthenticity. It paid seventy-five pounds a day and more at weekends. The company was run by a former Para captain, please ring the number below. Why not? I thought, and it might take the edge off my news to Julia. She knew I did not like working for Mohammed at Park Lane, but that wasn't enough of a reason to leave it like that. Not that I really had a choice.

At home and after the thin ice I was walking on, I rang the number in the advert and arranged an interview as soon as possible. I rented a small car and went back to Forest Hill in London, begging a room for the night from an old school pal, Ted, who was a lighting engineer in

Covent Garden. He was the one who first introduced me to the wonders of Queen's *A Night at the Opera* album.

I secured the job, gave the staff my measurements for costume and I was ready to be a star. They needed people like me that weekend so instead of going all the way back to Devon, I stayed in London and travelled to the BMI building near Heathrow for a weekend shoot. James Bond in *Tomorrow Never Dies* – a good start and some money in the bank, which would hopefully earn me some brownie points back home.

'Fuck me, lads!' was the exclamation I gave walking into the canteen and rest marquee for all the extras. In the tent I came across two good mates from my days in the Corp in Poole – Micky Duff from the SBS job in Portland SBS and Moz T from the base. I had no idea they would be there. I instantly felt I was on the right track, and we spent the whole weekend laughing and taking the piss out of all the princess wannabees in the tent.

I nearly shook Pierce Brosnan's hand as he was leaving the toilet on set, but I thought that was a bit inappropriate. And Teri Hatcher had always been a favourite since her Lois & Clark Superman days.

I carried on with the life as an extra for a few more shows and mini-series over the next month or so. Notably, *Coming Home* with Joanna Lumley and *The Unknown Soldier* with Gary Mavers. It wasn't keeping the wolf from the doors, but it was better than nowt, I thought. Joanna was a lovely person and we chatted in the make-up van about *James and the Giant Peach*, her with her hair in curlers and me getting my moustache removed to play a Naval officer. I was also getting paid a small consultancy fee to advise on Navy behaviour and how officers interacted. My last visit to Pinewood as an extra was for the stealth boat scene in *Tomorrow Never Dies*, in which my mate Micky Duff gets strangled by the chief thug in the same Bond film. 'It's OK, Mick,' I said. 'The main henchman in every Bond film gets it in the end.'

On a break, I was called by Julia who told me that I had a job interview for a cruising company in Kent in three days' time and I needed to get back home to prepare. I took the car back and found out that I'd be in a car pool with another interviewee from Plymouth and a Navy Chief.

After a long trip to Kent and a three-day interview process for the job of safety officer, I was given the news I was dreading, but still, nevertheless, pleased me. It was the last thing I wanted – more time away than the corps, and surrounded by women, which would leave my wife fuming. But I had no choice: I had no job and a bank account with a huge hole in it. We were haemorrhaging money by the day and this would solve the problem.

14

JELLY SHOTS AND BROKEN YACHTS

'Excuse me, Sir. But what are you doing?' The six-foot two-inch Dane turned and stared at me. I was wearing the white tropical uniform with gold shoulder flashes that was standard for security officers working on Royal Caribbean International (RCI) cruise liners. I politely waited for his reply. But the man stared right through me before slowly jabbing his finger over my shoulder. 'I'm going over there,' he mumbled. The only problem was that he was stark naked, and we were on the tenth floor of the giant liner, *Radiance of the Seas*, my next venture in the non-military world of work.

To make matters worse, a crowd of curious passengers had gathered at a safe distance to watch the proceedings. As I glanced around, I realised we were standing on a thick plate-glass floor, and, directly below us, the Filipino waiters and kitchen staff were staring in fascination up at the giant nude Dane. Christ, I'd better sort this out quick, I thought as one of the waiters winked up at me.

'Sir, you can't go over there. I cannot allow you to walk around the ship without any clothes,' I quietly explained. The Dane stared back at me and seemed not to hear what I was saying. At my side, two other ship staff were watching developments carefully. Our ship was berthed in New Orleans as part of a major convention weekend, and, as far as I knew, this guy was one of the convention delegates.

The man stepped forwards as though to brush past me. Without thinking, I caught his arm, trapped his leg with my leg, and threw him down on the deck with a judo move. Before he could respond, I had flipped him over on to his stomach and had his arms pinned behind his back so they could be shackled with the metal handcuffs we always carried with us. Two colleagues and I helped the Dane to his feet and led him, protesting and struggling wildly, to the security office.

After eighteen years in the Royal Marines I thought I had encountered every possible type of bizarre human behaviour. How wrong could I be. Tackling naked Danes was merely the tip of the iceberg when it came to what happened on some of the fanciest ships afloat. And, as with so many things in my life, entirely by accident, I had ended up working as security on cruise ships in 1997.

International Maritime Security (IMS) was the assessment agency I had gone to. It had been founded by Brian Parrott, a former brigadier in the Intelligence Corps. He was well known and a very highly respected guy, and IMS worked with some of the world's leading maritime operators, including cruise firms. They dealt in everything from anti-piracy to on-board safety and security procedures. They had profiled the best possible candidates for security work, and ex-Royal Navy and Royal Marine personnel were very high on the list.

More specifically, the world's leading cruise company, Royal Caribbean International (RCI), were now recruiting senior security and safety officers for a range of plush new ships they were set to launch, and I was delighted to be accepted for training with them.

I was thrilled at the prospect of a decent, well-paying job. RCI were a by-word for high standards in the industry, and the contract basically meant four months working at sea and then two months off at home. Unfortunately, my wife didn't share my delight. Julia did not see the point in my having left the Royal Marines to spend more time with her and the children only to head off again to sea on cruise liners. The curse of all my military experience and training was that they seemed to have no commercial application outside the security sector. RCI seemed to offer the obvious answer and I persuaded Julia that I had no other alternative.

It was hard work bringing myself up to speed with all the safety and security regulations that govern the operation of these cruise ships, some of which literally rank as floating cities. As a security officer, I was responsible for the entire security of the ship, both passengers and crew. As a safety officer – whose role can be separate or combined, depending on the cruise ship involved – you have to be au fait with firefighting regulations, evacuation procedures, health matters and industrial safety systems. The firefighting drills were hugely important, and it was my responsibility not only to organise crew training in tackling an on-board fire, but also work with portside firefighting agencies. Briefing a crew on firefighting exercises wasn't easy when you could be dealing with a group of fifty or so men who spoke fourteen different languages. But it had to be done.

My first ship assignment was to *Nordic Empress*, which operated on a Caribbean itinerary ranging from CocoCay, a private island in the Bahamas, to the US Virgin Islands and the British Virgin Islands. She had a crew of 800 and displaced 42,000 tonnes. At the time I thought she was quite a huge liner, but, of course, she has been dwarfed by the vessels launched since then. I had a two-week on-board training period where I was instructed in all the finer details of what was expected of me by an ex-Royal Navy matelot chief. I would be working as a safety officer; the security officer was a giant Filipino guy who didn't say a whole lot, and who usually covered the night shift.

RCI told me that on my time off I would initially be required to travel to Miami or London for specific training courses. I needed to secure a key qualification called a Standard of Training Certification for Watch Keepers (STCW 95), which was recognised worldwide as the benchmark for my new trade. Until then, it was effectively on-the-job training. While working for the four months' stint I would be paid salary-and-a-half, with the half expected to give me an income while I was off for the other two months, which I would not receive until the day I signed off to go home. A major benefit was that, while working, all my food and clothing needs were paid for by RCI. I don't think I've ever eaten so well as on board ship; to a large degree we would eat pretty much the same food as the passengers. And the leisure facilities were also open to us – cinema, gym, disco and theatres.

As a security/safety officer, I would have a dedicated security team answering to me. At the start, that comprised seven Filipino guards, but within a few years, as the whole issue of security became much more high profile, there were ten security staff, the bulk of whom were Gurkhas. After the September 11 attacks in New York, we were given access to state-of-the-art security systems ranging from portable X-ray machines to hand-scanners and from computer ID processing units (APASS) to vastly expanded on-board CCTV systems.

What most shocked me in this work was the antics of some people on these cruise holidays. The way some passengers got stuck into port bars and lounges would have done justice to a parched squad of the Parachute Regiment or Royal Marines. On board, we were responsible for people, so we stepped in if we thought things were getting out of hand or if someone was drinking enough to endanger themselves or others. But, once ashore they were often a law unto themselves. Some of the Mexican and Caribbean port bars were notorious for their drinks. Several plied passengers with 'jelly shots' – basically potent alcoholic cocktails set into a cold jelly mould, which caused havoc.

As safety/security officer, I was responsible for all embarkations and disembarkations from the liner. I evolved a policy of being at the gang-plank for all port day-trips to check off the passengers as they re-boarded. In one case, I spotted a seventy-seven-year-old grandmother totally out of her head on jelly shots staggering down the quayside. Just metres from the ship, she tripped and was too drunk to bring her hands up to protect her face. She plunged face down onto the concrete, I had to carry her on board so the medical officer could bandage her bleeding face and knees.

It never ceased to amaze me how, surrounded by such luxury and opulence, people still insisted on ruining their holiday through booze. My baptism of fire came only a couple of weeks into my contract on

Nordic Empress when I had to intervene with several ship security assistants after two young American women had sparked a row between their boyfriends and four young Puerto Ricans. The women – left alone by their boyfriends who were drinking at the bar – decided to amuse themselves by teasing four handsome Puerto Rican guys, getting them to buy drinks and meals for them. But the instant the American boyfriends arrived back on the scene, all hell broke loose.

The four immediately wanted to attack the Puerto Ricans, who quite wisely withdrew to their cabin. The two women protested their innocence to their boyfriends, and then proceeded to accuse the Puerto Ricans of having molested them. Within a few minutes the entire group was screaming and roaring up and down the corridor, wanting to kill the four Puerto Ricans. A burly Canadian first officer, Ron, was doing his best to keep the peace in the corridor when I arrived. One of the girls was claiming she had been sexually assaulted and all four were screaming at me to do something. All four were clearly drunk as skunks – but, because they had paid for a cruise holiday everything that went wrong was instantly someone else's fault. The major weapon that Americans tend to throw around is the threat of a lawsuit. In reality, I didn't have much power as a security officer. I didn't have full powers of arrest, though I could put a passenger or crewman in a detention cell for their own safety and could also order a passenger off the ship at the next stop if I deemed them to be a threat to myself or the ship. They would then have to make their own way home at their own expense. This was usually enough to calm tempers and make irate passengers think twice about the fuss they were kicking up.

I went into the cabin and spoke to the four Puerto Ricans through a Spanish-speaking crew member. They vehemently denied any suggestion of sexual assault and claimed that it was the women who had joined them by the pool and had flirted with them for the day. One woman had to be repeatedly told by a crew member to put her bikini top back on while at the pool. The problem arose only when the boyfriends arrived back from their marathon bar session. When I came out of the cabin and tried to explain to the young Americans the version of events I had been given, all hell broke loose again.

179

The four just kept screaming threats and promising lawsuits. Then they demanded to see Captain Lacteridis, but they had about as much chance of getting a meeting with the captain as I had of being promoted to brigadier-general. However, I felt the situation was serious enough to alert his deputy, the staff captain, who was a Swede, and a strict disciplinarian. The man arrived down in the corridor five minutes later – having interrupted his formal dinner – and wanted to know what the hell was going on. He was wearing a dress suit and was clearly unimpressed by what he saw. His frosty demeanour worked like a charm on the Americans and they instantly calmed down, started smiling, said it was all a misunderstanding and left the area. I was dumbfounded and the staff captain gave both of us a dirty look as if to say, why was I bothered with such a non-event as this. I learned that as safety or security officer, you had to take immediate control of the situation – you dictate what will happen, not some irate or drunken passenger.

Sometimes you felt it was a never-ending cycle. When we operated from Florida, holiday companies would sometimes run promotions in conjunction with local drinks firms. For $200 or $300, a person could get a short cruise and as much booze as a small water buffalo could consume. It was a recipe for chaos and we were often left to pick up the pieces. On one cruise we had to detain a middle-aged husband who had drunkenly decided to give his wife a hiding in their cabin. On another occasion, a group of thirty arrived on board – the men all seemed to be built like WWF wrestlers and the women were intent on wearing only thongs. For the entire time they were on board it was a misery. We were constantly asking the women to put their bikini tops on, the men were getting involved in fights and, when the entertainment director decided to host a formal dress ball, one of the group arrived dressed as a grizzly bear. The other guests were clearly unimpressed at having a grizzly bear destroy the etiquette of a formal evening. When the group threatened to descend into further drunken mayhem, they were finally warned that if they didn't behave, the entire group would be removed at the next port of call and they could find their own way back to Florida at their own expense. One guy then had the cheek to try and bribe an officer with the offer of a Rolex watch. We all heaved a sigh of relief when they disembarked – and we were shocked to hear afterwards that they were almost all policemen, doctors and firemen.

You knew in advance that certain cruise schedules were going to be heart-breakers. We could almost time the trouble when sailing out of Ensenada or Cozumel in Mexico. The 'jelly' tequila cocktails served in the port clubs here were absolutely notorious, and couples who just two hours before were hand-in-hand, pricing diamond rings and tanzanite earrings for each other were suddenly rolling around on the deck, screaming and tearing each other's hair out. The other major problem in these two ports was that passengers lost all sense of time in the port bars. They were either too smashed or busy to care about the ship's departure time. And, trust me, we left on time. Passengers who missed the liner had to make their own way to the next port of call. Or, if they were really lucky, they could pay a local boatman or the pilot launch to race them out of the harbour to the cruise liner before we picked up speed. The captain repeatedly stressed to me that he didn't like being hassled by late passengers trying to make such pick-ups, so I had free rein to be as tough as I liked on the passengers once they were back on board by checking their IDs endlessly.

Allegations of sexual assault was something that always seemed to rear its ugly head, usually in combination with elephantine levels of drinking by the parties involved. Cruises in the Caribbean and off Mexico are notorious for such reports, and every single one has to be sorted out by the security officer. The complaint is almost inevitably filed between 2am and 5am, and you're then faced by a furious father, brother or boyfriend who wants to kill another male passenger. At the very least, they want you to place the alleged offender in irons and await his portside delivery to the local constabulary.

I dealt with one tearful girl who was just fifteen years old – who had to be taken to the ship's medical officer by the time I arrived on the scene. I took a full statement from everyone involved, but bitter experience had taught me that there seems to be no such thing as a black-and-white case, and, in many instances, the occasional lie is thrown in by eye-witness statements from other passengers and the truth comes forth eventually, especially from the use of CCTV security camera footage from all public areas of the ship.

Sometimes the cases were tragic in the extreme. One woman who booked a cruise with her boyfriend was reported missing while we were at sea. She just vanished one night off Miami and no trace of her was ever found; the investigation took a dark turn when it was claimed that the couple had been arguing loudly in the hours before she disappeared. But there was never any hard evidence. After my investigations and company procedures were followed through, there were the consulates to deal with, our risk-assessment teams of lawyers and the FBI, who because of international state regulations were always involved with serious crime on US-based ships. I was told about three years later by the lead Fed on the case that despite repeated investigations, the file remained open and the boyfriend was still a suspect.

Throughout it all, crew training threatened to break my will. Every time we took on new crew, I had to run fire drills. Some crew were fine about it – it was an hour or so on deck in sunshine. Others, however, couldn't hide their boredom and it was difficult to get across the fact that fighting a fire at sea and running an evacuation drill was, quite literally, a matter of life and death. I did succeed in frightening the living crap out of all the younger crew members by explaining what would happen to them if they misfired or played around with the fire extinguishers. But, for the most part, it was like trying to push a boulder uphill. And my counterpart in the safety security side, Derek, a Portsmouth football hooligan, used to show the new joiners the end of a finger he had collected and preserved in embalming fluid and kept in a jar for his demonstration of the dangers of watertight doors.

The HR managers hated the lengths we went to in order to get through to them the dangers they faced. The drug issue on these cruises could never be underestimated either, particularly in certain parts of the world. Cruises from Alaska, Hawaii and eastern parts of the Caribbean largely avoided the worst of the drug problem. But those that operated in waters off Mexico, Jamaica, Haiti, Venezuela and Columbia tended to keep us on our toes. Very often, it would be the local police who would tip us off about passengers suspected of trying to buy or smuggle drugs.

One time, two beautiful young African American women were reported to us by the local Dutch Police, who were on exchange from Holland to their Caribbean protectorate. The coppers didn't have jurisdiction on the ship and also wanted to catch the whole procedure from start to finish, from going ashore to when they returned back on board the ship.

One of the officers liaised with me on the gangway and pointed the women out as they left. I had already used the security technology on board to flag them up on our system. He knew their names from his intelligence and I informed my guards to make us aware when they were leaving, but as clandestinely as possible. I then sent the smallest female Filipino guard ashore in the same tender to report back to me on their movements.

On their return to the ship I was on the gangway with the Dutch policeman and we stopped them. We escorted them to the on-board medical facility, where two Swedish nurses were ready for them and asked them to strip. When they were searched they were found to be carrying 50kg of cocaine strapped around their bodies underneath body-hugging wetsuits. The suits compressed the outline of the attachments and in a cursory pat down could not be detected.

The money offered by local drug gangs was clearly enticing enough for some to take the risk. But it was a very big risk. If people were caught, they were immediately handed over to the local police and faced a long sentence in a Mexican, Jamaican, Haitian or even a US prison. From what I have heard, British prisons rank as holiday camps compared to the conditions in some of these jails, though we tried to get them to the US as a preference, because we knew the sentencing was more stringent.

Crew members would cut their belts in half, fill them with cocaine and then stitch them back together again. They would cut thick flip-flops in half, hollow them out, fill them with a substance and then re-weld them with super glue. The tricks were endless.

I was constantly being warned off from doing hull inspections whenever we went to Ocho Rios, Jamaica. Certain older members of the senior crew had heard old rumours of divers being murdered under the water in this and other Jamaican ports, because they had obviously come across drug-smuggler divers under the ship.

It is a fact that divers did weld cages onto the hulls of ships while we waited in port in order to use them as stowage containers for contraband and drugs. These were retrieved when the ship arrived in a port and sold on the US market, where the street value increased the further north you went.

Sometimes, too, the pressures proved too much for some of the 'mules' – we once had a poor guy who took a dive off the rear of a fourteen-storey-high cruise liner. I don't know if the propellers got him or if he simply drowned, but it was another example and reminder that the glamorous world of cruising has a dark underbelly.

I worked on a number of ships: *Nordic Empress*, *Enchantment of the Seas*, *Radiance of the Seas*, just being commissioned, *Adventure*, *Sovereign* and *Monarch of the Seas*. *Radiance* was my third ship and I was part of her working-up operation; it was a thrill to design the systems and procedures that you knew the ship would employ throughout her entire cruise life. *Radiance* could cater for 2,100 passengers and she was so impressive she set in train a whole new series of superb cruise liners culminating in RCI's new *Oasis of the Seas* class, which boasts a whopping 222,900 tonne displacement and 2,700 staterooms, spread over 16 decks. Her major rival was the new *Queen Mary*, and a glittering new era of liners was ushered in. Every imaginable luxury is built into these floating palaces – they have their own library, cinema, casino, gym, swimming pool, climbing walls, concert hall, shopping mall, beauty centre, a bowling alley and even artificial waves for surfing. And they have the safety systems to match, making the job of her security and safety officer one of the most important afloat.

It was also traditional that the newest cruise liners immediately went onto the most prestigious and profitable routes, a fact that I would not complain about. I had always wanted to travel the world; now the liners I worked on would glide into Hawaii, Alaska, Baja, California, the Panama Canal, St Lucia, Mustique or Jamaica and the Caymans – and I'd lean over the rail and soak up the sights and the atmosphere. I have seen some of the most remarkable sights in the world – whales breaking the sea surface, volcanoes smoking on the horizon, the dawn breaking as you glide between two continents and dolphins arrowing ahead of the liner's bow wave.

As the company expanded and I went from ship to ship, I was increasingly being asked to do courses or take over various projects. It slowly ate into my home time, and, by the time I was transferring off *Radiance*, my marriage was on the rocks.

Frustrated, tired and lonely from problems at home, I made one of the biggest mistakes of my life, I started to take female crew to my cabin. One lady in question was Scandinavian and was working on the same cruise liner. She was single and a good few years younger than me. I'd always heard that married men were attractive to some women because they were 'safe' or offered a no-strings-attached kind of relationship. Perhaps it's because there is some kind of challenge in getting a man who effectively belongs to someone else. Whatever the reason, I was weak and gave in to the temptation. The affair was passionate but absolutely insane. Julia soon found out and I knew that I had committed the cardinal sin. For all our problems, I think we both wanted our relationship to work. But it never did. Needless to say, the fling petered out almost as soon as it started – and I was once again left tired, frustrated and lonely. Only this time I had the wreckage of my marriage for company.

I just wasn't at home often enough and Julia wanted a normal family life. I cannot say I blamed her. I was away at sea so much that she was basically raising the kids on her own. I shouldn't have done what I did. But retrospect is a wonderful thing.

15

SADDAM'S REVENGE

Having spent just over five years on liners, I arrived back in the UK to try and save my marriage, but it was beginning to look like a forlorn hope. It was back to minimum-wage jobs again and I felt I was worth more than that. A friend who worked in construction said he could employ me as a general labourer. The money wasn't bad. So, for the next six months, I mixed cement, dug holes, erected fences and laid patios. I then got another job as a brickie's labourer which, mercifully, paid a little bit more, though I wished I had stayed erecting fences.

By now my Royal Marine severance package was nothing but a distant and fond memory. We had a beautiful home, now back in Yorkshire, but the debts just seemed to be getting larger by the day. I couldn't ever seem to earn enough and was caught in an ever-descending spiral. Still, I enjoyed the construction work. I liked being outdoors and the camaraderie on the building sites reminded me of my days in uniform. What was great about it too was that there was very little bullshit. Unfortunately, what there was was a lot of rain. And you can't lay bricks in the rain. This meant that when it was raining and it was a typical English winter that year, I wasn't able to earn. The debts just kept getting bigger and bigger.

I was at my wits' end. I couldn't find any security work in Yorkshire or even within easy commuting distance. Finally, a friend in RCI contacted me and said that there was a job available for me if I wanted it. It was as the office-based manager for *Brilliance of the Seas*, their latest ship, and it would be in Weighbridge, London. I took the job, which lasted just long enough for me to help them get their licence from the regulating bodies, then I was surplus to their requirements.

Julia was adamant that if I went back to sea the marriage was effectively over. I didn't want to lose her and the kids, but I didn't see any other alternative, so I rang my friend and applied for my old job of ship security officer on the next liner available. Then I moved back into my mum's house until I was called by RCI for a ship assignment. I wasn't seeing my family much but was still paying bills at home. Mounting pressure piled on me to earn a decent wage and when the RCI appointment came, I went.

My heart sank in those days for many reasons. I was forty-one and my world had spiralled beyond any recognition and any semblance of normality at home; it was upside-down and the worst to date. I looked to the future, not knowing what it held, and it never was to be the same again.

I had once been at the top of the pecking order for assignments and had had the option of newly built 'super liners', but I now had to start all over again. I was assigned to *Monarch of the Seas*, and the cruise schedule was one that made most cruise-line employees grimace.

We sailed from Long Island in Los Angeles, down the California coast, stopping at San Diego, Catalina Island and then on to Ensenada in Mexico. Catalina Island is infamous as the centre of the vast US porn industry – not that I ever got a chance to see anything beyond blue skies and beaches. The *Monarch* was now operating at the 'cheap and cheerful' end of the cruise market, priced to appeal to all-comers. At the time of her launch in 1991, she was the biggest liner afloat and RCI's undisputed flagship. Now, supplanted by a new generation of giant sister ships, she was the cruise industry's answer to Benidorm and it was packed with wrinklies and clientele from the lower end of the pay scale. It was worst on the Friday-to-Sunday three-day cruise, when most norms of civilised behaviour seemed to be suspended. A significant number of passengers equated a good cruise with getting paralytic and violently ill. A large portion of the remainder added a brawl, just for good measure. Once, fire hoses had to be deployed on a pool deck to separate gangs of youths who were engaged in a running battle and terrorising other passengers.

After a few months, I was as depressed as I had ever been in my life. I had just received a letter confirming that Julia had served me with divorce papers, I had debts beyond my wildest nightmares, and no conceivable way of paying them off in the short term. I sat down one evening to try and figure out my finances and calculated that I would probably have to stay at sea for ten years just to sort things out financially. And those calculations didn't factor in education costs for my boys. I also knew that I was stuck on this cruise schedule until a vacancy opened up on one of the other more prestigious vessels with an easier itinerary and not so much bouncing.

It was so bad that I was forced to swallow my pride and seek financial and debt advice from the Citizens Advice Bureau (CAB). It was one of the worst days in my life. I had been a proud Royal Marine Commando who felt he could face down anything. I could have fallen into a downward spiral and become another victim of PTSD, which former servicemen suffer in their thousands now, but I have never been afraid to seek advice for things of which I have no knowledge.

And then, out of the blue in October 2003, I got an email that changed my life. In the Royal Marines I was friendly with a fellow sergeant called Taff A. We'd kept in contact after we had both left the Commandos as part of the defence cuts of 1996. Like myself, Taff had been drawn into the security industry, as it offered the best jobs for old warriors like us. Taff had set up a private security contracting company and he needed guys with serious experience. He had a contract offer in Iraq in the aftermath of the US-led invasion in 2003. Was I interested in working as a private security contractor?

Iraq? I was forty-two-years-old and it was almost seven years since I had last slung a rifle, but I had kept myself in pretty good shape, so I reckoned I was up to any physical challenge. I emailed Taff for more details and he explained that he was doing subcontracting work for a

British private military company who, in turn, were working for a giant US construction group. The pay – minus various deductions – would leave me with the sum of £6,000 per month before tax. All food and supplies would be provided for us in Iraq, and, given that the country was on a war footing, there wasn't much chance of blowing our wages on shopping sprees.

It was like manna from heaven. The money was good enough that even with just two years' work I would be able to deal with most of our debts, now my debts. It was a chance for a clean start. I had no great political worries about going. I wasn't going to Iraq as a mercenary – I was going to protect people, and, sometimes, buildings. My job in Iraq would be to save lives, not to take them. The Task training I'd got for bodyguard work would be a major advantage, and my years working with RCI were also a bonus, having given me a broad sense of fair play and understanding of over a hundred different national personalities. Back then, in October 2003, the insurgency hadn't really kicked off and the beheading of Western hostages was a nightmare yet to be experienced. In hindsight, it's hard to explain the fact that I didn't worry for a second about the potential dangers or the rights and wrongs of going to Iraq. I was a trained soldier, and this was precisely the kind of job I was trained for. Most important of all, it was a job that paid well. I instantly agreed to go.

I quit RCI and returned to the UK to get some gear for the Middle East. I'd worked in Hong Kong and for a very brief period in Brunei, so I knew all about the importance of having the correct gear: desert fatigues, light combat boots and plenty of cotton clothing for the sun and heat. I called to see Julia and the kids and the rest of my family. Julia was appalled that I was going to Iraq, but, by then, the marriage was over anyway. I travelled down to London and caught a train out to Heathrow where I was to meet up with some of the other contractors at the Royal Jordanian Airlines ticket desk.

The scene was like something straight out of a Marx Brothers or Laurel and Hardy comedy. There were dozens of ex-military types milling around, all trying desperately to look like tourists. Everyone had short-cropped, military-regulation hair or was shaved shiny, almost every forearm was festooned with regimental and unit tattoos, and almost everyone was wearing a short leather jacket. Me – well, I looked like I'd just stepped off the dance floor of an RCI cruise liner: I arrived in a pair of comfortable chinos and a silk Bermuda shirt that was slightly on the loud side.

Instantly, I was among friends. One of the first guys I spotted was an old Royal Marine mate called Yorkie F. We laughed at the motley crew all around us. The queue would have done justice to a French Foreign Legion recruiting advert. There were, indeed, ex-Legionnaires, and there were Croat veterans of the Yugoslav civil war, South Africans who had fought in the border war, former Soviet Bloc Special Forces troops drawn from Bulgaria and Ukraine. There were even a few grizzled former Rhodesian army veterans. And later there was an Irishman who had served with both the Irish Army and the French Foreign Legion.

We flew from Heathrow to Amman in Jordan, where we were met by yet another former Royal Marine Commando, Andy 'Dapper' D. Dapper was one of the senior liaison officers working with the Hart Group, the British security firm that Taff was subcontracting for. Hart was a serious player in the world of global security. Founded by Lord Richard Bethel, a veteran of the Household Cavalry and 22 SAS, Hart traditionally specialised in maritime security and was very highly respected. But the situation in Iraq had persuaded firms like Hart to branch out beyond their normal maritime role and they were now providing security detachments for key installations, civilian and political personnel, as well as convoys.

The last time I had met Dapper, we were involved in a pub brawl with each other in Norway where we were both on an Arctic warfare exercise in 1987. He was as shocked to see me as I was delighted to meet him. Dapper explained the routine: we would be split up into groups of between four and six, briefed on the situation in Iraq and our responsibilities, and then transferred to Baghdad overland from Jordan. The transfer would involve a fleet of about ten GMC taxis that would take us from the Jordanian border through Ramadi and Fallujah to the Iraqi capital.

My recollection of that twelve-hour journey was how boring and uncomfortable it was. We were allowed two stops in the open desert – to relieve our bladders and drink a can of lukewarm Coca-Cola. Little did we realise at the time that this roadway would, in just a few months, be dubbed the 'Highway to Hell', such was the ferocity of attacks on convoys and individual vehicles. The road ran right through the al-Anbar region of Iraq, the heart of the so-called Sunni Triangle. Hundreds would die here over the coming years, and only burned-out, blackened vehicles would mark the sites of their deaths. I can't believe now that we drove through it totally unarmed that day. Not even the Jordanian taxi drivers had weapons. Only when we arrived to within a few miles of Baghdad were a couple of AK-47s tossed on to the floor of the coach that would take us to our billets in the Red Zone of Baghdad. At this time, the deteriorating security situation had forced the Allied forces to divide Baghdad into various zones, which were colour-coded. The safest area was the 'Green Zone' and this is where the various embassies, charities, media organisations and Allied administrative centres were located. The 'Red Zone' was where you watched your back at all times – and personal protection was always an issue of serious concern. Needless to say, that's where I was based. There to meet us were Taff and Dave 'Monster' M., another Royal Marine veteran whom I had met on a navigational exercise in the 1980s.

The first day was spent getting acquainted with the AK-47. The Kalashnikov design was almost a half-century old, but it was still a fearsome infantry weapon. It was typically Russian – rugged, with no frills, and it was designed to operate in the worst conditions. The AK-47 was particularly highly regarded in Iraq for two reasons: it was as easy to get ammunition for it as it was to get a cigarette, and it fired irrespective of the sand and dust that blew everywhere. I didn't know it that November day in 2003, but, for the next five years, the closest relationship I would have in my life would be with that AK-47.

The very next day we transferred to Basra in the far south of Iraq. After the Allied invasion, Basra fell within the British zone of occupation, and this is where our security detail would operate from. The

US military were getting hammered trying to deal with the Sunnis in the north. Here in Basra, it was largely Shiite, and, for the time being, relatively peaceful. That would change soon enough as savage battles erupted between the Shiite militias for control of the city. En route to Basra we stopped for a quick lunch in al-Kut and got acquainted with al-Amara and al-Qurna on the way through, both having Hart Group bases in them, just before arriving as night fell in Basra international airport.

Once in the airport operational area, we were divided into our designated groups as per the locations we had just passed through since being in country and were then dispatched to join the rapidly expanding company and its ever-increasing demand for manpower.

I must admit, we had all heard tales of the different locations on the way down from Jordan and had our preferences. The head sheds (bosses) had different ideas and it felt a bit like being chosen from a line-up to play footie and hoping you would be chosen soon and go to the right team.

My initial contract was with a huge US construction company called Perini that had made its name building enormous casinos and hotels in Las Vegas. They had absolutely no experience in electrical construction of things such as pylons, power stations and generation sub-units, but they still managed to land a major contract, worth tens of millions of dollars, to help rebuild Iraq's infrastructure – and promptly hired an Indian firm as a subcontractor to do the actual work. Our job was to protect the construction sites and keep the workers and engineers from being shot or kidnapped. I would initially operate from Basra airport, across the Shatt al-Arab waterway, where Hart had a small complex of portacabins, and a small hotel in Basra called the Merbad. Taff, Andy and Dave were already assigned up country to Baghdad and I would remain in Basra with two other ex-Marines, Mark 'Fish' F. and Tony 'Ginge' P., both of whom I had served with in the Corps. Fish was the Sheik liaison rep and Ginge was running al-Qurna.

It was very much a crash course in local politics, operating procedures and the major dangers we faced. Basra was largely under the control of the British military, though there were also Ukrainian forces deployed here. Then there were newly recruited Iraqi police, who operated mostly at checkpoints on all major strategic road junctions and retail premises. None of us had much regard for the Iraqi police; we felt they were as liable to stand back and allow you to be shot as they were to try and help protect you. For the most part, we bullied them to either leave us alone or let us exit areas quickly. The nightmare scenario we all feared was being held up in traffic or at a petrol station by the police and instantly becoming a sitting target for insurgents or militiamen, only too willing to kill a couple of 'infidels'. To help us blend in with the local populace we operated in low-profile, soft-skinned (i.e. not bullet-proofed) vehicles. We also used all local Iraqi drivers and hired guns; not many were anything other than available to work for the yankee dollar. They couldn't shoot and were mostly youngsters with no military experience, though there was the odd exception: there were some older guys who had been in the Iran–Iraq War and had fought the Americans in the first Gulf War. What a crowd! Plus they were being chaperoned round the desert by a motley crew of ex-everything else from all corners of the world and not many spoke a common language.

Our work was also a course in survival techniques: how to spot if your vehicle was being followed; how to approach a junction without being shot at by trigger-happy British or American military; how to negotiate a convoy through a town or village without ever coming to a halt; and, above all else, how to develop that sixth sense that soldiers need to detect an ambush. My Northern Ireland experience definitely stood me in good stead in Iraq; you had to learn fast here, just like in Belfast. I learned to expect the unexpected. A dead donkey or water buffalo by the roadside might not be just harmless roadkill; such carcasses were to the insurgents what road culverts were to the IRA. They loved to place their improvised explosive devices (IEDs) inside a swollen, fly-infested carcass, and detonate it the second a military vehicle or contractor's car drove past.

An example of how bad the security situation would eventually become was evident from the first route we used to operate over from al-Amara to al-Qurna. In late 2003 and early 2004, the road was dangerous but still passable – by 2006 it was virtually guaranteed death for any Westerner to travel that way. We learned that al-Qurna was the legendary location of the 'Adam Tree' of the Garden of Eden. I can certainly vouch for the fact there were plenty of snakes – though mostly of the human variety – in that area.

Hart had evolved a system whereby the older, more experienced operators paired off with the new arrivals. It helped pass on operational knowledge much faster than in any briefing room. My partner was an ex-South African Special Forces guy called Johan K. He was younger than me, but had obviously spent his entire life in uniform in Africa or undertaking security contracts in the Middle East. And I was new on the block.

There were a lot of South African and former Rhodesian soldiers in Iraq, and, unlike the Europeans, they didn't seem to adhere to the soldier–officer divide. They all acted like normal non-commissioned ranks, whereas, in true blue-blood British style, our former officers tended to keep to themselves.

There were a few eye-openers. Working for RCI, I was used to the finest food. Over here, it was worse than the muck we'd eaten in the Commandos while on exercises. The hotel was particularly dreadful and I reckoned that the food there was as dangerous as the insurgents. Breakfast was a hard-boiled egg and a slice of triangular processed cheese wrapped up in a diamond-shaped kind of Iraqi naan bread known as a 'Simoon' (we called it 'fanny bread' because we opened it wide to stuff it with food and it looked like...... well you get the picture). Most times, we didn't get to have lunch so we shoved a few of our 'Simoon' wraps into our pockets for later in the day.

There was a half-decent family restaurant just down the road but even at this stage, in November 2003, just a few months after the Allied forces had been welcomed into Iraq as liberators, we were warned not to go to the restaurant alone and unarmed. We each invested in a Tariq, the Iraqi-made copy of the venerable Beretta 9mm pistol. We quickly learned what a wise investment this was. At night, as we bunked down in the hotel, the Basra skyline would be lit up with tracer rounds or heavy machine-gun fire as the militias battled each other or the Allied troops. And once darkness fell, packs of feral dogs would roam around the town and rip apart anything left out. Their howls and yowls made sleeping a major achievement.

It was a demanding job that quickly got a hell of a lot worse. We were usually on duty from 5am and there were no assigned vehicles or local teams. You just had to gather the best local team you could find each day on a first-come, first-served basis. The Iraqis were desperate to work as part of the security teams, largely because it guaranteed a relatively decent income in a country where everything had gone to shit. An Iraqi doctor was earning about $2 a day, while an Iraqi working with a security team could earn up to $7 a day. A lot of the Iraqis who wanted work had little or no military experience, and believe me it showed. But many were lovely guys who were simply trying to do the best for their families. A few of us started to give them proper training – crash-courses in how to hold a weapon, how to react to a challenge, how to protect a client and how to get out of a bad situation fast.

Not everyone was patient with them. Many of the South Africans and Rhodesians, in particular, brought their cultural traditions with them – having spent generations shouting at indigenous Africans, they simply applied the same technique to Iraqi contractors. The local security personnel became 'sand kaffirs', a phrase I loathed. Also, there was a huge divide in attitude between the older and younger security. Older guys, like myself, tended to adopt a more balanced, commonsense approach to the Iraqis. We needed these guys, and if they felt you were trying to work with them, they re-doubled their efforts to learn the ropes. Shouting at them or insulting them merely created a poisonous atmosphere – and made doing the job even more difficult. I found that if you treated the Iraqis with consideration and respect, it was repaid tenfold. Anyway, I reckoned that if you could be killed alongside a man, you might as well respect each other.

The tendency to insult the Iraqis often proved particularly dangerous. We had one young idiot from Johannesburg who picked a fist-fight with an Iraqi security guard – in the open and in front of dozens of Iraqi security contractors on whom we often depended for life-and-death advice. The Iraqi hadn't followed some petty rules – but there was a time and place to handle such things. I was forced to have a quiet word with a few of the older Afrikaners about it. I couldn't blame an Iraqi barrack-room lawyer later for shouting at his comrades to 'take down the white eyes' for their disrespect.

There was trouble from other sources too. Soon after, a young Algerian, who claimed to be an ex-Legionnaire, kicked the shit out of a young Iraqi, but when I inquired about the brawl, other disgusted ex-Foreign Legionnaires told me they didn't care if he got fired – the Algerian had lied and had never actually worn the Kepi. Maybe he didn't know it, but his problems were only beginning – there is nothing in this world so dangerous as an ex-Foreign Legionnaire who feels the Legion has been dishonoured.

The South Africans and Rhodesians were superb soldiers, which was hardly surprising, given that they had been fighting in various parts of Africa and the globe for more than four decades. They had fought many guerrilla wars and knew how to handle themselves when it came to a shooting fight. Almost to a man, they drank too much. But there were times I felt very sorry for them; they seemed like a proud, tough and fearless remnant of a world that no longer existed. Some of the Rhodesians had fought with the famed Selous Scouts unit in the 1970s, only to see Rhodesia transformed into Zimbabwe, and one of Africa's richest countries gradually descend into poverty and anarchy. A lot of these guys had lost their homes, farms and jobs, and simply couldn't return to Harare. It was equally tough for the South Africans. Their own government threatened them with arrest and prosecution if they did not leave Iraq immediately; they were deemed to be mercenaries for being in Iraq – which I don't believe any of us were – mainly because, as reservists, they were still officially considered to be part of their country's defence forces and shouldn't be chasing the dollar in foreign climes. Eventually a compromise was agreed, largely because there were so many South Africans on contracts in the Middle East, and they could return home without fear of arrest or prosecution. The pound sterling to the rand was about 12:1 at the time, so these guys could afford to buy a game reserve when they went home and some of them did just that.

Every single one of us knew what would happen if we were captured alive. Most of the South Africans drank to cope with it. For some, the pressure simply got too great. One guy I worked with took his own life while back home on leave in South Africa. He had other issues as well, but it all got too much for him.

We learned that Iraq was also attracting military 'wannabes', and if we didn't weed them out, they would probably get us all killed. These idiots were slipping past the recruiting officers. A number of nutters arrived from France whose only experience of wearing a military uniform was at a fancy-dress parade. Two more arrived who had also never even held a gun before, let alone fired one in anger – they had both been working as doormen at a Paris nightclub and thought the pay would be much better in Iraq. Others, who had a small bit of military experience, were almost worse. They had usually served in their country's military reserves and were now hell-bent on seeing some shooting action – those of us who had spent years in uniform simply hoped we could make it to the end of a contract without having to fire a weapon in anger. Christ only knows what some of these untrained guys would have done if they'd actually found themselves in an ambush and had to rely on military experience they did not have.

The other sore point for us former soldiers was the arrival of troops from Bosnia. A number of the ex-Foreign Legionnaires and some Brits had served on UN duty in Sarajevo and wanted nothing whatsoever to do with the Bosnian Serbs – they branded them 'baby-killers'. Several bluntly refused to serve on security teams with former Bosnian soldiers and threatened to resign if forced to do so. Soldiers who served with elite units like the Royal Marines, Paras, Foreign Legion and US Marines set very high standards for themselves and unit honour was taken very seriously. Hence, no one hated the crimes committed against civilians in the former Yugoslavia more than the British, French and American soldiers, who reckoned they should have been given free rein by politicians to end the carnage there the instant it started. My abiding memory of the small groups of Bosnians that arrived is that they kept entirely to themselves and ate more than all the other nationalities put together, mostly meat and potatoes.

Our security compound was a heady mix of AK-47s, military honour, testosterone and US-dollar bank accounts. There were days when I raised my eyes to heaven and wondered whether some of our own guys were as likely to kill us as the Iraqi insurgents with their IEDs and RPG-7s. But, as the conflict in Iraq worsened, the wheat was very quickly sifted from the chaff.

As well as looking after the US construction overseers and their Indian subcontractors, we would also occasionally have to provide an escort for convoys of US Corps of Engineers personnel. These were not military personnel, but wielded tremendous power because they could influence the spending on reconstruction contracts. Some were pretty OK – they had US military experience and knew what was going on around them. Others were from a different planet. They were in Iraq on a mission to save humanity and the earth. Frankly, my ambition ended with saving myself, my client and my security team.

Occasionally, we had to escort these convoys as far as al-Kut, some three hours' drive from Basra. The key was always to get back to base before it got dark. No one liked being in bandit country at night, particularly as the heaviest weapon we had at that point was an AK-47. Later, we would add a heavy machine gun to larger convoys moving through risky areas. If guys were caught in an ambush, it gave them some chance of being able to fight their way through. The problem was that there were very few ways of defending yourself against IEDs or RPG-7 rockets. The RPG (rocket-propelled grenade) – another Russian contribution to humanity – was notoriously inaccurate from medium to long range, but it was deadly accurate at short range, and, depending on the rocket head fitted, was capable of shredding any sort of soft-skinned vehicles.

Our US client was by now going from strength to strength. On the back of the Basra contracts they had secured further work in Nasiriyah and az-Zubayr, mostly rebuilding power pylons and electricity stations.

Az-Zubayr was situated towards Umm Qasr in the south, while Nasiriyah was a two-hour drive on the Basra–Baghdad road north. I hated the Nasiriyah contract because it entailed guarding convoys collecting heavy electrical goods from the Kuwaiti border. This was a three- to-four-hour drive at a tortuously slow pace along a road that was also heavily used by the US military. If you put a foot wrong, those guys were as likely to shoot at you as were the insurgents, who were virtually camped along the route.

What people don't realise about Iraq was that at this stage the insurgency was as much about money and criminal activity as it was a political protest against the Allied forces. I described it as the Ali Baba syndrome. For example, the Iraqis had stripped thousands of miles of electrical cable so the copper could be melted down and sold across the border in Iran. But now new power lines were being re-erected and had to be guarded by the very same tribesmen who had pulled them down in the first place. A lot of the Iraqis simply wanted to make a few dollars and, if they couldn't join the police, army or a private military company (PMC), they were just as willing to engage in a career as a roadside bandit – a modern-day Ali Baba, if you will. The trouble is that both a roadside bandit and a politically motivated insurgent ultimately want you dead, albeit for very different reasons.

There was nothing more certain to attract attacks and AK-47 rounds than a slow-moving convoy laden with million-dollar generators and power-station-control gear. If a criminal gang, or even a tribal group, could hijack such a load, they could make enough on the black market to feed their people for a whole year. Such an action became almost a badge of honour for some of the tribal chiefs, whose eyes lit up with dollar signs when they spotted a convoy. The attacks reached such a pitch that the US military took to bringing their people through in hundred-vehicle convoys, and if we came up against such a convoy, they were quite liable to shoot at us too. Even carrying Union Jack flags made no difference.

Sometimes, a private convoy like ours would be routed through the desert, particularly if a US military convoy had just been attacked on the main road. But here there was the constant danger of road-traffic accidents, which was how we lost most personnel the early stages. One lad was killed instantly crossing the desert in a dust storm that reduced visibility to less than 30cm; his vehicle drove head-on into an articulated lorry coming in the opposite direction. The unfortunate guy had been in Iraq for fewer than two years, and it was his third serious car accident.

Nasiriyah was a major pain for me. When the US firm got the contract, I was assigned, with a former French army officer, called Alain, and a US civilian engineer, to do a full recce of the power station site involved. It involved living in a tent at a nearby Italian army camp for a fortnight while the engineering assessment was being done. I was anxious that Nasiriyah worked out well because I had been promised promotion to team leader, which would substantially increase my wages. But it was sod's law. We were only on site three days when I came down with a horrendous dose of Saddam's revenge: I felt unwell, had dreadful stomach cramps, then felt light-headed and finally developed a thunderous dose of diarrhoea. For eight nightmarish days I tried to provide security for the engineering team while running to the stinking thunderbox (Portaloo) on site every fifteen minutes or so in the rain and darkness. On occasions, I was racing to the toilet through a foot of mud and sludge in my flip-flops. On one occasion I didn't make it out of the sleeping bag and lay there realising just how wet that fart was – but luckily, it was a borrowed sleeping bag, and I was delighted to give it back!

When the assessment was completed, I was shipped back to Basra, a move that didn't particularly please me because I thought I would be appointed on-site security officer. Alain got the job – which kept the influential French contingent happy – but I did get my promotion. I felt I had earned it, and I soon realised I would be earning my extra pay as well.

I was taking over as section leader from a Rhodesian guy called Ken B. He was a truly great bloke, but had spent a little too long in the field and was a little too fond of the sauce. He was replaced after an astonishing incident where he had decided to call into the Italian army camp in Nasiriyah with his security team just to load up a jeep with crates of Peroni beer to take back to Basra. The Italian army tried to limit the amount of booze he was taking, and it suddenly turned into a screaming match and a stand-off. Eventually, the Italian Carabinieri were called to the scene and arrested the private security contractors on the spot. While all this was going on, another security team was stalled, waiting with a convoy for the return of their missing security colleagues. It was the final straw in a string of events for Ken; his stint as leader was over.

One of the first things that happened when I took over was that we mercifully left our base at the Merbad hotel and relocated to five separate houses in Basra city. I felt this massively increased our security, and all road approaches to the area were blocked off and guarded at night by Iraqi personnel. In turn, we had to designate Western operators to watch the Iraqis throughout the night, as every so often an Iraqi security contractor would either fall asleep, go home to visit his wife or simply wander off for a drink or a smoke. Another – far more serious – trick was to drive past us on their nights off and spray one of our houses with badly aimed machine-gun fire. The purpose of that was to underline just how valuable Iraqi security guards were for our protection, and thus maintain their jobs.

And all the while, the security situation around us was going to shit. The number and sophistication of attacks against the convoys mounted at an alarming rate, and, from losing a few of our personnel to road-traffic accidents we began to pay a huge price in blood in armed attacks. The vacuum created by the effective abolition of the Iraqi army was filled by a lethal mix of criminals, lunatics, sadists, Iranian-backed militias and Iraqi insurgents determined to rid their country of infidels.

Our worst nightmares were about to be realised.

201

16

FALLEN COMRADES

'Drive, for Christ's sake, drive. Get the fucking truck moving,' I screamed. The Indian and Filipino drivers simply shrugged at me in confusion and smiled. But I knew we had only seconds before we'd be taken apart by the insurgents, so I jumped out of my own Ford Explorer, ran towards their lorries and with a series of desperate hand gestures and mimed curses got them to stop smiling and move their heavily laden trucks. All around me I could hear the 'thwack' of 7.62mm rounds slapping into the earth and bouncing off the walls. Two other members of the security detail, Ben and Jean-Michel, were in the lead vehicles, but now disembarked to cover the trucks. 'MOVE YOUR ARSES, NOW,' I bellowed. The message finally got through – the drivers stopped grinning and hurried to get the artics moving.

God almighty, we're going to have to try and disengage while driving at 40kph, I thought to myself. The lorries shuddered forwards at a roundabout and slowly began to pull clear of the ambush killing ground. Each one was carrying a huge cylindrical container, the size of a grain hopper, which we had picked up at the Kuwaiti border and were escorting to Burzegan, a desolate shit-hole near the Iranian border where a new refinery was being rebuilt.

We pulled away from the overpass where the insurgents had planned their ambush. The trucks were gearing up, but we were still moving at a painfully slow pace. Thank God, I thought, we still have the British military escort of two Land Rovers with GPMGs (General Purpose Machine Guns). At least they can give us some firepower to fight our way fully clear.

Behind us, one of the Land Rover gunners was giving the insurgents hell, blazing away with his GPMG. The other British escort had picked up the ambush before the insurgents had fully opened up on us – the sight of empty streets in the nearby town of al-Amara, without even curious kids around, was a stark giveaway that something was going to happen. The lead Land Rover had slowed at the first sign of trouble, unwilling to lead the convoy deeper into the fire zone. But the decision to slow and then bring the lorries to a complete halt could have been catastrophic if the RPG-7 hadn't overshot its target. If the lorry had been hit, it would most certainly have been crippled – and would then have blocked the escape route of all the other vehicles. The insurgents wanted us trapped so they could cut us to pieces at their leisure in their chosen killing ground. But what saved us was the inaccuracy of the Russian grenade launcher. The RPG-7 was a cheap and lethal weapon but was best used at close quarters. Even experienced troops found them difficult to aim with any accuracy from long distances – and the rockets, more often than not, missed their intended target, spiralling away to explode harmlessly.

Two RPG-7s had been fired at us, and miraculously both had missed. I couldn't believe it. If either had hit one of the lorries we would have been trapped in the killing zone. I was amazed that in the hundreds of rounds fired, we hadn't suffered a single casualty and all seventeen vehicles had made it back to base. After the firefight was over and the teams formed up on the other side of town safely away from the built-up areas, you could hear giggles and joyous banter from all the team members as the adrenalin slowly began to wear off. We were unscathed, and happy to be alive as a team. It was also the first taste of action for many, mostly the younger lads in the outfit. For most soldiers, when they meet death head-on and live to tell the tale, they're chuffed, not only at having survived but at having come through their first baptism of fire and effectively earned their spurs.

Tragically, we would not be so lucky in the coming months. This was 2004 and already the security situation in Iraq was going down the crapper. The British military were taking hell from the local Shiite militias, who wanted to secure control before the Allied withdrawal. A particular pain for the British Army were the Mahdi Army, the Shiite militia that backed the local religious guru, Muqtada al-Sadr. His father had been butchered by Saddam Hussein as part of the crackdown on the Shiite community. And it was Muqtada's name that was chanted by Iraqi guards as Saddam Hussein was led to the gallows. In the north, the Sunnis were wreaking havoc on the American forces, and elements allied to al-Qaeda had injected a vicious and brutal element to the conflict with their video-taped beheadings of prisoners. Making life even more intolerable was the fact that the Iranians were supplying logistical and technological help to the insurgents, especially in the design and manufacture of shaped charges, specially made improvised explosive devices (IEDs). Within a few months, these had evolved to such a lethal level of capability that all but the most heavily armoured targets were being sliced apart in roadside ambushes.

If Iraq had seemed like easy money the previous year, now it was proving anything but. In the coming three years, almost a dozen guys I worked with – many of them good friends – paid the butcher's bill in Iraq in a series of firefights and ambushes. The only small mercy is that none was taken alive and forced to face the horror of spending their final moments in an orange jumpsuit before a video camera. Throughout it all, I was charged with running one of the many security operations for Hart in Iraq, and each day sending out lads that I knew might not make it back to base alive.

The first major loss we sustained wasn't in a firefight at all, but in a convoy blow-out in the desert. A Scottish guy, Ian L., had worked with me on a contract in al-Amara where we were providing site security for an Indian company re-erecting 400Kv power pylons. As the contract came to its close and the line was finished, I had the job of back-loading all the equipment, stores and spare weapons to Basra. It was a tough job, as much owing to the remote location as to the fact that the local tribe we had struck a security deal with had insisted on not only taking wages but trying to steal everything in our compound that was not nailed down. Ian and I made it through the rest of the contract without incident, apart from having to just watch the local Arab tribe come in with trucks and filch everything. There was nothing we could do, save watch them. There were only the two of us, the perimeter fence had partly gone and the rest was on the back of the sheik's truck for scrap or his camel compound. And then, as Ian was driving back from dropping the client off at the Kuwaiti border, the team he was travelling with suffered a tyre blow-out.

Apparently, the Iraqi driver slammed on the brakes with the car doing close to 110kph after the blow-out, the worst possible reaction in the circumstances. That stretch of highway was built almost 3m up from the desert floor to prevent flooding, and the car shot off the roadway like a skateboard. It flipped over six times before coming to rest on its roof. The driver and an Iraqi guard both died before they could be rushed to hospital. I was at Basra airport when I heard the news and I could not believe it. It emerged later that the tyres weren't rated for the extremes of temperature that are typical in Iraq – freezing in winter, scorching-hot in summer. The rubber simply couldn't take it and fatally weakened. Luckily, Ian was in a separate car and arrived back shortly afterwards.

By mid-2005, the risk of convoys being ambushed was a daily occurrence. In April, I moved up to Baghdad and the surrounding districts. I was detailed to send two security teams to escort a convoy from Abu Ghraib in Baghdad to al-Hit, a small hamlet just outside Ramadi and smack-bang in the middle of the notorious al-Anbar region of the Sunni Triangle. The lads didn't like it because they knew this was close to the no-go area of the Sunni militias. Most of the kidnappings of Western contractors who subsequently ended up being beheaded on camera occurred in this general area. But we simply had no choice – without convoys to supply them, the Iraqi police, the Allies and the construction teams just could not work. And it was our job to ensure the convoys got through and that the civilian personnel were protected. We had a job to do – the guys might not have liked it, but they knew the convoys had to be protected. We all knew the risks.

I was in the Logistics Movement Control Centre in the Green Zone in Baghdad, acting as Hart's security representative, when the word eventually came through that the convoy had been hit – and hit hard. We had special electronic locators attached to the security teams so we could follow their progress from the control centre, and each team was also equipped with radios and mobile phones to let us know their progress. The second we knew there was trouble, we got to work getting help to them. But in this case it was too late. The convoy had driven into a carefully planned ambush where a group of more than fifty insurgents had torn into the vehicles with RPGs, several roadside bombs and small-arms fire. The convoy comprised ten vehicles – six heavy trucks and four security cars, none of which was armoured. There were twenty-two personnel involved – six truck drivers, four international security guards and twelve Iraqi security personnel.

There was a US quick-response military unit in that zone, but it took five hours before the ambush site was fully secured. By then, several of the truck drivers, half the Iraqi security guards and two of the four international security personnel were dead. The two security personnel killed were Nick Coetze, a likeable South African, and Akihito Saito, a former member of the Japanese Air Brigade and the French Foreign Legion.

Akihito had tried to fight back when the ambush was sprung, but was apparently killed by small-arms fire. By the time the ambush site was secured, there was no trace of either Nick's or Akihito's bodies. The insurgents would usually deliberately take the bodies, and then photograph and release any personal items, like passports or security passes. The bastards later posted photos on the internet of Akihito lying dead by the roadside. The removal of bodies served two purposes: it fucked with the minds of other security contractors, and it could be a useful source of income. Insurgents demanded thousands of dollars for the return of bodies, playing on the anguish of desperate relatives and friends, who only want their loved one's remains back so they can give them a proper burial. For many of these poor lads, the only grave they ever got was a lonely piece of desert.

Sometimes, this cruel policy backfired on the insurgents in that some security contractors were really pissed off by the treatment of their friends and more determined than ever to do their jobs well. There was also the chance that, in an ambush, they could repay a little debt to any insurgents who crossed their gun-sights. One of our two security contractors who survived the al-Hit ambush, came back to Iraq after a short leave in Britain and resumed contract work. I bumped into him in Basra in 2006 where he continued working for another private security company – but with extra determination and motivation. Now it wasn't just the money for him – it was personal.

These deaths were a grim signal of what lay ahead for our security teams. I had personally been very lucky with the Burzegan convoy, and, until al-Hit, Hart had been fortunate to have their convoys either avoid or successfully fight their way through ambushes. But the mood of the whole country was changing. In al-Kut, a sprawling town a couple of hours' drive outside Basra, a Shiite rebellion a few months earlier had left our small local security team trapped in the Hart HQ building, which was directly across the road from the local hotel. The office was surrounded by a perimeter wall and heavy gates. We had three international security contractors on the premises – a Briton, a New Zealander and the team leader, a big, bearded South African called Greg B. We got a radio call to say the city was in open rebellion and that an armed mob had surrounded the Hart premises. Greg was brash and very confident and when he said they needed evacuation we knew the situation must be very serious indeed.

The team was told to move to the roof of the building while we tried to organise an air evacuation for them. Only I knew the precise location of the premises – which was a new position and I had only been there the week previously on the way back from Baghdad; it was different from the original one we had in the town. We tried to guide a British Sea King helicopter to the scene by means of a map grid reference. The pilot successfully located the house, but the volume of gunfire that greeted him made a winch evacuation absolutely impossible. The pilot was also acutely conscious of the dangers of RPG-7s and did not want an Iraqi version of 'Blackhawk Down', the notorious battle that had taken place in Somalia in 1993. The US, with other UN forces, were trying to stabilise the East African country which had descended into total anarchy. A group of US Rangers and Special Forces troops were trapped in a built-up area of Mogadishu by hundreds of gunmen led by a Somali warlord. They lacked armoured vehicles and so couldn't force their way out. Repeated efforts to evacuate them by Blackhawk helicopter failed. Two helicopters were shot down during the evacuation attempts – both by RPG-7s – and three others were badly damaged. In a bloody operation to evacuate the troops, which ultimately required reinforcements with tanks and armoured personnel carriers, 18 US troops were killed and 73 others wounded. A staggering estimate of 1,500 Somali gunmen and civilians were killed in what the US later called 'The Battle of Mogadishu'. The Somalis referred to the bloodbath as 'The Day of the Rangers'.

The chopper circled the house at 270 metres to monitor developments. For some inexplicable reason, one of the Iraqi security guards had opened one of the outer perimeter gates, and the crowd immediately flooded into the building. As the three lads tried to back up the stairs to the roof and negotiate with the mob, Greg was shot in the upper leg. The other two lads dragged him up to the roof and the mob didn't want to risk rushing the stairs because of the assault rifles of the two uninjured Hart operatives.

It was tragic. The chopper couldn't risk a landing because of the danger posed by RPGs, while Greg bled to death from a ripped femoral artery. When it was clear that Greg was dead, the other two lads decided their only chance of survival lay in a roof-top run. They scrambled across several rooftops in the darkness before they were able to sneak into a Hart jeep and flee the town, disguised as Iraqis, wearing a dish-dash (a long garment) and a shemag (headscarf), which was standard dress for the local population.

Several months later I moved locations from the Green Zone control centre to the Abu Ghraib warehouse, where we had four teams based. I was put in charge of the teams and their movements. It was the same base that the previous team had departed from with such heavy losses. For the most part we were undertaking around ten different security contracts at any one time. These could range from convoy escort duties to personnel inspection and protection of locations, as well as static security and managerial jobs. As the country edged towards total mayhem, the security companies realised that they had no alternative now but to invest in armour protection for both vehicles and personnel. At the start, Iraq had allowed the security contractors a sort of buffer or honeymoon period. Now, the honeymoon was over and the vast increase in IED use and the hugely effective Iranian-designed shaped explosive charges made armour absolutely essential for everyday security operations, though not even the best armour could protect you from the shaped charges.

Convoy protection was the bread-and-butter for every security contractor outside the Green Zone who was not on a static security operation (e.g. protecting a building). At the start of the war, convoys had posed a risk, but were not a third as dangerous as they were now. Convoys were being hammered regularly by the insurgents, who had evolved special tactics to cripple, isolate and destroy the security apparatus and thus the US plans for rebuilding the country. As the attacks grew in regularity and ferocity, reports flooded in of contractors we had worked alongside being killed and maimed in convoy ambushes. I was now watching friends of mine coming back from convoy security duties covered in blood and bandages – and they were the lucky ones. By my second year in Iraq with Hart, some contractors regarded convoy duty as akin to a death sentence.

Two weeks into my new assignment, our worst loss occurred in June 2005, when one of our convoys drove into a carefully prepared killing zone at al-Habaniyah outside Baghdad in the heart of the Sunni Triangle. I was in charge of the organisation of the convoy, which was being led by Yves M., a veteran of both the French and Croat armies; he was married to a Croat woman and, like me, was in Iraq to try and make enough money for a new life on civvie street. I got on really well with Yves, whose personality seemed too small for any room he was in. He was extravagant, confident and exceptionally generous with anyone he dealt with. Yves was also particularly mindful of the Iraqi security guards he worked with, and was hugely liked and respected by them in return. Today, I can close my eyes and still picture Yves strolling into the Hart control room and nonchalantly saying, 'Geoffrey, baby, I have a small problem' in his typical Charles Aznavour voice. Very little fazed Yves, and he was undoubtedly one of the most popular and respected team leaders in Hart. He was the kind of guy it was a pleasure to work alongside.

As one of our most experienced operators, Yves was to take charge of the convoy to al-Habaniyah. He would have a strong security presence with him: Sean L., a South African; Denis B., a former French Foreign Legion Chef (sergeant-major); and Paddy O'Keeffe, my Irish mate, who had also been in the Foreign Legion. I had already served with Paddy on a static security contract on the reconstruction of Saddam Hussein's Court of Justice in Baghdad. These guys all knew their stuff and were among the best operators we had. The lads would also have two full teams of Iraqi security contractors, as well as four vehicles, one of which would be equipped with a belt-fed Russian-made squad machine gun (PKM). I knew the lads did not like the route or the destination. The timing also left a lot to be desired, with the convoy planned for almost one month to the day after the al-Hit convoy had been hammered. But we simply had no choice.

To be honest, I didn't like matters much either, but there was no alternative. If the lads did not take the convoy through today, another security team would have to take it through tomorrow. I knew that, and so did Yves and his team. But it still didn't stop Yves telling me that he had serious concerns about the mission. Typical of Yves, despite his reservations, he was not refusing to take the convoy through. But the Iraqis absolutely freaked when they heard the destination was al-Habaniyah, and immediately refused to go. A lot of the assigned Iraqi contractors simply walked away. It took more than an hour to round up enough replacements to allow the convoy to leave and I had to muster all my reserve Iraqi guards and threaten them with 'Fuck off home now then' before they agreed. As Yves drove out of the compound, he shouted, 'Allahu Akbar' or 'God is great', to try and rally the Iraqis and boost morale. It was a poignant gesture by a very brave man.

A couple of hours later my control centre in the Green Zone got a call from Yves saying they had just reached a US military checkpoint on the approach to al-Habaniyah. A few minutes later, there was radio contact and a garbled message saying that they had just been ambushed and the team was leaving the line open so that we could listen in from the control centre. Yves was shouting that there were casualties – then the line went dead. My project manager in Baghdad rang me to say that the convoy had been attacked and that he feared the worst. Frantically, we worked the phones and radios to get help to them from the US military, but the area was deemed so risky that even the US military would not send a patrol in without full armoured support; and that took time to organise – time which, tragically, our lads simply did not have. The seconds seem to stretch into hours. At the base, the control centre team were desperately trying to get the US military to the scene in strength. We had heard from Yves' radio calls that the convoy was facing an increasingly desperate battle for survival. Yves was shouting for help – and the clatter of gunfire was clearly audible in the background. The fact that the line had since gone dead was grimly ominous.

I took a deep breath and desperately tried to focus on getting help to Yves and his team. I worked every contact I had, but the military were bluntly refusing to rush headlong into the area – the insurgents had forged a terrible reputation locally and the US were not going to risk their own troops without proper support or some idea of the size of force they faced. I looked at my watch and realised that Yves and his team still faced having to hold their ground in the several remaining hours of daylight. If the convoy was stranded and they were surrounded, it would be an impossible task. I closed my eyes and silently prayed for a miracle – that either the insurgents would withdraw before they overran the convoy or some US unit would arrive to offer desperately needed extra firepower. It was a race against time – and we began to fear the worst.

In the end, only Denis B. and Paddy survived. Denis was cut off at the rear of the convoy and just when he thought he was going to be gunned down with his Iraqi driver, they managed to hijack a car and drive back to the safety of the US checkpoint. The two had made a pact that, rather than be captured by the insurgents, they would turn their weapons on themselves. Before they needed to do this, a Toyota Hilux pick-up rolled up with two old Iraqis inside and the lads hijacked the vehicle and sped away to the US position. Incredibly, Denis and his Iraqi guard got a less than warm welcome at the US checkpoint and were immediately arrested until their identities could be confirmed.

Paddy was less fortunate. He was caught at the front of the convoy where the main killing took place. The insurgents used rockets and heavy machine-gun fire to disable first the security cars and then the trucks. Then, one by one, our lads were killed as they tried to defend the convoy and the Iraqi drivers in their care. There were later reports that more than fifty insurgents had targeted the convoy, and they had placed their attack in the perfect killing zone.

I was faced, for the first time in my life, with effectively being helpless while my mates were dying. There is nothing worse for a soldier than knowing your mates are fighting for their very lives – and you are somewhere else and totally powerless to help. I spent my whole life training to be 'the best of the best'. I could handle virtually every firearm ever made. And here I was, stuck in an office, trying to help defend my mates with nothing more than a telephone. Part of me wished I was with Yves, Denis and Paddy with an AK-47 in hand – but my training kept me focused on doing my job for the lads. I had to get help to them as fast as possible – that was my mission. I felt like screaming down the phone at the officials who kept stalling until they had the correct force assembled – just one bloody patrol might have been enough to scare off the insurgents before they butchered our men. But the US commanders had learned the hard way that a convoy ambush could just be the bait for a bigger ambush targeted at Coalition forces themselves. So the US weren't going to rush into anything near al-Habaniyah half-cocked. But by the time they were ready to move, Yves, Denis, Paddy and the Iraqi security team could be dead and on the way to a lonely desert grave. I was praying they would be okay while an overwhelming sense of foreboding formed in my gut. I knew it was going to be bad.

I was told the whole story afterwards. The insurgents used a tall building to site their heavy machine gun, and this dominated the entire convoy. Under cover of the heavy fire, the insurgents started to infiltrate the convoy vehicles – the worst nightmare for any security contractor.

Once the insurgents are in among the convoy, the security team are suddenly faced with an impossible situation. If you engage an insurgent among the convoy, you are now just as likely to kill one of your own team members. There are multiple fleeting targets, you have only a fraction of a second to decide between who is an insurgent and who is a friend and you can no longer move between sheltered firing points within the convoy. And as you move to engage targets within the convoy, you expose yourself to the gunmen on either side of the roadway. The reality is that once the convoy is infiltrated, the security team are little more than dead men walking.

Yves was killed when a heavy round pierced his body armour while he was on the radio desperately calling for help. Sean L. died when, as he stood beside Paddy, a round caught him below his body armour. He collapsed and died without a sound. Paddy kept fighting until the last Iraqi security guard beside him died from a bullet through the forehead; he kept fighting till he ran out of ammunition, and then desperately ran to pick up a weapon dropped by a dead insurgent. He realised his only hope was to try and make it to a machine gun still in Sean's wrecked car and bring it back in action.

As he ran towards the car, he was struck in the arm and leg by bullets. Knocked to the road surface, he managed to drag himself to the car, only for another round to catch him in the body armour and blow him off the elevated roadway. Paddy fell almost 4m down into an irrigation ditch. In desperation, he crawled, bleeding, through muck and filth into a partially collapsed drainage pipe, waiting all the while for the insurgents to find him. But they never came. They presumably saw him take the round in the torso and fall off the roadway, so they must have thought he was already dead.

Paddy stayed hidden in that stinking, dark pipe for several hours until he heard the sound of a US armoured convoy arriving to check on the shattered convoy. But the US military were taking absolutely no chances and called in an air strike to ensure that no insurgents were lingering in the area. Paddy later told me how, having staggered up on to the roadway when the air attack was over, he was met by the swivelling barrel of the chain-gun on a Bradley armoured personnel carrier. God only knows what the US soldier thought as he pointed his weapon at the figure covered in blood, mud, sewage and cordite standing in front of him. Paddy promptly collapsed on the roadway from his wounds. But he was alive.

Back at Hart HQ, we were in stunned denial. No one, in their worst nightmares, had ever dreamed of a situation like this, despite the fact that the security situation in Iraq had gone down the toilet over recent months. A well-defended convoy, led by one of our most experienced and capable operators, was successfully ambushed, cut off and then hacked to pieces. I couldn't believe it – I thought we had lost everyone, from the civilian drivers to the entire security team. What the fuck had gone wrong? How on earth did the insurgents get this kind of firepower together so fast?

I kept replaying all our preparations to see if there was something we could have done differently. But the truth was, we had done everything right – it was just that there was no possible preparation for the type of ambush the convoy had faced. Once they drove into that trap, there was little or no escape. I couldn't get Yves' face out of my mind. He was a bit like me – hoping to make enough money in Iraq to give his family a fresh start back home. Without knowing any of the details, I was sure Yves had died fighting to protect the drivers in his care. He was that kind of guy – the type of soldier you always prayed you'd have on your shoulder when the shit hit the fan. When Denis B. turned up, I was stunned, but delighted and relieved. My hopes suddenly rose that other members of the convoy team could have escaped the slaughter.

Maybe a few of the lads had managed to get away into the open fields? But, after hearing the initial outline from Denis of precisely what had happened, my hopes faded just as fast. The convoy security team had faced an ambush that resembled a perfect killing zone – and a subsequent assault mounted by a vastly superior insurgent force. The poor bastards never had a chance, I thought to myself; the second that fucking lead lorry stopped they were dead men. When the word filtered through later that the armoured US rescue mission had picked up just one more survivor – Paddy O'Keeffe – I let out a sigh of relief. The convoy mission had been a disaster – but as least we had Denis and Paddy back.

I met Paddy the next day as he recovered in hospital in Baghdad's international zone. I only had to look at his scarred face to realise just how bad it must have been. But there was no time for sentiment. We had to find out precisely what had happened and whether anyone else might have survived the carnage. I also wanted to learn whether there was anything we could have done to better protect the convoys. Paddy outlined events to me and a Hart security team, as well as intelligence analysts from the US military. As I heard the details of the ambush, I realised how lucky we were that anyone at all had survived. The insurgents had hit the convoy at precisely its most vulnerable point as it slowed to negotiate a tight bend in the road. Their selection of fire points had left the convoy security team at a hopeless disadvantage and, even more ominously, they had deliberately targeted the security team's vehicles to ensure no one escaped the carnage. It was a far cry from the random shots that convoys used to attract just eighteen months before. These guys knew what they were doing.

I was very disturbed too by Paddy's account of what followed the ambush. As he lay bleeding in the drainage ditch, Paddy heard the insurgents swarming over the convoy and executing any of the drivers or security contractors who were badly injured but still alive. Then, he heard a car race up to the scene, the sound of muffled voices, a slamming door or boot lid, then the car racing off across the desert. We realised that this must have been the removal of Yves' and Sean's bodies. In the confusion and the hurry to clear the ambush site, they forgot about Paddy.

Paddy recovered and left Iraq. I was delighted to see that a book he wrote on his Iraq experiences, *Hidden Soldier*, turned out to be a best-seller in Ireland. But I was shocked to learn that, after a two-year break at home in Ireland and in Australia, he had returned to Iraq in late 2008 to resume work for Hart. I think it speaks volumes for the courage of the guy – and the fact that, in our trade, it is very hard to escape an industry where your skills are at a premium. When you spend as long as we have in uniform, it is very difficult to find a permanent slot on civvie street.

A few days after the ambush, the contract at Abu Ghraib was cancelled for Hart and another company was shipped in to take our place. The remaining teams went to Basra and some were put on other jobs, while the rest went home until there was another position for them. I myself went to the HQ house in Baghdad to help with the logistical recovery – this meant helping to identify the remains of the guys who were recovered from the ambush site.

As long as I live, I will never forget what I had to do over those next few days. We drove to Balad airbase, north of Baghdad, where the remains of some of our personnel were placed in two twenty-foot-long refrigerated containers. You are always apprehensive when a body bag is opened up, particularly if it involves the remains of someone you worked alongside, drank with or maybe even shared family stories with. But I knew that these body bags were going to contain some particularly horrific sights.

I had to try and identify eighteen charred remains from the gun-fight and convoy burning. As if that wasn't bad enough, the bodies had been further damaged by the US air strike to clear the area of insurgents. Most of the bodies were totally unidentifiable. I will never forget what I saw that day – and simply couldn't equate the blackened, broken bodies with the proud young men I had worked alongside. If a body was partially recognised by the foreman of the trucking company or by the Iraqi security survivors, they were taken away in the back of an open truck to be given directly back to a grieving family. Tragically, not all were recognisable, but at least the families had something to mourn. Yet even this wasn't allowed for the families of Yves and Sean.

The next year was every bit as bleak for Hart and myself. I lost two more of my closest friends in Iraq to the lethal new IEDs and shaped charges that the Iranians had taught the insurgents how to make. Seb B. was a giant Briton, who had made his home in Andorra on the French–Spanish border. He was a former French Foreign Legionnaire and we joked that he had the biggest appetite in all of Iraq. If you weren't careful, Seb would eat his own dinner and then clear your plate as well. But he was great company and a guy everyone enjoyed spending time with. He died when the security jeep he was travelling in was hit by one of the new Iranian IEDs outside Diwaniya. The vehicle was shredded in the explosion and Seb was killed instantly. He never stood a chance.

Another good friend was Morne P. He was a South African and had spent most of his time in Iraq working in and around Basra. We all considered Morne to be lucky because he stayed working in the south while the rest of us transferred to Baghdad where the worst of the violence was centred. He was also a really decent bloke, and always had time for a chat and a laugh. Poor Morne was undertaking a routine convoy escort on the motorway out of Basra when an IED was remotely detonated just as his vehicle was passing. He was killed instantly in the resultant fireball. What shocked all of us was that the attack came on a roadway that we used on a regular basis and was deemed one of the safest routes in Iraq.

Sometimes, being killed instantly in an IED attack was the lesser of the evils security contractors faced. Another lad, Johan, a South African contractor, suffered horrific injuries in an ambush in 2007. He should have died within twenty-four hours but, largely thanks to the high-tech medical facilities available via the US military in Iraq, he survived – barely. The poor guy spent nearly a year on a ventilator before his family finally ordered the machine to be turned off, and he died in November 2008.

The hallmark of Iraq was that you never knew when you were in extreme danger. Two other mates of mine had an incredible escape when the Baghdad café they were having a few drinks in was targeted

217

by suicide bombers. One bomber went to the souk, the local market-place, and the other walked over to the café. The two explosions killed dozens of civilians but, incredibly, both the Hart lads survived. In the aftermath of the twin bombings, the ground around the souk looked like it had been spray-painted in blood. One of my mates, Mike F., was physically blown up into the air by the force of the blast. But, amazingly, he walked away with only a few cuts, grazes and shattered eardrums. A military explosives expert later said that what saved their lives was the fact that the café was actually made of canvas tenting. It allowed the explosion to fully dissipate upwards, otherwise the boys would have been killed instantly.

Surrounded by so much death, horror and carnage, it is incredible to recall how people functioned, let alone retained a sense of decency and humanity. Above all, I never cease to be amazed at how the security teams – many of whom had lost close friends and colleagues – retained a sense of humour and wicked fun.

I suppose I had a cushier number than my colleagues on the two major occasions when it mattered. My job back at base was basically one of co-ordination and administration. I helped run the show – but, I suppose, I was lucky that I didn't have to go out with the convoys. I tried never to forget the fact that if I did my job right I'd dramatically increase the odds of our security operators making it safely to the end of their tour of duty. But that didn't alter the fact that, as the convoys rolled out each day, I silently prayed that they'd have a routine, boring journey and that the lads would make it back safe to the Hart compound. Never a day went by when I didn't wish I was with my rifle in hand if the shit ever hit the fan. Old habits die hard, I suppose, and once you're a Marine infantryman, you're always an infantryman. All the operators knew that I had done my own share of legwork – so they respected me. And they knew that my main priority was getting them whatever help they needed to get the job done – and they trusted my instincts.

On one occasion, I was part of the team at the old B'aath Party headquarters, which was being refurbished into a court complex and where, in a few months, the trial of Saddam Hussein would be staged. We were there to protect the construction workers and engineers, and twenty-one of us operated on a series of three watches. One of the security contractors was a lad called Ritchie from London. He fancied himself as a bit of a Del Boy and, being the senior man on the contract, I was the immediate target for some of his pranks. I woke up one morning to find my trainers missing, and, a couple of hours later, I received a ransom note. As I stomped around the construction site in borrowed boots, I was stunned to find photos of my trainers on posters taped to walls all over the building – complete with a new ransom note and a death threat. In one photo, the trainers were blindfolded! It may sound like a schoolboy prank, but it was the kind of thing that kept us sane in a country fast becoming a lunatic asylum.

Probably the closest I came to dying in my five years in Iraq was at Baghdad airport as we were working on a security contract connected to the imminent 2006 general election. I had just met with two other security teams for a chat, then walked back to my car. I sat in my vehicle – and suddenly it seemed like the very air was sucked from my lungs. I thought my ears would burst. It was a blast wave from a car bomb that exploded less than 100 metres away. Almost by instinct, I forced myself down into the footwell of the car for shelter and I could feel the heat of the blast wave as it swept over us. As I crouched there, stunned, bits of masonry and metal began to fall around the car and carpark, like some form of grisly rain. All around me I could see shrapnel holes from the car bomb.

I jumped out of the car to see what I could do to help. I can best describe the scene as like something from Dante's *Inferno*. A smouldering engine block was wedged by a huge crater in the tarmac metres from where I had just been talking to the other Hart lads minutes beforehand. The entire place seemed to be covered in broken glass and twisted pieces of metal. As I looked around, I spotted the steering wheel from the same car almost 150 metres away. Then, slowly, the cries and screams for help began. I stared over at the security checkpoint in front of the airport and realised, in horror, that there had been two men stationed there. Now, one was literally a mass of red congealed jelly. Later, in front of the security post, was found the upper torso of a uniformed man lying on the concrete footpath. In shock I recognised the uniform and realised it was the ex-Royal Marine who was on security duty at the main gate to BIAP (Baghdad Intn'l Airport). Later, I also heard that the lower half of the poor guy was found more than 100 metres away.

My abiding memory of that horrific day was the sight of two Iraqis staggering towards me. An acrid smoke cloud surrounded the front of the outer airport checkpoint and these two men came out of the smoke like spectres. One man seemed to be supporting the other, who had what looked like a nosebleed. But, as he staggered closer, I recoiled, realising that the entire lower half of his face had been blown off. He was moaning piteously through the shattered remains of what was left of his lower jaw. My team of security guards took him and transferred him immediately to a local Military hospital. I never heard what happened to the poor bastard – yet another statistic on Iraq's unending list of the maimed.

What shocked me most was the general view that this had not been a particularly costly attack. The perception – certainly from the media and anyone reading a newspaper – was that the injured should consider themselves lucky, in that they were still alive. However, when you saw at first-hand what a car bomb could do to a human body, the injured were anything but lucky. They were treated as little more than a statistic: 'Twelve injured in car bombing at airport.' But the awful reality was that the dead were probably the lucky ones. The injured, in this case, had to try and live with legs, arms, jaws and even eyes blown off. And then be treated long-term for their injuries in hospitals that were short of medicines, doctors and nurses. Rehab programmes simply didn't exist in Iraq when I was there.

In the subsequent security lockdown at the airport, I ended up spending four hours with the other Hart lads who were still in the vicinity. The US military were doing a full security shakedown and no one was allowed to enter or leave the airport zone until that was completed. Passengers inside in the terminal were forced to wait there until the all-clear was given. Eventually, my international teammate,

Dave S., arrived out of the passenger terminal demanding to know what the fuss was all about! I could only stare at him in disbelief as we drove out of the carpark where bits of car, concrete and human debris were still visible.

That car bomb genuinely rattled me. For at least a fortnight afterwards I grimaced at every car that pulled up beside me or applied its brakes. It was a normal human reaction to having missed death by such a small margin. The problem with car bombs is that, even if you detect one, they're usually in such close proximity that they'll still vaporise you if they're detonated. But I couldn't let the apprehension show and, a few weeks later, I had to travel back to the airport on another security job.

Dave travelled with me and, as we were stopped at the new security arrangements at the airport, one of the sniffer dogs got excited about a car directly behind us in the queue. Dave must have realised my unspoken concern and smiled: 'Don't worry, Geoff, there's an armoured plate across the rear of this jeep.' I looked at him in disbelief and replied: 'You dumb bastard, that plate will be the very thing that cuts our bloody heads off if there's another car bombing.' Dave thought the whole situation was hilarious, and, after a while, I too just had to laugh. After that, I happened to be near two further car bombings, and Dave steadfastly refused to travel in a car with me – and a lot of the Hart lads joked that I was 'a Jonah' or 'car bomb magnet'. Wherever I went, a car bombing seemed to follow.

The Abu Ghraib contract finished and I was then back in Basra on convoys and a member of a team once again. The leader positions were all taken at that time and because of the impromptu end to the contract, we were either sent home or joined in where we could with the other contracts. I wasn't ready to go home, so I joined in with another team, ready for countrywide convoy duties.

My Hart Group contract in Basra lasted just one more month before I was due to go home. The whole place was a maelstrom of competing political and tribal interests. Sometimes the way contracts were awarded made absolutely no sense, and the political in-fighting was almost as bad as the insurrection.

To be honest, I had had enough of Hart by this stage. I loved the guys and they had treated me really well over the years, but I felt that they were headed purely down the armoured convoy route. I had seen enough of that – and had lost too many friends in the ambushes that made convoy operations a living nightmare.

I had tremendous respect for Hart and how they operated. My background meant that I was always happiest among the ordinary 'oppos' (mates) or security personnel. I wasn't an officer – I was basically one of the lads. It wasn't easy working in Iraq, surrounded by so much death and violence. I tried to look at it logically – and focus on just doing my job. All of us knew precisely what was involved in coming to Iraq – we all had a job to do and accepted the risks involved. I never felt personally responsible for any of the lads lost on convoy ambushes, because I knew I wasn't responsible. I did what I was paid to do to the best of my ability, protecting them and ensuring they had everything they needed to get the job done. But sometimes it was all down to fate, luck and the will of the gods as to who got to go home safe at the end of a tour. And, while it may sound cold, I kept my personal emotions for my family at home.

I left Hart Group, ready to move on and looking for a change. A good mate called Stevo from the same village as me and who had just left the Marines and the SBS recently, just happened to be in Basra; he was with one other guy called Johnno. They were starting a new contract with a small company called Peak Group and they wanted a third member to make the team up and fit into their rotation for leave periods. They were a great bunch of lads at Peak Group – mostly ex-Marines, with the odd sprinkling of Paras and Guardsmen. Peak was a very small company, low-key in its operations, and worked from a discreet villa in the Red Zone of Baghdad.

The Peak Group contract suited my plans. I had three weeks at home, then came back to Basra with Peak, fitting right into a new contract, which was mostly office-based. Unfortunately, it lasted two months then ceased to exist. Stevo was pining for the Corps and joined back up and Johnno went somewhere else. I, however, went to Baghdad to meet the other lads in my new company and stayed over the Christmas period. At the end of the festivities, I managed to get myself on a new contract for the rebuilding and refurbishment of an electrical sub-station.

I ended up spending nearly eighteen months in Camp Falcon, which was just off the infamous Route Irish (one of many nicknames for main highways, for military reasons). I was looking after security with five other Peak guys. The job was to check all the Iraqi contractors coming into work each day, as they rebuilt the sub-station on the outskirts of the camp. It was simple work, but we were still the target of mortars and rockets, which hit the base on a daily basis. Mortars and rockets were bad, but what everyone worried about most were the vehicle-borne improvised explosive devices (VBIEDs) that were a daily occurrence on Route Irish, outside the base.

This was the main route to Basra and the south from Baghdad and the north, and was now the undisputed number-one target for all insurgents in the region. Every day the workers risked their lives. Despite our best efforts and the detailed instructions we gave them about how to improve personal security on their way home, one or two of them would be picked off on a regular basis and our workforce reduced more than we would have liked. We even lost two Iraqi security guards, murdered simply because they were working for 'infidels'. The poor bastards were only trying to feed their families – and they paid for it with their lives. The fear of being caught was very real for them, but the money was a stronger pull. They would not even tell their neighbours for fear of being snitched on to the militias.

After eighteen months, I moved on to another contract to provide security for a team of South African telecommunications engineers who were working for a subcontractor who, in turn, was working for the US army. That made them prime targets for kidnappings and murders – so wherever they went outside their protected safe house we were in close proximity and heavily armed. I had learned that the Iraqi criminal gangs specialised in this kind of thing. They would kidnap a Western contractor and sell him to the highest bidder, be it the company he worked for or the Islamic insurgents who would then use the poor bastard for leverage or one of their gruesome beheading videos.

On bodyguard duty, you learned to keep a low-profile, move fast and never establish a routine of movements. I insisted that my clients varied their routes and the timing of their operations; whenever we moved we did so hard and fast. I also developed eyes in the back of my head – always on the lookout for anything suspicious. Even something as simple as a vehicle that looked out of place could tip you off to a potential threat.

There were a couple of incidents where I was sure we were being followed and watched. But our erratic, unpredictable movements made it difficult for anyone to anticipate what we were doing – and I also made sure that anyone following us knew we were heavily armed and ready to rock'n'roll if the need arose. I had also drilled it into all my drivers that they never stopped for anything unless I told them to. The trick was not to make it easy for potential kidnappers who were desperate to make money but weren't willing to die for it.

My final task in Iraq with Peak was to assist in a hostile security takeover for Zain, the biggest telecommunications company in the Middle East. Their previous security company, who had looked after all the management and buildings of Zain, was run by a local hoodlum and he wasn't about to relinquish his hold on the contract – there were millions of dollars involved – but the bosses of Zain were starting to feel intimidated by him and his henchmen and wanted him out.

We all knew that Peak's takeover had to be achieved quickly and quietly. If this thug knew we were coming he would have ample resources to cause major problems – and the last thing anyone wanted was a shootout between two groups who were supposed to be protecting people. The US and Coalition authorities approved our plans – they didn't like the idea of private military fiefdoms being set up in the country because of the future problems they would cause.

After months of planning, we got the go-ahead from the US government and Zain bosses. Discreetly, we got tooled up and ready to take over three compounds in a simultaneous operation. I was going to the switch room with two other Peak lads; about thirty Peak Iraqi security guards, supported by the other British contractors, were going to a small sub-station and the Zain HQ compounds. It was daunting to realise that hundreds of armed men were convoying through Sadr City at dusk to take over a heavily armed compound from an opposing security company.

It didn't go to plan. We secured part of the compound successfully from the Iraqi private security guards who obviously weren't being paid enough to confront a well-trained and heavily armed security force. But it was a different story at the headquarters section located within the main compound in Monsoor. Even with the Iraqi army and a senior US officer to back our case, the Iraqi security personnel at the HQ building would not allow our security teams entry. Their security group was known as the Babylon Eagles – and, despite sounding like a US football team, they didn't like their 'turf' being challenged by anyone. The Babylon Eagles were concerned at losing such a potential 'cash cow'. Because it was effectively a matter between two private security groups, the US officer did not want to take sides and quietly told us he was not going to intervene directly. It resulted in a stand-off, which dragged on throughout the night. Eventually, the Americans were growing concerned that the stand-off could pose a security risk for everyone involved – not least that it could erupt into a gun-fight – so they demanded that a solution be found. As with so many other things in Iraq, it ultimately boiled down to hard cash. The call came to abandon the switching station that we had taken the night before and hand it back to the other company.

When the matter was resolved months later, the Eagles refused to hand the switching station over to us directly because they felt it would involve them losing face. So it was handed back to its owners – and we then assumed security responsibility a short time later from Zain directly. The rumour later went around that the original security firm only agreed to walk away after they received a substantial cash inducement. The pointlessness of the whole thing made me sick – given the bloodshed all around us it was hard to credit the fact that an Iraqi security firm were only concerned about money and not protecting lives. But that is what it was all about – the almighty dollar. I left Iraq a few days later and wasn't sad to go.

I had gone to Iraq expecting to get work for one year. In the end, I spent almost five years on numerous contracts in the country. I saw hope turn to horror and suddenly a faint light of hope emerge again. I saw good people die for no good reason and I witnessed at first-hand the depth of evil that some humans were capable of. I saw greed and kindness in equal measure. I watched, every single day, as Iraqis struggled through every imaginable pain and indignity in the hope of a better life for their children. I observed the innocence of young American and British soldiers slowly transformed into cynicism and fatalism by the brutality all around them. I saw men making millions on contracts that others fought and bled for. Above all, I saw a people living in abject poverty in a country that should rank as one of the richest on the planet.

So I was not sorry to leave in 2008. The main reason I left was that Iraq, like other countries, was creating a tidal wave of bureaucracy to cope with its problems. Instead of tackling problems in a straightforward manner, politicians and military commanders alike created layers of bureaucracy as a solution. For instance, as a private security guard I was armed with an M-21 and a Glock 17 and was driving an armoured car and escorting senior US Marine colonels in uniform – yet I still could not get into a military barracks, because I had the wrong markings on my security badge. Ex-Coalition military personnel were treated as Aliens by the American military (their words). And European countries not in the US-led Coalition were officially regarded as TCNs – third country nationals. For the South Africans and French, who formed a sizeable part of the security contractor community, it was a policy they found insulting and demeaning. And British ex-Marines, who had been in the war a couple of years previously, were now not allowed around the country and into bases if their badges were not US-authorised. Mel Brooks's film, *Blazing Saddles*, said it all quite well with the line, 'Badges! We don't need no stinking badges.' This summed up how we all felt about the Americans' big brother attitude. The insanity of Iraq was that while the country going to hell all around us, you almost needed a badge just to take a crap. Iraq was very much a place where the inmates had taken control of the asylum.

I left Iraq having accomplished what I had set out to do. I had made enough money over the five years to pay off my debts back in the UK. I had also saved up enough of a nest-egg to start my own business up in Yorkshire. I had lived very frugally during my time in Iraq. Some of the lads went mad with their cash, spending it on lavish holidays, girlfriends and cars. I saved every single penny I could. When I came home, I had the fresh start that I had craved. But I also came back from Iraq conscious of the fact that I was a soldier – and that what I was best at in life were the demands of a military career. Despite the carnage and heartache all around me in Iraq, I had rediscovered something that I had last known when I had worn the Green Beret of the Royal Marine Commandos – a niche in life. I was a Commando, I was good at what I did, and I missed the adrenalin of my old life.

17

ENDEX ... OR NOT QUITE

Back in civvie street, I still dreamed of life on the edge in some dangerous part of the world. Military life gets into your veins and is a huge draw. Thirty-four years after I stepped off the train at Lympstone, I found it really hard to leave army life behind, no matter what the dangers. In fact, the danger was probably the main attraction.

As a Royal Marine I loved the thought of being sent at a moment's notice to a far-flung part of the globe. All my life I loved the idea of a new adventure, a new challenge and a new port of call. A friend once told me that adrenalin is every bit as addictive as heroin or alcohol – and it's an addiction that, probably, I hadn't quite seen the last of.

I found it a remarkable journey. I saw places and sights that I never thought possible. I saw the magic and wonder of nature from the Middle East to the far-flung frozen reaches of Alaska. Unfortunately, I also saw the very best and the very worst of humanity. I still considered myself an optimist. I believed in a better tomorrow even though, at times, I wished there were a few changes I could make to some of my yesterdays.

Yet, strangely, one of the things I didn't regret was going to Iraq. Those of us who worked in private security in the country took a lot of flak, not least from the media at home. We were accused of being mercenaries, guns for hire. The death of a US or British soldier always made the nightly news, yet when a private security contractor was killed, there were very few headlines. Not unless the death was particularly gruesome or, as in the case of one US firm, if the contractors were killed by a mob and their burned body parts hung from bridge girders. I'm not sure if it was the fact that the media didn't think some of these deaths were worth reporting or if it was a case that they felt we deserved what we got for choosing to be in Iraq in the first place. But it was pretty hypocritical because a lot of the same media outlets were bloody glad of the protection provided for themselves by private security contractors when they were in Iraq. I know full well that the actions of some private military companies – a lot of them American – didn't win us too many friends. For many of them, it was very much a case of balls over brains – too much firepower in your face. But most contractors preferred lower-profile operations; a true success for us was if insurgents didn't even know we were there in the first place.

My time in Iraq was spent protecting building sites, power stations, oil plants and escorting convoys of mostly civilian personnel. In my five years there I never undertook any offensive action, never once fired my gun except to protect someone in my care. I don't see how those are the actions of a mercenary. I saw at first-hand how desperate ordinary Iraqis were for a normal life, for simple things like being able to go shopping to the souk without the threat of a suicide bomber blowing you to smithereens; how they were prevented from visiting relatives in another neighbourhood because it meant passing through an opposing sect's area. If you ran the risk of crossing another sect's zone simply to see a loved one, you were virtually guaranteed to become a hostage for ransom. Or, more than likely, your body would be discovered lying in a drainage ditch or gutter, complete with drill marks to the feet and head. At one point in 2006–7, up to a hundred tortured and mutilated bodies were being discovered on rubbish heaps with domestic garbage every single week in Iraq. So much for freedom and democracy.

And I saw at first-hand the courage of the men I worked alongside. Men who knew, that if their convoy was attacked and they were killed, their body would probably be dragged off to an unmarked grave in some godforsaken part of the Iraqi desert. They knew full well the pain such a death would cause their families and loved ones. But they

229

still went on convoy missions because they knew the job simply had to be done, and they didn't want to let down their comrades. I also saw how Western contractors fought to protect Iraqi drivers and security contractors working with them. These poor guys more often than not ran the risk of a death sentence just for turning up for work. In Basra, for example, five local women came to clean the bedrooms and toilets of our base inside the airport complex. The five were murdered one evening when they returned home from their cleaning duties. They were butchered simply because they chose to work for Westerners – but they had no other work.

Iraq seemed to bring out the very best and the very worst in people. I suppose that's why I'm glad I experienced it – it was humanity in the raw. I witnessed blind hatred and anger that made me glad I had a loaded assault rifle at my side. I saw despair and anguish in equal measure, as families counted in blood the price of their new democracy. Yet amidst all the hatred and sectarian strife, I saw enough courage and decency to restore my faith in humanity. I saw aid workers risking everything to help people they didn't even know. And, admittedly on very rare occasions, I saw compassion and kindness that made you stop and wonder – from a simple gesture of compassion from a total stranger after an ambush to the way Iraqis who had lost almost everything still insisted on trying to show hospitality to others through a meal or the offer of tea. In Iraq, there were very few black-and-white situations. Amidst the tidal wave of visceral hatred, it was still possible to see kindness in ordinary people whose only prayer was for a better world for their children. At times it reminded me of Northern Ireland and you wondered why people bothered to stay amid the carnage all around them. But then you realised it was the hope of a better tomorrow that kept them going. That and the fact that this was their home. I worked and lived alongside Iraqis for months at a time – and I heard from them what they wanted for their families and country. To be honest, it was no different from what I wanted for my family and my country.

I regretted the mates that I lost in action. Sometimes, as I walked along Flamborough Head and the cold wind roared in from the North

Sea, I would close my eyes and picture their faces. I saw the faces of the lads who did not make it back from Northern Ireland, Hong Kong, Norway, Iraq and the Falklands. Some of them I could see as clearly as if I had met them just yesterday. And, to a man, they were all young, as I used to be.

I guess soldiers have asked the same question since time immemorial. Why me? Why did I make it home when they didn't? Why did I make it through situations when the law of averages was against me? In San Carlos Water, in Belfast, in Norway and in Baghdad, I was in situations far more dangerous than many that cost the lives of my friends. I will never forget the sing-songs on the way through the South Atlantic to the Falklands in 1982 where we all sang about going home in body bags. I still don't know whether it was 'devil may care' courage or simple, youthful stupidity. A few of the lads who sang those songs ultimately did go home that way. But not me. I have always considered myself a laid-back, good-humoured character. But there are times when I wonder if your fate in life is dictated simply by being in the wrong place at the wrong time. The odds-on are high in places like Iraq, but then, the adrenalin rush is equally high. And there's a deadly attraction in that too.

From my earliest days growing up, I've learned that humour can sometimes defuse most of life's situations – and being able to laugh at yourself is a vital part of staying grounded, I think. When I became a Royal Marine Commando, I was proud as punch of myself and decided to get a tattoo to mark the event. I went to the best tattoo artist in Plymouth – a guy famed in Navy ports around the world. He was a brilliant artist – but he wasn't quite so good at spelling or counting. On my left arm I got a tattoo of a magnificent Viking warrior in honour of my Nordic ancestry. On the other arm I got a Royal Marine insignia. Unfortunately, the Viking warrior had five fingers and a thumb on his clenched fist – and the Royal Marine insignia bore the inscription 'Comado', with the 'n' and second 'm' mysteriously gone AWOL.

So what did the future hold for me and my six-fingered Viking Comado warrior, and for people like me? My mate Paddy O'Keeffe wrote about his near-death experience in Iraq and the prospect of hanging up his gun, settling down and finding a niche on civvie street – but he went back to Iraq to work as a private security contractor. I couldn't help but think that, having spent thirty years of my life doing military-type work, the security industry was not quite finished with me yet. There is always something around the next corner that is dramatically different and enticing to what was around the previous corner.

I loved being back at home and it was great to recharge the batteries. No matter where I've wandered in the world, Flamborough has always been home and a special part of me. But I got the feeling that itchy feet may not be too far off on my horizon. A call from a friend about security work on an oil pipeline project in Kazakhstan had me picturing myself there before he even finished the offer. The winter of central Asia couldn't be all that much worse than that of northern Norway where I froze through most of my younger years, could it? Another mate rang me about anti-piracy patrols off the coast of East Africa following a spate of hijacking of freighters and tankers by Somali bandits. Again, I thought: Why not? I guess that once you're a Commando, you're always a Commando …

18

PIRATES

I spent two years back in England and set up a successful UPVC factory with my business partner Martin. I worked hard in establishing the company, but actually running the thing on a daily basis wasn't for me. It was too sedate, too much everyday-life. On top of that, the winter of 2009 was particularly harsh and recession had set in. I was also going through tough personal trials, and my elder son Aaron had left the north to go back to live with his mother in the south again, which iced the misery cake for me. I felt it was the right time to move on.

I put feelers out into the world of security and contacted other like-minded former servicemen, looking for the buzz of the unknown. Slowly word filtered out and interested parties started to get back to me. I was offered numerous jobs back in my old stomping ground of Iraq, but the thought made me far from excited, especially the prospect of Yank bullshit and red tape.

Eventually, I received a phone call from the guy who originally got me work out in Iraq back in 2003, Taff A. He had switched jobs and was in with the Maritime boys. He had been doing anti-piracy work off Tanzania, Somalia, the East Coast of Africa and the Gulf of Aden. Somali piracy was rife at this time and the big shipping companies soon realised that by having armed security on board they could reduce their insurance bills. PMLSC, Private Maritime Liaison Security Contractors, or a derivative thereof, was the official name for the former military guys now involved in anti-piracy. Taff was again subcontracting, this time to PVI (Protection Vessels International), set up in 2008 by ex-Marine Dom Mee, and nearly one thousand former Royal Marines were on the books. Who would have thought it? I reminded myself of the code I lived by, that of experiencing different things in life every day, refusing a run-of-the-mill existence. I was ready for a new and different adventure, and this time it was, in my opinion, less dangerous than Iraq had been. After signing the UPVC business over to Martin, I left Yorkshire and embarked on my next mission.

It was only a week after getting the call that I flew to Muscat in Oman. They wanted me there on the Saturday; it was now Thursday. After a two-day delay and a frantic shop for essential private security attire, i.e. baggy cargo pants, blue polo shirts, some fresh smellies and some foofoo (deodorant and talc), I set off to the airport carrying extra team kit for the lads already there. I was taking a night sight, an Iridium satellite phone, four sets of body armour and four helmets. Luckily the small matter of £800 in excess baggage was paid for by my new team leader Dave S. I met him at the airport and we split the weight. Dave was a former Royal Marines Weapons Instructor and had already been with the company for a while by then.

We arrived in the blazing heat of Oman and acclimatised as quickly as possible by wearing shades, shorts and flip-flops, trying to forget the shitty winter of 2009–10 that we had just gone through in the UK.

Three days later and my first trip out, four of us hopped on a tug from the harbour with our team kit and a weapon each, ready for what was supposed to be twenty days of escort duties on a car transporter for one of the company's clients. We had two Tikka hunting rifles, a Sig Sauer 2022 sports pro pistol and a Mossberg pump-action shotgun, with about 300 shells.

Preparing the ground for us to go in and out of ports around the whole of the Indian Ocean and Middle East had been quite a feat in itself. Many of the other companies doing the same kind of work as ourselves were attempting to fend off pirates unarmed, owing to issues with permissions and poor logistical support; they were armed only with a rocket flare and laid-down procedures and drills. Trying to repel a group of well-armed men in fast boats using a flare and a fire hose sounded ludicrous to me and I was glad that we were armed with a variety of strange, but deadly weapons.

The tactics used by the unarmed ships, such as increasing the speed of the craft, zigzagging manoeuvres and spreading razor wire around the upper decks (an inconvenience to the crew as some were in and out of the high-risk area constantly), did work sometimes. Perhaps the most vital of all the ships' security features were an alert and vigilant crewman on lookout from the bridge wings and a good strong sweat-box to lock yourself into.

We set sail to Mumbai, India, and after a briefing to the crew and taking them through some anti-piracy drills, we settled into the mundane task of watch-keeping. We did three hours on, nine off as a rule, but through the riskier areas increased to two of us on watch on a six-hour-on six-hour-off basis. If it wasn't for the glorious weather of the Indian Ocean and the fact that the ship was really large, being a car transporter and thus allowing us to patrol the upper decks, it could have been a pretty dire period of boredom.

We did not get off in the port of Mumbai, nor did we get off in the other ports we visited, other than Durban, but merely stayed on watch in the ports and observed the cars being on- and off-loaded by local drivers. From Mumbai we headed south out of the danger area of the Somali latitude, roughly the equator, and then headed due west to the east coast of Africa towards Kenya where the next stop was Mombasa.

The journey was uneventful, except for the endless cabin parties held by the ship's cook in the cabin next to mine. He was a huge Bulgarian and his assistant, the ship's steward, a small Indian. Uneventful, that is, until we reached the waters about a day's travel out of the Kenyan port. We were doing 21 knots and had a freeboard of about 15 metres, so we were no pushover of a target. Although, having said that, a car transporter very similar to ours had been taken just the year before and spent time at anchor off the Somali coast, until a ransom of four million dollars was found by its owners.

I was on watch with one other on the bridge when a crewman spotted a ship on the horizon. It was about 12 nautical miles away and had stopped. It was the size of a small cargo ship, not in itself suspicious, but it was strange for a ship this big to just stop so far mid-ocean. We watched it on the AIS (the ship's automatic identification system).

What was suspicious was the small white bow wave headed our way from the ship, which could only belong to that of a speedboat, or skiff, as they are known. We decided that there was a genuine threat to the ship and started the drill procedures. We called the captain to the bridge and the other two team members. Next, we sounded the ship's alarm bells and the crew were mustered in their designated meeting place and a roll call was carried out.

If the threat level were to increase, the crew would then head off to a secure area called the 'citadel', inside the ship. This was a safe room without any windows so that the crew would be safe from any stray RPGs and small-arms fire. It had to have plenty of food, water and some means of communication with the outside world.

While the crew were mustering in a safe place in the depths of the ship, the rest of us – the captain and four-man security team – were preparing to repel all boarders, just like in the days of old. Captain Jack Sparrow is the bad guy, remember. The book and film *Captain Phillips* was a lesson in how not to stop pirates taking over your ship, and following BMP4 (Best Management Practices for Protection against Somali Piracy) guidelines was mandatory.

The bridge was our stand-to location and where we kept all other equipment, such as extra ammo, binoculars, body armour and plastic-lined helmets. We got a quick brief from the Team Leader (TL), and the three team members went to the stern of the ship to wait for the approach of the skiff.

We stood there on the top deck at the rear of the ship for forty-five minutes as the small skiff did a large semicircle to our rear and approached from the stern, leaving the mother ship where we last saw it. The mother ship was slowly moving off into the distance in the opposite direction and we increased speed to 21 knots plus.

One small-boat wake was still quite prominent in the beautiful crystal seas and clear sunshine. Being one travel day out from Mombasa in the Indian Ocean, we kept moving. We stood there waiting in the blazing sun, sweating like crazy and psyching ourselves up for what was to come. We got increasingly impatient and stood there smoking, frustratingly saying, 'Oh for god's sake, get a move on will ya.' We were wearing body armour and blue Kevlar helmets and the plastic interior padding of the helmet made the sweat run down our foreheads and into our eyes. We soon discarded them as not practical for our purpose at this time; we weren't being shot at yet and we needed good vision to see the target for clear warning shots.

As the single skiff approached, we could see the crew clearly and got ourselves into firing positions. As you can imagine, lying down on the upper deck of a steel ship is like putting yourself in a frying pan and voluntarily sizzling off your outer layer of skin. Paul and Matt lay there sweating and searing their legs in their shorts, with the sweat rolling off their bald pates and trickling into their eyes. They both had Tikka hunting rifles and I had a Mossberg pump-action shotgun with solid shot cartridges.

I took up position behind the large uprights of the ramp cables, used to offload the cars, and stayed standing; I had enough cover from fire and view and needed more freedom of movement to re-cock the weapon after each shot when needed.

Eventually, the craft came within effective firing range and we requested permission to fire warning shots. By now, there was absolutely no doubt in anyone's mind about who the guys in the skiff were and what their intentions towards us were, and if we were doing 21 knots, they must have been doing at least 30 to be able to catch us at all.

A similar ship might have been taken the year before but we weren't about to let it happen to us. We were not merchant seamen; we were armed security, veterans, with time served fighting battles in foreign countries. We could be killed if captured, or handed over to Al-Qaeda in Somalia (Al Shabaab), or badly beaten at the least. So they would not be getting on our ship, not on our watch.

We had all the advantages: height over the enemy, a stable platform and high-powered rifles with telescopic sights. Matt was in the standing position. He fired off the first round when the skiff was at around 0.7 nautical miles away, which is a good distance. We saw the round hit the water in front of the boat and a plume of water rose in front of the boat. Nothing happened. They either didn't notice or didn't understand what it was. They just kept on coming. Matt was to fire again after we got permission to let go another round.

The boat had come a couple of hundred metres closer now and Matt was still standing. This time, the round went over their heads; having been on the receiving end of 7.62mm rounds whizzing over my head, I was more than aware of what the crack of misplaced air would have been like for them. Still they kept coming.

Paul was lying down behind a hatch casing, using a dirty old rag to constantly keep the sweat from his eyes, and as the skiff got to about 200 metres and with permission from the TL Dave, he let off another. This sent up an even bigger water spray in front of the boat and it immediately swerved to the side, as if trying to avoid the spout of water that was in front of it. All it did then was come back on course and carry on towards us. We could clearly see two people standing in the craft, but the practice was for up to five other men to be in the bottom of the boat crouching down, ready to come out once close.

One skiff this far out was not the norm; they usually went about in groups of three or four, and came onto the sides with extendable, lightweight ladders to board. The sides of a car transporter, however, were far too high for a ladder without rocket-propelled grappling hooks, so they would climb up the fixed ladder that a vessel of this kind was fitted with at the rear. But because a similar vessel had been successfully taken the year before, the crew on this ship had sensibly cut off the stern ladders, making it difficult, though not impossible to get on board that way. Of course, we also still had the obligatory razor wire all around the external edges, but this could still be overcome by a determined, desperate band of Jolly Roger latter-day pirates.

Once back on course, the skiff just kept coming and it made us wonder what incentives the pirates had been promised by their commanders to make them keep going and what made them so desperate. Anyway, we were ready for our next step as they came within range of my pump and now that the warning shots, as per international law, were out of the way, it was just a matter of waiting for them to get under the rear so I could unleash hell on their heads.

We decided to give them one last chance to back off, so Matt fired the fourth warning shot over their heads and this, surprisingly, seemed to do the trick. Whether we hit one unawares or they decided that this was the point at which they should stop we'll never know; they suddenly stopped dead in the water and we quickly sailed off towards our next port.

The captain and crew were of course very happy with this outcome because at this point the piracy attacks were at their peak in the Indian Ocean. There were thousands of cars on the carrier and the recovery of the crew alone is profit in the millions for a successfully pirated, vessel and its crew.

There were no more attacks on us on that trip, but many on others in the Gulf of Aden and Arabian Sea. There are still some private security companies doing the same job in the same areas unarmed. I simply wouldn't do it. I have been accused of being reckless on occasion, but I would risk-assess that as being a foolhardy errand. There have been security personnel on ships who have had to hide in the citadel with the crew, because they have had no means to prevent the inevitable.

I spent five years in Iraq when Abu Musab al Zarqawi was chopping off heads with a rusty, blunt spoon and I wasn't going to be some other terrorist's chucky egg with my head bashed in and my brains scooped out.

The events I have just described coincided with the Middle Eastern uprisings in Egypt, Yemen, Bahrain, Syria and Libya. The Arab Spring was a positive hope for everyone in defeating so many tyrants, dictators and poor rulers. But these were some of the places we needed to embark and disembark from one ship to another. Many of the ships that travelled through the Suez Canal en route to Singapore had no security on board. The whole maritime trade was at risk, and transiting inland was also fraught with problems.

Some of the ships taken as booty were then used as mother ships, to store or tow the skiffs, which enabled them to travel vast distances from Somalia for weeks on end. They were known as a Pirate Action Group, or PAG, and were often included in daily reports to all mariners, but unless they were caught doing something illegal, the Coalition forces were very reluctant to interfere with their progress and were an ineffectual deterrent.

While on a small chemical tanker, I had the opportunity to talk to one of the crew who was a Turkish motorman. I was interested to know the ins and outs of a ship hijack and crew kidnap from someone who had experienced it first-hand. He had spent 137 days in captivity, at anchor, off Somalia on the sister ship of the one we were presently on. He described the ordeal to me as it unfolded and I prompted him for more or less the complete story. His account follows:[1]

'On 28 December 2009 at 5.30pm on a clear, sunny day off the Horn of Africa, north of Somalia, we were about two days out to sea in the IRTC (Internationally Recommended Transit Corridor). The ship was travelling at its maximum speed, roughly 11 knots, and I was down in my cabin area, when we heard the ship's alarm bells and the internal intercom system.

The captain's voice came over loud and clear. He said that the ship was under pirate attack and we were to muster in the allotted primary secure area, as per our drill procedures.

We had no security on board and the procedures for anti-piracy measures were pretty basic to say the least.

The whole crew, minus the bridge and engine duty watch,

---

1   I have withheld his name for his own protection, partly from reprisals from shipping companies and partly because he and his family still live in Mozambique, Africa.

240

mustered and waited for the next set of instructions from the captain on the bridge, and the chief officer checked us off the crew list to account for us all. Two men at this time were missing.

The ship was moving through the IRTC in an easterly direction from the Red Sea towards our next port of call in Thailand, nearly 5,000km. Normally you go with a naval escort through the corridor; there are just two routes, easterly and westerly, and these marked by lines on a chart. On this occasion we were without an escort, as we didn't wish to wait for the convoy times. The area is so vast, you could go for weeks without seeing any naval presence.

We had taken the usual precautions while in the high-risk[2] area, such as attaching razor wire all around the upper deck, on the edges and leading up to the superstructure. We had rigged fire hoses, open and ready to trip the main pumps to create a water wall over the sides. We had locked all the doors leading outside and established an anti-pirate watch from the bridge wings to give early warning.

At 4pm, there had been a suspicious sighting of a fishing boat in the area, a large one of the kind that pirates sometimes use as a mother craft. There are frequent sightings of these vessels, using their own waterways, and if they are doing you no harm, there is not a lot you can do other than steam on.

---

2   The high-risk area was once designated as purely the area of the Gulf of Aden, between the coastlines of Yemen in the north and Djibouti and the whole length of the Somali coast to the south and down the Somali basin. But now, no ship is safe inside a nominal box that stretches from Latitude 15° North in the Red Sea, the UAE in the Persian Gulf at 26° North, Latitude 10° South, north of Madagascar, and Longitude 78° East, through the southernmost point of India, pretty much the whole of the Indian Ocean, comprising the Maldives and the Lakshadweep islands in the east and the Seychelles in the south.

At 5.30pm, this same suspect craft lowered a smaller boat into the water and it came straight for us at high speed. It happened so fast it didn't give the bridge watch much time to put into action all the counter-measures. The fire hoses were turned on to create a water wall over the sides, making it difficult for the pirates to see where to place their ladders. Zigzag manoeuvring was employed to create more wake and disturbed sea, so as to make it difficult for the attackers to hold the boat alongside and climb their ladder. Lastly, a mayday call was put out on VHF radio, Channel 16, to anyone listening.[3]

In the small boat, or skiff, there were only two men visible, the coxswain and the leader in the bow with an AK-47. We didn't see the other five crouched down in the boat at this time; they hide from view in case there are armed security on board and they don't want to make themselves a target, or because maybe they think that they can get closer if we only see the two of them, mistaking them for innocent fishermen.[4]

---

3   If there is time, a threatened ship can also contact UKMTO (United Kingdom Maritime Transport Organisation), in Dubai, to have them dispatch help. The problem is that at sea the maximum speed any warship can do to come to your assistance is 20–30 knots per hour and if you are over 30 miles away that's a whole hour. That gives the pirates plenty of time to get on board and take control; they can do it in five minutes.

Even a helicopter would have to warm up and go through safety procedures before they could get in the air. Plus, once the pirates are on board, the military will do nothing to interfere, in case the pirates decide to hurt or shoot any of their hostages, which in turn would lead to major political reprisals.

4   Once they are close enough, they may spray the ship's side with automatic weapons, or fire a Rocket Propelled Grenade (RPG) at the bridge in order to intimidate the captain enough to make him stop.

The bridge officers may decide to fire rocket flares at the pirates as an added deterrent; sometimes this does work. If the sea is rough enough, the ship can get up sufficient speed to make boarding difficult, plus zigzagging, combined with the razor wire, can make them think twice. Not in this case though. Our vessel was a small tanker and we

The rest of us were down in the muster area when the captain called us all up to the bridge. The pirates were there with their guns and we were all mustered on the starboard bridge wing to be accounted for and like I said, there were two crew missing at this time and we did not know where they were.

It turned out that they were terrified of the approaching pirates and had hidden themselves on board. One was in the lifeboat I think, I am not sure about the location of the other.

There were twenty-six of us and we had to stay there under armed guard while some of the pirates searched us for mobile phones and any other devices. Their leader made the bridge officers steer the ship on a course for the Somali coast and our fate for the next few months. They fired a burst into the air to remind us that they had weapons and to make any of the braver ones think twice. The skiff was released to be recovered by the mother ship.

All this was done by a bunch of rag-tag individuals wearing scruffy, dirty t-shirts, shorts and flip-flops. Just the same as seen on any piece of newsreel from any war-torn African country.

The leader of the pirates then went with the captain to his office and I presume stole all the ship's cash. They were there for about an hour and this is where they discussed the work routines and how he wanted the crew used.

---

have a low freeboard, that's the height of the ship's side above the sea level and it will differ with the amount of cargo carried or type of ship.

Once alongside, the lightweight ladder is hooked over the ship's side and the pirates stream out from the bottom of the small boats and climb the ladder as quick as monkeys up a tree. They sprint to the superstructure, where all the accommodation, bridge and access to the controls of the ship are. Once they're on the bridge, that's it, the ship is lost. Locking the bridge doors has no effect and won't stop a spray of 7.62mm calibre bullets.

It was decided that all the crew would stay in the cargo control room together. There was a toilet and shower in the area. The captain would stay in his cabin, the cook would do the cooking and we would all be designated jobs to do. Mostly the jobs consisted of mopping the stairs and keeping the ship clean and were also designed to keep us occupied for the period of the incarceration. This was not done until after we were established in the anchorage, so they could have more control over us.

We were a mixed crew of Eastern Europeans, Indians and Filipinos, Russian, Bulgarian, Estonian, Hungarian, Romanian and Ukrainian.

We were allowed to get some sleeping kit from our cabins, one at a time, but the pirates slept in them, mostly in shifts and just left them as untidy as pigsties. It goes without saying that we had all our personal possessions rifled through; no doubt the booty was divided later.

The bridge officers would do watches on the bridge, which after we were at anchor, meant nothing more than an anchor watch, ensuring the ship didn't drag its anchor and become grounded. The engineers would do watches in the engine room so we had the necessities provided by the generators.

Once we were at the anchorage, which was at a location halfway down the East Somalia coastline, more pirates came on board, at least sixteen altogether; these were to be our guards for the duration. They wore rough paramilitary camouflage uniforms and worked in two separate shifts of twelve hours on and twelve off. Six slept while six were strategically located around the ship and four more supervised them. There was one on the roof of the bridge, one on each bridge wing, one in the bridge, one outside our confinement room and one at the end of the corridor, acting as backup. The other four supervisors roamed about as they pleased.

After the first two weeks, food started to get low. The pirates did boost our rations with some rice to keep us alive, as it was in their interests to keep us healthy for the ransom demands. But this wasn't enough and if four of us had not been given the task of fishing for four hours a day, there would not have been nearly enough to eat.

During the whole of the 137 days that we did this routine, the pirates did not mistreat me and we all kept ourselves to ourselves, none of the crew wanting to unnecessarily rock the boat. The only occasion that I witnessed any real violence was when the pirates accused the chief engineer of hiding money in the engine room. They got really irate and searched the area very thoroughly, also beating up the second and third engineer. When the chief wouldn't tell them where the money was they really hurt his legs badly by twisting them somehow. I later saw him hobbling about like an old man. I don't know how badly they were damaged and I don't think they ever found any money, nor do I know why they ever thought he would keep any in the engine room.

Occasionally, the man who led the assault on the ship, the boss, would visit us and stay for a few days. A few days into the routine, the negotiator came on board. He was nicknamed 'Carlos' and was of mixed African-Asian race. He talked to the captain and our shoreside owners and this apparently was the first time that our office even knew that we had been taken. Carlos told them that the ship was under their control and that they wanted US$15 million for the ship and crews' safe release. And so it went on. We caught many fish in those days at anchor and mopped the floors till they bled.

They did let us contact our families three times in the whole period, so they knew we were alive and well. Eventually we were told that an agreement had been made and we were to be released for a sum of US$5 million.

On the last day of our imprisonment, a small plane overflew us. We were told to muster in a long line on the upper deck as they went over, so that they could look and check that we were all okay and in good condition. Then the plane went over again and dropped two waterproof cylindrical canisters, which we presumed were stuffed with money.

Once the money was checked and all was to the pirates' liking, they left the ship. The captain checked his ship's email system, now it was up and running again, to see what his orders were. He was instructed to go to a rendezvous position, where he was met by representatives of his company, on one of our patrol boats. We then proceeded to give the ship an armed escort back to Salalah in Oman.'

Because so many ships were being taken from these waters and the ransom demands were so high, by 2012 the shipping insurance companies began to insist that ships should travel through the high-risk areas (HRA) of the charted areas with an escort.

In 2006, between the latitudes of 10° North and 10° South and in the HRA a total of 239 ships were either hijacked, shot at, boarded or nearly boarded. In 2010, when piracy was at its peak, that number was 445, and in 2011, the number went down to 266. The number of ships taken with armed security on board were down to none. Better naval practices and armed security on ships greatly reduced the number of ships being taken, but there is still the odd one that does not follow the Best Management Practices, or BMP, edition 4.

Violence to crew and passengers in 2006 was 317 with 188 taken hostage and 15 being killed. In 2010, that number was 1181 taken hostage and 8 killed. In 2011, that number had reduced again to 495 taken hostage and 7 killed. In 2012 it had reduced again.

Eventually, piracy died out along the Somali coastline and was redirected to the Gulf of Guinea on the west coast. Oil bandits and gangsters were attacking ships sailing in waters off Sierra Leone and Nigeria, only this time, the pirates killed everyone and stole the oil. Each ship would have to anchor and seek protection from the local Navy. The few private contractors that went to the west coast were not armed due to the rules of those countries. But still, they went.

Somali piracy died out for a number of reasons. The Americans made a series of raids by jets destroying boats, communications and infrastructure. They put a bigger presence on the ground using control teams and helped the local governments take back control of the coastline. And also, we like to think, no ship was ever taken again after armed teams were deployed onto them for escort duties.

Piracy in the region started when local Somali fishermen, wishing to stop foreign fishermen stealing their catch, took one ship as a protest and gained world attention. The rot set in and the financial benefits from kidnap and ransom on the high seas far outweighed any reward from a good haul.

I can sympathise with fishermen and their cause, coming from a fishing coastline in East Yorkshire, not far north of Hull, but anything in this world taken to an extreme is never the correct, moral or long-term answer to anything.

After the ordeal of being at the whim of pirates and being denied their freedom, seamen, once released from their kidnappers, sail on to calmer waters. After a year off and having spent their small amount of compensation and back pay, most of these merchantmen will return to sea.

That's assuming they are employed by a reputable company. Some unscrupulous shipping companies, based in the Far East and subcontinent, who cannot be reached to deal with the issues of a missing crew and paying hefty ransoms, will consider the loss of the ship and crew a sacrifice that they are happy and willing to take.

19

THE NEXT CHAPTER

I rose through the ranks of PVI from team member to team leader and on to superintendent team leader, where my job was to travel with the teams on the ships we protected. I managed 95 ships of all varieties. Finally I went back to being team leader when the piracy threat started to wane. I flitted in and out of the UK, as the work diminished – our teams could be waiting for weeks on floating hulks of rust for a ship to protect – and the job we did combined with US and Coalition raids in Somalia forced the money to a pittance.

One such occasion in 2016, I was on a cargo ship and had just left the eastern end of the IRTC when the captain called me to his cabin for what I thought was a standard update of some kind. He told me that my ex-wife had rung and wanted me to get back to her as it was urgent. Strange and rare as it was, I had had stranger calls to stranger places.

The news I got devastated our world. My beautiful elder son Aaron had been killed in a road accident. I was struck mute and for a pragmatic person having this news there are no words.

I told my office by satellite phone and they asked the captain and his company, who was on a strict passage plan, what they could do. They came through and the ship re-routed north to Salalah in Oman, where a flight had been arranged back home.

I spent the entire trip back unable to function, not thinking, catatonic, frozen in mind, believing it was a dream, a mistake, something that would change, not possible.

Anyone who has experienced grief, especially the loss of a child, will know that the feelings cannot ever be described enough on paper, so I will not even try to do that here.

I left the job with more of a whimper than a bang and one of the last transits I had was on a small cruise ship from Muscat to Aqaba in Jordan. I was still crying at the drop of a hat and would spend hours wandering in my head aimlessly; this job was not helping with all the quiet hours alone on bridge wings.

I had spent six years being a security officer on cruise ships from the late 90s to 2003 and swore I would never do it again; I had moved on, but I could see the writing was on the wall for anti-piracy and one year later I left Tiverton as my base and had an interview to go back cruising for Marella and with Columbia Cruise Services. I was successful and presently work for Marella Cruises, the British part of TUI Cruises.

I am still amazed when people ask, 'But surely there's no trouble on cruise ships?' And I have to explain that with 2000 guests, all in one place, all in party mode with easy access to cocktails, like a week-long wedding reception, you still need security. They all have the ability to fight when they let themselves go!

I am here now, updating you, living with my younger son, who is doing well after the tough times he went through losing his big brother, and wishing he succeeds ever so much.

The End

AFTERWORD

In 2009, shortly after this book was first published, Lieutenant Ricardo Lucero contacted the author and thanked him for coming to his rescue on that fateful day in San Carlos Water in 1982 and requested the return of his helmet and flight suit.

And one month following this first contact, Lucero's family and a British journalist living in Argentina followed up the contact on Facebook, by sending press cuttings, informing the author that Ricardo Lucero, then a crop duster in rural Argentina, had died after crashing his plane into a tree in bad visibility. It seemed a futile and strangely ironic close to a great pilot's life and at such a coincidental time.

In February 2009, I was one of the many millions of subscribers to the phenomenon of 'Facebook'. I was not addicted and could browse quite happily once a day or once a week even. It allowed me to catch up with many former Marine mates, whom I hadn't heard from or seen since the late 70s and early 80s. I was also using it to let people know about my book. One day out of the blue, I got a message from a guy in a strange uniform, which I recognised nonetheless.

It was a message very to the point, written in broken English using Google Translate and apparently sent from Argentina. It turned out that it was the pilot that I had saved from that watery grave in San Carlos Water twenty-eight years previously, none other than Lieutenant Ricardo Lucero. Ricardo asked me if I was ok, thanked me for helping him from the water and enquired if I knew where his flight suit and helmet were. He told me that his family were very pleased that he hadn't been drowned that fateful day and they wanted to personally thank me for rescuing their dad, uncle and friend.

I had wanted to keep the helmet as a souvenir all those years ago, but it had been shamelessly taken from me by the corporal marine from the LCU. I informed him, that as far as I was aware, the helmet and suit were in the Royal Marines Museum in Southsea, yet this was a guess as I just wasn't sure of their location and hadn't visited it since I was in training learning to be a Royal Marine all those years back.

Ricardo told me that he had found me through a military historian in Argentina. I found it strange timing, so close after the release of my book. I later found out that it may have been the efforts of Ralph Riegel in trying to set up a meeting between us both in Argentina, as part of my book launch publicity programme. Anyway, he didn't really correspond a great deal after that; perhaps the answer regarding his prized possessions was not what he was hoping for or maybe he was finding Google Translate a struggle.

A number of Argentinians, however, began contacting me all of a sudden, all through Facebook and all telling me that they were pleased that I had rescued their father, friend, uncle and comrade from the water in the Falklands. Ricardo must have told them the story over the years, plus they would have seen him in media footage of the time under armed guard, entering the dock of HMS *Fearless* and on his way to being interviewed in a nice military fashion by the intelligence guys of the Royal Marines.

Ricardo's family and friends wanted to tell me just how grateful they were and I found it gratifying to know that I had kept their large, close family together. They all wanted to thank me for his life in person, if possible.

At this point, a local journalist from Bridlington, Judy Broadbent, found the story behind my book fascinating and managed to get me a full centre spread in *The Sun* newspaper, which in turn led many former military men and women to ring me up and explain their links to the stories in my book.

A local from Flamborough Head and a former Royal Navy helicopter crew member hunted me down and told me how pleased he was to see the Wessex helicopter on the back cover of the book. He had worked with Marines in the jungle of Brunei on this type of aircraft.

Another woman left me a cryptic note from her husband. I rang them back and found that the guy in question had read the article and was sure that he was the very artilleryman who had shot Lucero's jet down with his Rapier missile.

On another occasion, I was sent a small amount of money towards visiting the pilot in Argentina; the donor thought this was my next natural course of action and to be honest it had crossed my mind after Ricardo had got in touch.

I was also contacted during this time by a journalist in Argentina, called Laurence, who acted as a kind of go-between. She was English and married to an Argentinian. Her ability to judge the mood in Argentina was vital. She also thought I should visit the family and friends of Ricardo, maybe make a thing of it. It was Argentina's Bicentennial and also a spiky political period between Argentina and UK politicians.

Cristina Fernández de Kirchner, the Argentinian president at the time, was not doing well in the polls and was stirring the old Malvinas pot again, mainly owing to the rediscovery of oil fields there. Like we didn't know they were there in the first place!

I was ready to visit and was looking forward to it; it was important to get the timing right in view of work commitments, weather, politics and also future book sales. I also was really looking forward to visiting South America and the family and friends of Captain Ricardo Lucero.

Then out of the blue, I received a message on Facebook from Laurence. I was totally shocked and couldn't quite believe what I was reading. I thought it was a sick joke, but it wasn't.

I was sent a digital image of a plane crash in Argentina. The translation said that the pilot had died tragically after flying his crop duster into a tree one morning in the fog. I found it hard to believe; why now? Twenty-eight years without a word, then I get contacted through Facebook, then Ricardo dies in a tragic accident.

I sent my condolences to the family via one of his pilot mates and was inundated with replies from his family, telling of their thanks for all the years together they had had with him and for my part in keeping them together, so to speak.

There were those who considered that Ricardo may have been taken out by someone, to prevent the reunion and all it might symbolise: human courage and reconciliation between two former enemies. A government plot of sorts.

APPENDIX

THE ROYAL MARINES

The Royal Marines trace their origins back to 28 October 1664 when 1,200 soldiers were recruited for service with the Royal Navy, to be known as the Duke of York's Maritime Regiment of Foot. Britain's oldest regiments – the Coldstream Guards (1650) and Household Cavalry (1660) – were formed just the previous decade. The Duke of York's Regiment was funded through the Admiralty's budget and, for almost two hundred years, were the only dedicated, long-service soldiers in the Royal Navy.

Because of Britain's repeated wars in the seventeenth and eighteenth centuries, and later because of colonial expansion, the Royal Marines became a cadre of very experienced, battle-hardened troops. One of their most famous actions came in 1704 when Royal Marines, assisted by Dutch Marines, took Gibraltar, despite frantic Spanish attempts to defend the strategic island. The battle left two legacies: the single battle honour traditionally displayed by the Royal Marines 'Gibraltar'; and a long-standing link with the Dutch Marine Corps.

The Royal Marines dramatically expanded during the nineteenth century as the Royal Navy faced massive new commitments to support Britain's overseas colonies. The Royal Marines were also the 'teeth' in Britain's imperial policing programme, fighting against Napoleon's troops until 1815, Algerian pirates in 1816 and the Turkish Fleet in 1827. In the nineteenth century, Britain refused to follow the lead of either France or Prussia/Germany and maintain a large standing army, instead, Britain relied on the Royal Marines even for civil duties – supporting the Royal Irish Constabulary in Northern Ireland in the 1880s and even helping provide security during bitter industrial disputes in Britain in the 1830s.

By the 1890s, Britain was engaged in a naval race with imperial Germany and the Royal Navy expanded – so, too, did the Royal Marines. Every British vessel larger than a destroyer had a Royal Navy detachment, and, on major vessels, it was Marines who operated the gun turrets. A Royal Marine won the Victoria Cross at Jutland for ordering his blazing turret on the battle-cruiser, *Lion*, to be flooded before its magazine could explode, and Royal Marines also fought at Gallipoli in 1915 and at the Zeebrugge landings in 1918.

By 1940, the Royal Marines had expanded to a force of 80,000 men, and, on Winston Churchill's direction, they once again adopted the role of an elite, hardened strike force. In 1942, the Royal Marines formed their first 'Commando' units, capable of maritime landings but effectively designed for extended land-combat operations. The Normandy landings in 1944 were led by 5 Royal Marine Commando, and three out of every four British landing craft were operated by Royal Marines on D-Day. The commandos were at the forefront of the drive to Berlin in 1945. As Britain adjusted post-war to the winding down of empire, the Royal Marines were involved in operations ranging from Malaysia to Borneo, and from Korea to Suez. Royal Marines also deployed to Cyprus, Aden and Northern Ireland. Along with the Parachute Regiment, the Royal Marines were central to the Falkland Islands operation and were involved in some of the heaviest fighting. In Northern Ireland, they did regular tours of duty from 1969 during the Troubles. The Royal Marines also served as the primary recruiting ground for Special Forces members of the Special Boat Service (SBS) which is the maritime equivalent to the SAS.

But it was the 1990s that witnessed one of the most hectic deployment schedules for the Royal Marines since the nineteenth century, despite the fact that, with 7,500 personnel, the Royal Marines are now just one-tenth of their WW II size. Up until 2006, the Royal Marines have fought wars, undertaken disaster relief, peace enforcement and even civil protection operations in the Gulf (1991), Kuwait (1994), Bosnia (1995), Congo (1997), Montserrat (1998), Kosovo (2001), Sierra Leone (2004), Albania (2003), East Timor (2005), Iraq (2003) and Afghanistan (2006). And they continue to do so today.

However, the core role of the Royal Marines remains that of a highly trained, light infantry force, capable of rapid maritime deployment. That role has been dramatically underlined by the Royal Navy's commissioning of a series of new landing and support craft, including the helicopter assault ship, HMS *Ocean, Bulwark* and other specially designed helicopter, commando carriers. These craft aim to support the rapid – and potentially long-term – deployment of Commando units in various global trouble spots.

THE FALKLANDS

Located 600km from South America and 11,000km from mainland Britain, the Falkland Islands, comprising two main islands and almost 210 smaller islands, are barren, desolate and windswept. Their fate was originally settled as part of the minor subtext to treaties signed between Britain, France and Spain during the wars of the eighteenth century. Originally settled by a British pirate, the Falklands then witnessed a French colony being set up in response to Louis XV's loss of Canada. The French eventually sold their claims to Spain, and, in 1770, tensions over who actually controlled the islands led to an armed stand-off.

Ironically, the first military action – a Spanish landing in 1770 – resulted in twenty-three Royal Marines having to surrender after being surrounded by almost two thousand infantry. Just over a year later, the islands were returned to the British, though problems re-emerged when, fifty years later, a newly independent Argentina claimed 'Las Malvinas' islands as part of their national territory. Britain, who had abandoned the islands in 1775, moved to reassert control, and a small Argentine garrison was evicted in 1833. For a time, retiring Royal Marines provided the garrison until, in 1850, ex-Marines were recruited to launch the islands' major industry: sheep farming.

Over the next century, the only time the Falklands hit the world headlines was when a German imperial naval squadron, under Admiral Graf Spee, raided the British telegraph station during World War I – only to stumble across a vastly superior Royal Navy force and be destroyed. In the 1950s and 1960s, repeated Argentine claims to sovereignty of the islands were referred to the United Nations. Painstaking negotiations were thrown into turmoil when, by the late 1960s, it was apparent that the islanders, leery of Argentina's political turmoil and the savagery of paramilitary groups, wanted to remain a British colony.

In March 1982, under mounting political pressure domestically and having disastrously misread British political intentions, the military junta ruling Argentina ordered the implementation of Operation Rosario: the seizure of the Falkland Islands. South Georgia was taken first, and the main island invaded on 2 April. The islands' outnumbered and outgunned garrison, despite a valiant stand, quickly surrendered. General Leopoldo Galtieri celebrated a remarkable triumph – for less than a week, when it became clear that British Prime Minister Margaret Thatcher would fight to reclaim the islands. A hurriedly assembled Royal Navy task force sailed into the South Atlantic. On 25 April South Georgia was taken and, on 30 April, a maritime exclusion zone was declared around the Falkland Islands.

On 2 May, the Royal Navy nuclear submarine, HMS *Conqueror*, sank Argentina's World War II vintage light cruiser, *General Belgrano*, as it was deemed a threat to the task force. The 14,000-tonne cruiser was hit by two Mark 8 torpedoes and sank in just over thirty minutes, prompting speculation that her internal watertight doors may not have been closed. The cruiser was attacked while outside the maritime exclusion zone – a fact that subsequently caused a major political headache for London. A total of 368 Argentine sailors died and 700 were rescued, the casualties accounting for almost half of Argentine losses in the entire Falklands campaign. It was quickly apparent that Argentine aircraft held the key to the Falklands – sinking enough Royal Navy ships or even the crucially important British carriers could swing the campaign. On 4 May, an

Exocet missile struck HMS *Sheffield*, crippling the destroyer, which later sank. On 21 May, British troops landed at San Carlos Water, marking the effort to retake the main Falkland Islands. Argentine air attacks damaged several Royal Navy ships, but missed the British carriers and thus failed to disrupt the landings of elite British forces led by the Royal Marines and Parachute Regiment. Special Forces, including the SAS and SBS, had already been on the Falklands for several weeks. The battle of Goose Green was fought on 27–28 May, and when British Paras took the Argentine positions, the battle for the Falklands was virtually over. On 13 June, major parts of the Falklands capital, Stanley, were retaken and, on 20 June, Argentine forces in all outlying posts surrendered.

The fighting was marked by two major new weapons: the Sea Harrier jet and the Exocet missile. The Sea Harrier provided the British with an aircraft that could secure air dominance and operate without the support of a traditional aircraft carrier. The Exocet, launched from Dassault Super Étendard fighter-bombers, offering the Argentineans a lethal anti-ship capability. But, whereas the British had sufficient Sea Harriers for their needs, the Argentines had too few Super Étendards and too few Exocets. The traditional 500kg bombs they ultimately relied on did not have low-altitude fuses – though, if triggered, the bombs could prove devastating, as the Royal Navy discovered. In the weeks after the successful recapture of the islands, British commanders admitted that, had one of their carriers been sunk, the entire operation could have been thrown into doubt.

The conflict, which was never officially deemed a war by either side, cost 258 British lives and 649 Argentine over 74 days of fighting. Just three civilians were killed. Argentina's Constitution still lays claim to Las Malvinas.

HONG KONG

Home to almost seven million people, Hong Kong now ranks as one of the world's most powerful trading cities. However, for more than a century, it was a bitter bone of contention between Britain and China. In the mid-nineteenth century, Hong Kong was a booming port, not least because of China's surging trade with Europe. Tea, pottery, jade and silk were flowing from China to Britain – and the British, to reverse the unfavourable balance of trade, wanted to ship opium into China from its colonial holdings in India and Afghanistan. The Chinese – rightly worried about the social consequences of expanded opium dens – objected, and in 1839 war gave Britain the excuse to seize Hong Kong and force Beijing to sign the controversial lease agreement. This resulted in the seizure by the Royal Navy of Hong Kong in 1841. Further tracts of land around Hong Kong were seized in 1860, following the Second Opium War. In 1898, Britain secured a 99-year lease on mainland territories close to Hong Kong Island, further escalating development of the port.

By 1930, Hong Kong was the busiest port not only in China but in the entire Far East, outside Japan. It served as an administrative centre for Britain's numerous imperial interests in the Far East, as well as a strategic port for the Royal Navy. However, the city was seized by the Japanese on the outbreak of World War II, in December 1941. It took the Japanese just seventeen days to capture the mammoth port. It was only returned to British control in 1945 in the closing weeks of the war. China's civil war and the resultant victory of Mao Tse-Tung and the Communist Party marked a watershed in Hong Kong's development. The city was flooded with immigrants, fleeing the communists, and with businessmen relocating away from Mao's influence.

Over the next thirty years, Hong Kong became the touchstone of Chinese dealings with the West. As Hong Kong boomed, thanks to its textile and manufacturing industries, China found that the colony was a valuable source of foreign currency for the People's Republic of China (PRC). Beijing decided to establish Shenzhen, just inland from Hong Kong in the PRC, as a special investment zone. This copper-fastened Hong Kong's growth, while also greatly expanding the port's influence into the PRC itself.

In 1984, London and Beijing signed the Sino-British Declaration and it was agreed that Hong Kong would be handed over by the British to full Chinese control in July 1997. With the land leases within two decades of expiring, the British had no choice. From a military point of view, Hong Kong was virtually indefensible, and the tiny British garrison, mostly made up of Royal Marine detachments, was faced by the Chinese People's Liberation Army, which, with more than three million soldiers, ranked as the world's biggest fighting force.

Britain agreed to the handover, which was completed after a lavish ceremony on 1 July 1997 with the former Tory Minister, Chris Patten, serving as the last governor. In return, Beijing agreed to run Hong Kong as a special administrative region for fifty years, with full business, economic and financial guarantees. Along with the former Portuguese colony of Macau, Hong Kong is the only such 'special' region within the People's Republic of China.

NORWAY AND NATO

At the height of the Cold War, Norway was, along with West Germany, regarded as the likely frontline in any Soviet invasion of Europe. Norway, as a member of the North Atlantic Treaty Organisation (NATO), was required to provide bases for exercises aimed at defending Europe from Soviet aggression. These included both submarine and air force bases.

The NATO policy was two-fold: to prevent Norway from being overrun in any invasion and, almost as crucially, to protect the North Atlantic air and sea approaches through which military convoys between the US and Europe would have to be attacked. NATO planners were mindful of the lessons of 1939 when Britain and France disastrously misjudged the importance of Norway, and the successful invasion of the country by Adolf Hitler's Wehrmacht provided a platform from which Britain and her vital Atlantic convoys were attacked right up until 1945.

To defend Norway, the US helped fund modern aircraft for the Royal Norwegian Air Force, and the US Navy, alongside the Royal Navy, worked closely with the Royal Norwegian Navy, both on anti-submarine and anti-aircraft operations. NATO forces also had to train for the unique demands of fighting in the country's challenging Arctic environment. One of NATO's key units was Britain's Royal Marines and their specialist Arctic warfare unit, Four-Two Commando. For almost fifty years, Four-Two Commando trained how to fight, manoeuvre, hide and survive in one of Europe's harshest environments alongside other NATO units and the Royal Norwegian Army.

NORTHERN IRELAND

The restoration of the Northern Ireland Assembly in 2007 and the historic power-sharing deal between Ian Paisley's Democratic Unionist Party (DUP) and Gerry Adams's Sinn Féin, effectively ended almost four decades of sectarian strife that came close to tearing Irish society apart and made Ulster a global by-word for terrorism.

The seeds of the conflict were sown in 1922 when Ireland was partitioned following the War of Independence between British forces and the Irish Republican Army (IRA). Twenty-six counties formed the Irish Free State (later Republic) and six Ulster counties made up Northern Ireland. The latter had a Protestant majority who refused to be incorporated into any Dublin (i.e. Catholic-dominated) parliament. The Northern Ireland state-let was run from a parliament at Stormont, but also sent MPs to Westminster.

The partition of Ireland caused a furore among Republican activists in the newly created Free State, and provoked a vicious civil war which left a much bitterer and bloodier legacy than the War of Independence. However, despite a brief 'border' campaign by lingering Irish Republican Army (IRA) elements in the 1950s, which was crushed – somewhat ironically, by the Dublin authorities – Northern Ireland remained relatively stable until the late 1960s.

'The Troubles', as they were euphemistically dubbed, erupted in 1968 when a civil rights campaign by Catholics over biased housing policies in Northern Ireland provoked a violent Unionist backlash. Unionist and Loyalist elements claimed the civil rights campaign was threatening long-standing Protestant rights – and ultimately saw it as a way of bringing Northern Ireland closer to the Republic. The conflict quickly escalated, with extremists coming to the fore in both Unionist and Nationalist camps. As sectarian violence spiralled, British troops were deployed in 1969 to try and contain attacks. Initially welcomed by Catholic communities for protecting them from Protestant paramilitaries, British troops suddenly found themselves the focus of increasing hostility from both communities.

On 11 October 1969, the first RUC policeman was shot dead, then, on 10 March 1971, three off-duty British soldiers were found shot dead. The introduction of internment by Westminster proved a disaster, with the majority of those arrested being Catholic, and the measure effectively proved a recruitment bonanza for the re-emerging IRA. Ironically, the IRA had been discredited in the early phases of the violence because of their inability to protect Catholic communities from Loyalist violence. In January 1972, thirteen Catholic demonstrators were shot dead at a civil rights march in Derry by the Parachute Regiment – the so-called 'Bloody Sunday' killings. This immediately created a major split between the minority Catholic community and British troops, and recruitment for the IRA again soared. The British Embassy in Dublin was burned by a furious crowd and the IRA launched the first of its bombing campaigns on mainland UK.

Violence spiralled to horrific levels over the course of the next decade and repeated attempts to negotiate an end to the sectarian strife were frustrated – most famously when the Sunningdale Agreement collapsed after a Unionist-Loyalist strike, co-ordinated by Rev Ian Paisley. IRA attacks increased in sophistication and lethality owing to the import of arms and explosives from the Soviet Bloc via Libya. The IRA unleashed a bomb attack against the Parachute Regiment at Warrenpoint, killing eighteen troops, including members of the Queen's Own Highlanders. It was one of the greatest losses of life suffered by British forces during the conflict.

The savagery of the conflict continued to escalate with the notorious Shankill Road gang emerging as a Loyalist 'death squad', who kidnapped and tortured to death Catholic civilians. The IRA, for its part, launched a bomb attack against a Remembrance Day crowd in Enniskillen, and then bombed the Shankill Road, the heartland of Loyalism. The IRA also conducted a savage war against any members of the Nationalist community seen to be even mildly supportive of the security services.

By the 1980s, politicians in Britain, Ireland and the US launched repeated initiatives to try and resolve the crisis, and the 1985 Anglo-Irish Agreement, while derided by many at the time, created valuable new co-operation and dialogue between Dublin and London. In 1993, Ireland and Britain signed the Downing Street Declaration and co-operation on Northern Ireland reached new levels. The IRA announced a ceasefire and, in 1998, Britain and Ireland endorsed the Good Friday Agreement, which effectively consigned the constitutional future of Northern Ireland to majority democratic agreement. Britain repealed the Government of Ireland Act (1920) and the Republic dropped its territorial claim to Northern Ireland. Despite occasional setbacks, the paramilitaries finally got the message that the population was sick of the violence and wanted peace.

Tortuous negotiations over a power-sharing agreement between Unionists and Nationalists ultimately took nine years to conclude. The irony was that the main Unionist and Nationalist parties (the Ulster Unionist Party and the SDLP) were displaced by their formerly radical rivals, the Democratic Unionist Party (DUP) and Sinn Féin. Rev Ian Paisley became Northern Ireland's First Minister at the revived Stormont Assembly with Sinn Féin's Martin McGuinness as his deputy. These men – once committed foes – developed such a good working relationship they were dubbed 'the Chuckle Brothers'. While occasional flashpoints have occurred, the deal has, to date, held, and Northern Ireland now contemplates a peaceful future.

The Northern Ireland conflict eventually claimed more than 3,500 lives, of which 499 were British soldiers. If Northern Ireland-based regiments, RAF and Royal Navy personnel are included, the figure becomes 716. An estimated 377 IRA or Republican paramilitaries were killed. Loyalist paramilitary deaths amount to an estimated 149, while

341 British and Irish policemen were killed between 1969 and 2007. More than 1,800 civilians lost their lives. Despite overwhelming public support for the peace deal, splinter paramilitary groups on both sides have vowed to fight on. The head of Ireland's police, Garda Commissioner Fachtna Murphy, warned in 2008 that these groups continue to pose a threat despite the fact that they are starved of funds, weapons and public support.

Today in Northern Ireland, several splinter groups have been formed as a result of splits within the IRA, including the Continuity IRA, which is still active in the dissident Irish Republican campaign, and the Real IRA.

IRAQ

Few nations on earth have witnessed the bloodshed that Iraq has encountered over the past two thousand years. The Hittite, Assyrian, Babylonian, Persian, Greek, Roman, Byzantine and then successive Islamic empires all fought fierce battles for control of the vital Tigris and Euphrates valleys of Iraq, which have been hailed as the cradle of civilisation.

In early 2003, US-led Coalition forces poured into Iraq having claimed that President Saddam Hussein had failed to comply with United Nations directions about weapons of mass destruction (WMD). The invasion appeared, to many, to be unfinished business that the US authorities had with Saddam dating back to his invasion of Kuwait in 1990 and the subsequent Gulf War in 1991. President George H. Bush had ordered Coalition forces to drive Iraqi troops out of Kuwait in 1991, but signally failed to topple Saddam's regime by halting Coalition troops just inside the Iraqi border. This became a factor in the US presidential election which George H. Bush lost in 1992 to Bill Clinton. However, his son, George W. Bush, was US President twelve years later when a fresh Coalition assault was mounted on Iraq starting on 20 March 2003. After initial setbacks, the Coalition forces pulverised Iraqi resistance, and Saddam's regime collapsed from within. Saddam went on the run. The so-called 'shock and awe' military doctrine of US Vice-President Dick Cheney and US Defence Secretary Donald Rumsfeld appeared justified.

A few months later, Saddam's two sons, Uday and Qusay – his heirs apparent – were both killed after refusing to surrender to US forces. Saddam himself was captured on 13 December 2003 hiding in a hole in the ground near a farmhouse and was later put on trial for war crimes. He was convicted and sentenced to death by an Iraqi court. The Iraqi Government later refused calls for the execution to be delayed, pending appeals. Saddam's hanging, on 30 December 2006, caused outrage after video footage was released on the internet which showed the dictator being taunted by Shiite guards as he stood on the gallows just seconds from death. Secret footage was subsequently released of the dead dictator's body lying on a hospital gurney after the execution.

Long before the execution, hardline members of the former Revolutionary Guard, the B'aath Party members and an increasing influx of fundamentalist Islamic fighters from overseas began to increase pressure on the already-stretched Coalition forces. Violence was also sparked by criminal groups who realised that kidnapping and robbery were very profitable businesses in the new Iraq. A growing number of suicide bomb attacks was followed by increasingly sophisticated ambushes using improvised explosive devices (IEDs). These shaped charges were lethal to all but the most heavily armoured vehicles, and the lightly armed Coalition troops, many driving Humvees and Land Rovers, suddenly appeared very vulnerable. The Coalition's reliance on the high-tech weaponry at the centre of the 'shock and awe' doctrine was now of little help in dealing with the insurgents, and Coalition manpower became a major issue, with US forces struggling to balance commitments to Iraq with those to Afghanistan, the Middle East and Korea. The bipartisan Iraq Study Group in the US, led by former US Secretary of State James Baker, was highly critical of the policies adopted and warned that a fresh approach had to be developed in Iraq.

But the attacks on Coalition forces went hand-in-hand with attempts by insurgents to fan hatred between Iraq's Sunni and Shiite communities. The conflict became so bitter that mosques were attacked; injured patients were abducted and killed if they were mistakenly taken to a hospital controlled by the rival sect. The sectarian violence led to thousands of Iraqis fleeing their homes for the safety of enclaves controlled by their own religious grouping. By October 2006, the US was losing troops at a rate not witnessed since Vietnam, with 102 killed that month alone. British casualties in southern Iraq had also begun to rise. The Bush Government – following a virtual collapse in Republican support in the November 2006 US mid-term elections, which cost the party control of both the US Senate and Congress – then signalled its determination to pursue new strategies to ease tensions in Iraq, insisting that 20,000 extra US troops could help secure Baghdad. It was suddenly realised that Coalition forces in Iraq were stretched too thinly.

Despite widespread scepticism, the so-called 'troop surge' under General David Petraeus, the US army's leading counter-insurgency specialist, proved a startling success from mid-2007. Its impact was bolstered by the decision of US commanders to cede some security tasks to Iraqi tribal leaders, who, tired of the bloodshed, were desperate for a return to normality; those who were hesitant were paid for their tribal support. The two initiatives achieved what many had thought impossible, and squeezed the insurgents and foreign militants into marginal activity. Today Iraq is enjoying its most stable period since 2003. Armed violence persists in different forms, but it is sporadic, fragmented and localised. However, the country remains fragile and divided, and its people face an array of deepening challenges that the state is struggling to address.

PRIVATE MILITARY COMPANIES

The global security industry, ranging from the domestic security sector through to the private military industry, is estimated to be worth in excess of one trillion dollars, rivalling even the total cost of global healthcare.

Under the Geneva Convention (1949), a mercenary is not accorded the rights of a combatant or prisoner of war. The convention deems that a mercenary is a soldier who fights for private gain and has no direct political or ideological connection to the conflict. However, the legislation that governs this area – Protocol GC1 (1977) – has not been signed by numerous countries, including the United States. Under the strict definition of the Geneva Convention, since the US-led Coalition handed over power to the Iraqi Government, armed personnel employed to assist the Coalition are legally regarded as security contractors unless they declare that they are not resident in Iraq. In a notoriously difficult area to define, the broad agreement has been that personnel involved in protection duties for convoys, hospitals or key VIPs are security contractors. Those who take an active or non-defensive role in the conflict are regarded as mercenaries.

Despite the United Nations adopting a special Mercenary Convention in 1989, it has been argued by neutral and non-aligned countries that the legislation totally ignores the growing use of Private Military Companies (PMCs) by sovereign states.

The Iraq war is the first major conflict in which PMCs have come to widespread public attention though they have been involved in conflicts since the 1970s, mostly in Africa. The best-known PMCs are Executive Outcomes, which hit the headlines over its work in Angola and Sierra Leone, and Sandline International, which was involved in controversial contracts in New Guinea and Sierra Leone.

The advantages of PMCs to governments are significant: a country can effectively minimise the risks to its own military personnel, distance itself from a specific conflict, reduce the cost of involvement in any war zone and, in certain cases, avoid adverse publicity while ensuring a specific political goal is achieved.

In Iraq, the first PMC to make international headlines was Blackwater-USA, which had four security contractors killed outside Fallujah in March 2004 while they were protecting a food convoy. The vicious desecration of the bodies by insurgents – one of which was burned, dismembered and then hung from a bridge – is believed to have been a key factor in the Coalition's decision to try and stabilise the Fallujah pocket. Weeks of savage fighting followed.

Ironically, despite the growing controversy over the work of PMCs in conflict zones, the UN has itself worked with PMCs – for example, the awarding of a logistical contract to Executive Outcomes for sub-Saharan Africa. A key British Foreign Office consultative report admitted that, in the modern world, it was cheaper and often more effective for a government to hire a PMC than assign its own troops to an overseas project. However, former UN Secretary-General Kofi Annan ruled against using PMCs to support future UN missions and opted to retain the time-tested formula of using mandates to secure troops from UN member states.

ABOUT THE AUTHOR

GEOFF NORDASS

Born in Bridlington and raised on Flamborough Head, Yorkshire in 1961, Geoff Nordass joined the elite Royal Marine Commandos in 1978. He served tours of duty in Northern Ireland, Hong Kong and Norway as well as the Baltic and Mediterranean on HMS *Fearless*. He was mentioned in dispatches for the courage he showed in support of a joint SAS/SBS mission during Operation Corporate, the retaking of the Falkland Islands from Argentine forces in 1982. He later qualified as a RN diver and a parachutist before deploying in support of the Special Boat Service (SBS). He then introduced the new combat hovercraft (LCAC M) into service with the Royal Marines.

Having left the Royal Marines in 1996, he worked as a bodyguard for Mohammed and Dodi al-Fayed before a brief career as an 'action extra' in films including James Bond's *Tomorrow Never Dies*. He then spent six years as a security officer for Royal Caribbean on the most luxurious cruise ships afloat. From 2003 to 2008, he served as a private security contractor in Iraq, overseeing some of the most dangerous missions in the war-torn country. He then left an action-based life for a more sedate life in the UK, setting up a factory with his business partner Martin.

This proved to be too quiet and in 2010, he once again left the shores of England to be part of the fight against modern-day piracy in the Gulf of Aden and the East coast of Africa. Which he did for eight more years before hanging up his SLR once more to go back to the more stressful life of cruising, where he still gets slapped about by drunken, half-crazed passengers. Though admittedly, the main reason was because he knew that life on a cruise ship is much more intense on the audit- and paperwork-side and he needed to fill his mind with the mundane. It was necessary to prevent his grief taking hold – the loss of his eldest son in 2016 at the age of 21 will be forever his greatest sorrow.

RALPH RIEGEL

Ralph Riegel is the Southern Correspondent for the *Irish Independent*. A graduate of DIT-Rathmines, he was external examiner for the CIT MA in Journalism. He is the author of ten books, five of which were bestsellers.

Printed in Great Britain
by Amazon